Michael Innes

RECOGNITIONS

Recognition: Mystery Writers

Bruce Cassiday, General Editor

Michael Innes

George L. Scheper

Ungar / New York

1986
The Ungar Publishing Company
370 Lexington Avenue, New York, NY 10017

Printed in the United States of America

Library of Congress Cataloging-in-Publication Data

Scheper, George L., 1939–
  Michael Innes.

  (Recognitions)
  Bibliography: p.
  Includes index.
  1. Innes, Michael, 1906–   — Criticism and
interpretation. I. Title. II. Series.
PR6037.T466Z87   1986   823'.912   86-11412
ISBN 0-8044-2806-9

To my parents,
George Louis Scheper and Anne Znojemska Scheper
and to Dianne,
in honor of "the great Mystery" (Eph. 5:28–32)

Contents

Preface: Death as a Game

In introducing her monograph on Dorothy L. Sayers, Dawson Gaillard begins by citing G. K. Chesterton's dictum about the implicit bargain that ought to stand between writer, reader, and critic of detective fiction: "If it is the first rule of the writer of mystery stories to conceal the secret from the reader, it is the first duty of the critic to conceal it from the public. I will therefore put my hand upon my mouth." Gaillard then adds, "As a writer of detective fiction, Dorothy L. Sayers fulfilled her part of the bargain. Please be warned, however, that as a critic, I do not put my hand upon my mouth. In order to demonstrate relationships among Sayers' works, I must often tell on the criminal. To avoid premature knowledge about the plot, the reader is advised to read the work before reading my discussions."[1]

The same considerations are operative in the present volume, and naturally it would be preferable — as indeed it always is — for the reader to consult the text before the criticism. And yet other factors come into play in the case of Michael Innes that perhaps obviate the need for such a caution. For one thing, Innes has written almost fifty volumes of detective fiction, so it is not likely that many readers will have had occasion to read, let alone reread, all of these before perusing this book! It is an inherent aspect of Innes's qualities as a mystery writer that one is simply less concerned about his "endings" than one is with those of other writers of the genre. In fact, in what must seem at first a strikingly paradoxical assertion, it can be argued that it is Innes's very reputation for having somewhat "lame endings" that is actually the hallmark of his real preeminence as a detective novelist. For the run-of-the-mill detective story, as critic Dennis Porter has so aptly put it,

is like a conjurer's trick or a fairground haunted house: all the eerie
and mystifying effects, into which the spectator/reader enters with such
more-than-willing suspension of disbelief, turn out in the end to be all
a matter of trick lighting, mirrors, and papier-mâché masks. "The
reason why run-of-the mill detective stories do not warrant a rereading
is that almost all the pleasure for the reader is in their hermeneutic
dimension, in the suspense of not knowing. Such novels," Porter concludes, using Roland Barthes classificatory scheme, "are mere *textes de
désir.*" Like pornography, that is, they hold our interest only through
a kind of erotic anticipation, while at the end, "Postcoital sadness occurs because there is for the moment nothing more to know or feel."[2]
Whereas, in the case of "mainstream" literature, reader interest and
pleasure remain in the telling itself, not simply the anticipated out-
come; such works are, by contrast, *textes de plaisir.*

Herein is the legitimate complaint of those readers and critics who
find most detective fiction disappointing: it is almost impossible for
the long-awaited revelation, no matter how ingenious the device, "to
make the reader feel," as Edmund Wilson put it, "that the waiting has
been worth while."[3] Innes himself is manifestly aware of this problem
and refers to it from time to time in his own detective fiction. For instance, Miss Priscilla Pringle, the rather dotty mystery-writing protagonist of *Appleby's Answer* (1973), acknowledges at one point, as
she anxiously watches a fellow passenger on a train finishing the final
pages of one of her own novels, that "Deep in the constitution of the
detective-story there is a large liability to end flatly or badly, and
readers who have perused some 200 pages with satisfaction are often
enough disproportionately censorious as they make their way through
the score or so of pages with which it concludes. It is as if the ungrateful
creatures were suddenly persuaded that they have been chewing straw"
(p. 14; Compare *Stop Press* [1939], p. 264).

Far from trying to outdo himself and everyone else in attempting
to overcome that propensity with ever more ingenious concluding devices, Innes simply accepts and ignores the problem. His own endings
are apt to be jokey and bizarre, "fantasticated," to use his own favorite
expression; they are a constant reminder that Innes simply has no intention of writing "realistic crime fiction"—which, in any case, as he
argues in an essay on his craft, is work for Aeschylus, Shakespeare or
Dostoevski, not the writer of detective romances:

I am myself horrified at being credited with writing Crime Fiction — and for complex reasons. Partly, it is a matter of my training as a student of literature. Aeschylus could write Crime Fiction — and Shakespeare and Dostoevski and (in a way) Dickens. But it isn't for lesser talents. . . . A world in which everybody is liable to murder anybody else (and this is the prime datum of the thriller) can't but be so full of guilt and misery that only Aeschylus, Shakespeare and the others rolled into one could hope to cope with it. If, that is to say, it were allowed to be any sort of *real* world. . . . Nothing *real* must be allowed in. Let your guilt and misery, for instance, be real and you crack the mold of the form.[4]

Thus, instead of the "authentic" smells of Chandler's mean streets or the mundane sweaty workings of the 87th Precinct, what one gets in Innes is more like the following, the description of the death of the superannuated Oxford scholar Dr. Undertone, a crucial witness at one stage of the proceedings of *Operation Pax* (1951). The story of Dr. Undertone's manner of dying in his college rooms is recounted by his faithful manservant: the old man had ordered an extra chop for dinner, drunk a couple of glasses of burgundy, and then flown into a rage:

A terrible rage, miss. It was fearful to watch. "You rascal," he said. The Doctor often addressed me like that, miss. He was a good honest-spoken gentleman of the old school. "You rascal," he said, "when did you uncork that wine?" And he stood up, all swollen and purple in the face. "How often have I told you," he said, "that burgundy must breathe?" And then, miss, he fell dead. It was what you might call a very peaceful end   (p. 248).

In short, what Innes offers instead of crime fiction "realism" is a whole corpus of the finest and most literate *detective novels of manners*, novels, that is, in which the whole, and considerable, pleasure is in the telling itself, "the pleasure of the story rather than the pleasure of the chase," as Erik Routley has put it.[5] In other words, like "real" literature, and unlike pornography, fairground haunted houses, and all too many detective novels, the books of Michael Innes are *textes de plaisir*, not mere *textes de désir*.

So, about that matter of revealed endings. . . .

Not to worry.

Mechanics

Throughout the work, references to Michael Innes's novels are not foot-
noted; page references are given in the text. To identify to which edition of each novel the page references refer, consult the Innes bibliography at the end, where the edition of each novel used for citation
is indicated by an asterisk (*). Use of other sources is designated by
standard footnoting.

Acknowledgments

I wish to thank the librarians of the Enoch Pratt Free Library and The Johns Hopkins University libraries in Baltimore; my editor, Bruce Cassiday, for his conscientiousness and patience (thanks, Bruce); Dianne Ganz of Montgomery College for reading and hashing over the manuscript with me; my colleague Peter Cenci of Essex Community College, for many stimulating hours of conversation on the subject of detective fiction; and Jim Hitchcock, an old friend and classmate from Princeton Graduate School and now of St. Louis University, for similar conversational riches all too many years ago. And to my children, Jeanne and David, thanks for your patience and self-reliance, and an apology for all the missed J-V Girls' basketball games, sessions of Dungeons and Dragons, and sundry other worthwhile family activities that I absented myself from in pursuit of the present project.

1

Michael Innes/J. I. M. Stewart: Don's Delight

For almost fifty years, connoisseurs of the mystery have been hailing Michael Innes as far and away the finest writer among the practitioners of detective fiction. Even those who prefer the hard-boiled detective story or the police procedural to the very British, very civilized sort of detective novel of manners that is the Innes hallmark concede that he is the master stylist. Indeed, his wit, his erudition, his gentle good humor, donnish manner, and mandarin prose — all so antithetical to anything like a "realistic" crime story — are what chiefly delight his adherents. With the publication of Innes's first novel in 1936, Nicholas Blake (mystery pseudonym of poet C. Day-Lewis, himself the author of a highly literate series of detective novels) commented that Innes "commands such a battery of wit, subtlety, learning and psychological penetration that he blows almost all opposition clean out of the water" (*Spectator*, 30 Oct. 1936, p. 770); and with the publication of Innes's second novel, the *Times Literary Supplement* reviewer judged him "in a class by himself among writers of detective fiction" (3 July 1937, p. 496). Since then, Innes has been characterized variously as "English, bookish, jokey, and bizarre. . . . *donnish*" (Michelle Slung), indeed as "the donniest of the donnish school of detective story writing" (H. R. F. Keating), as "the finest of the Farceurs" (Julian Symons), and as "the most puritan of detective novelists," marked by a "deliberate espousement of mental aristocracy," and yet with an "increasing capacity for being extremely funny . . . creating scenes of rabelasian extravagance" (Erik Routley).[1]

Innes himself some time ago described his own detective fictions as being "on the frontier between the detective story and the fantasy;

1

they have a somewhat 'literary' flavor but their values remain those of melodrama and not of fiction proper,"[2] and in a more recent essay he modestly declares that in adhering to a mannered, artificial approach, "I was only being faithful to that first *ethos* of the 'classical' English detective story as a diversion to be lightly offered and lightly received."[3] As masterpieces of the genre that has been called the "detective novel of manners," Innes's stories generally have little to do with Raymond Chandler's mean streets or the world of real crime in other than a parabolic way. "After all," Innes recalls someone as once saying to him dryly, "when you come to think of it, murder is a pretty rotten sort of thing."[4] Or, as a character expresses it in one of his short stories: "Sexual promiscuity, drink — and of course a very low mentality all round. That's the main positive correlation with homicide, you know."[5] Altogether a sordid business — in real life. Whereas, in the formal British detective novel, murder is quite a different sort of thing, in which the body is found by the butler bringing the port into the baronet's library "While — don't forget — the snow was falling softly in the park outside."[6] Robert Graves and Alan Hodge put it succinctly: such mysteries "were no more intended to be judged by realistic standards than one would judge Watteau's shepherds and shepherdesses in terms of contemporary sheep-farming."[7] They are, that is, essentially *pastoral* works, dealing, as will be shown, in certain kinds of idealization. It is in the matter of literary excellence that the distinction of Innes's work stands. Erik Routley, one of the few critics to comment at any length on Innes, acutely observes that "For the old intellectual puzzle Innes substitutes intellectual wine-tasting, the pleasure of the story rather than the pleasure of the chase. . . . For him narrative is vastly more important than plot and character." Among the pleasures of an Innes story, Routley elaborates, are that it is "written with a precision appropriate to its author's craft, and draws on the largest vocabulary of any author in the business. Innes takes a fastidious pleasure in long and perfectly balanced sentences, in the rhythms and values of words and syllables. . . . The impression you always get is that of a first-class senior common room raconteur with a sense of humour, to whom you listen just for the pleasure of hearing it happen."[8]

It has surely never come as a surprise to readers of Michael Innes to learn that this is the pseudonym of an Oxford don, a literary scholar of note who is also, under his proper name of J. I. M. Stewart, the author of numerous works of "straight" fiction. The author himself prefers to keep the Innes and Stewart names and their respective works quite distinct. Anyone familiar with both will readily recognize in the mysteries the novelistic skills of Stewart, and in the novels the imagination of Michael Innes. The key things—the narrative voice and the sense of values—are quite congruent. (Throughout the rest of this biographical chapter, the author will be referred to as Stewart, except for specific references to the publications and characteristics of Michael Innes; elsewhere in the book, conversely, the author will be referred to as Innes, except in relation to Stewart's professional career.)

Stewart says he adopted a pseudonym ("Michael Innes" is an adaptation of his middle names, Innes Macintosh) simply because it seemed the appropriate thing for an academic to do—and because there was such a strong tradition for so doing (C. Day-Lewis as Nicholas Blake and Bruce Montgomery as Edmund Crispin being two of the best-known other examples). The irony was that detective fiction was a form of light reading much favored by intellectuals at the time and was therefore quite "respectable."[9] At any rate, he has always remained firmly committed to the pseudonym—in fact, he professes to have been annoyed that American copyright law required the Stewart name, however discreetly, to appear on the Innes publications. As to whether the pseudonym ever provided any real anonymity, Stewart reports that at first a number of people thought that the author of *Death at the President's Lodging* (1936), the first Innes novel, was actually Nevill Coghill, the eminent Chaucerian and Oxford don.

Considering its consistent level of literary excellence, the Innes/Stewart output is prodigious; since 1936, the date of the first Innes mystery, to the present, there have been forty-five detective novels and three collections of short stories—almost one a year. And since 1954, the date of the first J. I. M. Stewart novel, there have been twenty novels and five collections of short stories under the Stewart name, an average of about one Stewart work of fiction every sixteen months. Moreover, in the course of his academic career, Stewart has published eight scholarly books and monographs, including the final volume of the Oxford History of English Literature (*Eight Modern Writers* [1963]), and numerous editions, introductions, articles, and reviews.

Because of the manifest "donnishness" of his stories—university settings, high-table conversations, literary and artistic allusions—one often gets the impression from the biographical notices that the one overwhelmingly relevant aspect of Stewart's life is his career as a don.[10] But other factors are perhaps equally important, though less evident. For instance, there is the rather surprising hint that Stewart is really an *expatriate* writer. This is so for at least two reasons.

Early in his professional career, Stewart held a post for ten years at the University of Adelaide in South Australia, and it was during this period of "antipodean exile," so to speak, that the first dozen Innes mysteries were written. While many of that first group, and some later ones as well, do use an Australian setting or Australian characters to advantage, it is usually as an exotic episode or bit of background, rather than as "home." The *central* locale of most of these stories remains the traditional English country-house or university setting. Thus, for quite a long time the author was writing of "a society remembered rather than observed — and remembered in terms of literary conventions which are themselves distancing themselves" as he worked.[11]

This nostalgic feeling comes across with especial force because of a second and more important way in which Stewart has always appeared as an expatriate. He is a Scot, born and bred in Edinburgh, who experienced a relatively brief foray into Oxford society only as an undergraduate at Oriel College, before being called to his professional duties, first to Leeds and then to Australia, until at last recalled to Oxford as a Fellow in 1949. The situation is summed up nicely in Innes's essay on his detective, John Appleby:

> I think a species of naive nostalgia was at work. English life and manners had a compelling fascination for me — and the more so because, as a Scot who had scarcely crossed the border as a boy, my experience of them had been comparatively brief. And at once keen but impressionistic![12]

The Scottish background and Stewart's situation as a Scot in England are therefore crucial to our fullest appreciation of the Innes/Stewart fictions. John Innes Mackintosh Stewart (a veritable pibroch of a name, conjuring up the skirl of bagpipes) was born in Edinburgh on September 30, 1906, the son of John Stewart, a lawyer and Director of Education of the City of Edinburgh, and Elizabeth Jane Clark. He says he was born "just outside Edinburgh and almost within the shadow of the centenary monument to the author of *Waverley*."[13] Oxford and Edinburgh, Stewart readily agrees with Lord Macaulay, are two of the three most beautiful cities in Europe

(Genoa was Macaulay's surprising third), but unlike Oxford, which is in no way remarkable for its natural surroundings, Edinburgh, Stewart says, "suggests overwhelmingly that nature and art have been for long at work together in a subtle partnership."[14] The dramatic positioning of the Auld Reekie above the Firth of Forth, the Castle and "boldly sculptured" forms of the surrounding hills silhouetted against the lowering Scottish sky, the ongoing dialogue between the twisty, medieval Old Town and the prim Georgian New Town — all constitute for Stewart the grand city of his childhood memories, along with the famous Edinburgh wind that always seemed as though it would puff down the city's monuments, "like the house in the story my mother used to tell me while this very wind was alarmingly rattling my nursery windows in the New Town."

This city of his boyhood Stewart remembers as exercising a powerful pull on his imagination; the topography and poetry of Edinburgh, he says, are a terrain that condition a Scot's temperament, and he tells an autobiographical story to illustrate the point. He recalls childhood picnics from which he could see the soaring cantilevered railway bridge built in 1889 over the Firth of Forth: "I believe that it came a good deal to command my infant imagination." But the great day when he first actually *crossed* the bridge was a bitter disillusionment: "The train in which I was at last privileged to travel simply pursued a level course *through* the bridge. I had expected it to swoop grandly up and down those tremendous metallic slopes." The point was that the romantic young Scot expected the train to soar and plunge, to behave with the same operatic exhilaration as the topography of the city itself.[15] The Scots, in short, for Stewart, are "proud and independent," but possessed of "extravagant expectations."

Edinburgh was an "East-Windy, West-Endy" sort of place, says Stewart, with reference to an old jibe about the city. Patrician in style, but stubbornly and proudly middle class in its values, it always managed to convey in the severe façades of the massive gray-stone houses "an unmistakable impression of exclusiveness, of well-bred reserve." And in the Edinburgh Academy, the school that epitomized this "Modern Athens," Stewart received his boyhood education. The overall regimen of the school was essentially philistine, Stewart recalls:

> philistine in a fashion closely reflecting one side of the Edinburgh character. We worked all morning and through the afternoon, chiefly at Greek and Latin, presented bleakly and without

frills. . . . Then we were required to put much effort into tough
and often disagreeably muddy games. After that we went home on
our bicycles — a stiff, uphill progress, more likely than not. ("An
Edinburgh Boyhood," p. 67)

There was one "salvation and glory": the Scottish National Gallery. "It alone nourished in me, as it must have nourished in others,
a simple sensuousness — aestheticism, if it must be called that — which
found little encouragement elsewhere in the Modern Athens." As Osbert Sitwell reported that he had gained his education during holidays
from Eton College, so Stewart reflects that "I got a modicum of mine"
inside those rooms with "Italian light on Scottish walls." Two or three
of the Academy boys, he remembers, would, almost guiltily, steal
moments inside those embracing walls:

> Outside, Edinburgh was gray and cold — and under the cloud rack,
> or dimly through the fog, we ought probably to have been watching
> the First Fifteen defeating Fettes or Loretto at Rugby in a sea of
> mud. Inside, color and warmth were all around us, as if we had
> been miraculously transported into some great luminous shell
> through which Mediterranean sunlight poured.   ("An Edinburgh
> Boyhood," p. 68)

It was to be a lasting influence, manifest in the fictions of both
Michael Innes and J. I. M. Stewart. A sensitivity to art and a quite
respectable competence in art criticism is apparent in Stewart's *The
Last Tresilians* (1965) or Innes's *A Private View* (1952) or *Money from
Holme* (1964). Stewart had even thought at one point of making art
history his career — but he could not afford it.

Finally, while Edinburgh has basked in its image as the Modern
Athens, it might with equal aptness, Stewart says, be dubbed the
"Belated Bath." Since the Settlement Act of 1707, Edinburgh has had
to accept the role of a *provincial* capital, with wealth and opportunity
perceived as lying south, across the border. Hence, Stewart says, in
ultimately seeking his fortune in England, "I am far from singular. The
Scots have always been wanderers." So on the one hand there was the
imaginative tug of Scotland, and its family associations; but on the
other hand, there was the pull of England, and that, ironically enough,
was given impetus by the Edinburgh Academy, a monument to Scottish pride, established by Sir Walter Scott. Most of the schoolmasters

were "Oxbridgians," whose natural expectation was that their business was to prepare the ablest boys for admission to those august institutions. "Such was the prestige of our powerful neighbor." Yet, he adds, given the beauty and poetry of Edinburgh, "It seems odd that I ever wanted to leave it." In short, "Why go away?" Stewart's answer to his self-posed question takes the form of a story:

> Cathedrals, little Norman churches, the two "great universities": I saw them for the first time when I was seventeen and made a bold foray with my parents across the border. The effect was overwhelming. I took one look at Christ Church's Tom Tower, and before my mother had verified in her guidebook that it was the work of Sir Christopher Wren, I had decided that within its shadow was my home.   (p. 70)

And so the die was cast. He won a scholarship to Oriel College, where his classmates included Christopher Isherwood and W. H. Auden (whom he remembers as the "Shelleian" character of the crowd).

Stewart reports that "At Oxford I had a great Elizabethan scholar as my tutor; he got me a first class in English and then I went to Vienna for a year to recover. After that I had the good luck to fall in with Francis Meynell, and for him I edited the Nonesuch Edition of Florio's *Montaigne*; this in turn got me a job as a lecturer in the University of Leeds."[16] This early academic connection with Montaigne points us in the right direction; the qualities Stewart saw in Montaigne — "a distaste for the prosaic enthusiasm and learned triviality of the schools" and an intelligence "free, roving and comprehensive"[17] — are precisely what can be seen in Stewart himself. Leeds, meanwhile, was a highly respectable university in a grim industrial town. Innes in later years offers comic images of life in such a "redbrick" university in several of the mysteries; "Nesfield," in particular, in *The Weight of the Evidence* (1943), is modeled on Leeds. The cafeteria trays, the institutional coffee, the inelegant accommodations, and the hordes of working class kids must all have seemed a far cry from Oxford, where in Stewart's day breakfast was still brought up to the students' rooms by scouts, and dining hall and common room were still attended by elaborate rituals. But Innes's satire in *The Weight of the Evidence* and in *Old Hall, New Hall* (1956), another "redbrick" tale, is gentle and even fond. It was also at Leeds that Stewart met, and married, Mary Hardwick. As he tells the story, "I was recommended to two excellent lodgings by the professors who appointed me; in the one there was already a lodger, a young woman; in the other not. I made the natural choice and a year later the young woman and I were married."[18] She was a medical student who went on to become a doctor and did infant welfare work when they moved to Australia.

Stewart spent five years in Leeds and then made the important move to Adelaide, South Australia. "When I was twenty-seven," he writes, "my former teachers sent me out to Australia to be a professor of English literature. I was to be a 'full' professor, they explained — which at least suggested that I had been sufficiently stuffed with books. But I had never *written* a book. So I celebrated the occasion by writing and publishing a detective novel";[19] it was called *Death at the President's Lodging*. He went on to produce a dozen mysteries during the ten years he spent in Australia. As Stewart put it in an interview, albeit with tongue in cheek, he first undertook the writing of detective fiction out of a "failure of nerve" — by which he meant that he had arrived in Australia without any real sense of academic or scholarly direction, and no money (he recalls how he and his wife would hoard a few pence to afford a Sunday paper or a chocolate at the end of the week). So the job took him to Australia, but it was Inspector Appleby who enabled him to return to Great Britain. Meanwhile World War II had intervened, and his wife put in work as a wartime physician. It was not until just after the explosion of the atom bomb that the family was able to book passage on a steamer back to Britain, and a job at Belfast.

During the Australia years Innes's output included a couple of volumes extraordinarily long and complex for the detective genre. "This suggests," he writes, "more application than, I fear, actually went into the activity; one is rather freely inventive when one is young, and the stories seemed to get themselves on the page out of odd corners of my mind at odd times and seasons."[20] His habit in those days was to devote a couple of hours before breakfast to the writing of the detective stories; in a comment he made at the time, in 1942, he explains, "For nine months of the year, and between six and eight o'clock in the morning, the South Australian climate is just right for authorship of this sort. . . . Sometimes I lie on the beach in the sun and wonder if I mightn't some day write something else."[21] Many years later he reiterated, unassumingly, that "a detective novel takes about four weeks to write, or three weeks if confined to an hour or two before breakfast, so it gets tucked into a routine as readily as fishing or gardening or billiards."[22]

It is in these first years that some of the most remarkable Innes stories were written. After his first novel — a highly convoluted variant of the locked-room puzzle in an academic setting ("I made the whole thing more fantastic than you'd believe," he said, almost thirty years later) — Innes's next several books were extremely ambitious, seeming to attempt a fusion of the conventions of the mystery story with the realistic characterization and plotting of the mainstream novel — a tendency particularly evident in *Lament for a Maker* (1938) and *Stop Press* (1939) — although Innes himself came to believe that such a combination of straight and detective fiction ultimately did not work.

The other Innes novels of the Australian period tend to be "thriller-fantasias," a mode that has become more or less the Innes hallmark. Far from being Christie-like puzzle stories, these narratives have the color, atmosphere, and action characteristic of thrillers, including some remarkably told flight-and-pursuit scenes, but these are combined with plots and characterizations that reveal themselves ultimately as comic and fantastic. A good example of this, and a key work for getting down a good bit of the Appleby family background (it is the novel in which he meets and woos Judith, an artistic member of the eccentric Raven family) is *Appleby's End* (1945), full of the picturesque atmosphere of a wonderfully dotty rural England with characters called Heyhoe, Hoobin, and Rainbird, and towns called Drool, Snarl, Linger, Boxer's Bottom, and Abbots Yatter. Also, while Innes is almost never topical in a realistic way (his is not, he says, "a real world, controlled by actual and contemporary social pressures, any more than is, say, the world of P. G. Wodehouse"),[23] the war years and postwar atmosphere did contribute to a motif of international intrigue in a number of the Innes novels of the forties (for example, *The Secret Vanguard* [1940] and *From "London" Far* [1946]).

The postwar years 1946–48 Stewart spent at Queens University, Belfast, a locale that seems not to have left a very strong impress on his fictions — although a very effective use of Irish setting does occur in *The Journeying Boy* (1949), which indeed Innes thinks of as perhaps his best novel. But it was at this time that he produced his first important scholarly publication, *Character and Motive in Shakespeare* (1951). It was the work that established Stewart's scholarly credentials. Stewart has candidly said that he wrote the book not because he had anything "burningly new" to say about Shakespeare, but to help secure an appointment at Oxford. Despite that typically self-deprecating assessment, *Character and Motive* remains quite a worthwhile contribution to Shakespeare studies. It is — and this is perhaps characteristic of Stewart's natural instinct for dialectic — really a dialogue with what were at the time certain influential critics of the "neohistorical" school of criticism, for whom inconsistencies of character or implausibilities of motivation in certain plays were to be "explained" by the conditions of Shakespeare's theater, the expectations of the Elizabethan audience or Shakespeare's fidelity to one or another contemporary literary convention. Against such suggestions, Stewart argues carefully and persuasively on behalf of the realistic psychology of the plays, right up to the point where — as in life — character touches upon the irrational, the mysterious, and the mythic. It is a very donnish book, not so much the presentation of the results of original scholarly research as rather a sort of tutorial in which Stewart patiently upholds the central humanistic traditions of criticism. Some of these matters of Shakespearean literary criticism were later deftly woven into the plot of Innes's *Hamlet, Revenge!* (1937).

At the time Stewart was at work on *Character and Motive in Shakespeare*, Michael Innes made a rare foray into a literary venture other than detective fiction: a series of three radio plays for the BBC's Third Programme. The first was one of a series of "Imaginary Conversations" conceived by Rayner Heppenstall; script contributors, in addition to Innes, included Sean O'Faolain, V. S. Pritchett, Herbert Read, and C. V. Wedgewood. Innes's contribution involved a conversation between Samuel Johnson and Lord Monboddo, as a sort of traditionalism vs. scientism debate.[24] Innes's second and third radio plays dealt with Shakespeare, specifically *Hamlet*. The first, "The Hawk and the Handsaw," is a brilliant piece in which a physician (Dr. Mungo) recalls to the Danish court of King Fortinbras how forty years earlier he had sought to cure Hamlet of his melancholia and obsessions. The flashback dialogue between Dr. Mungo and Prince Hamlet amounts to a masterful presentation and critique of the psychoanalytic interpretation that had recently been brought forward by Ernest Jones in *Hamlet and Oedipus*. Mungo, that is, would persuade Hamlet that the ghost and its message are a projection of Hamlet's guilt-ridden unconscious mind, specifically of his murderous Oedipal feelings toward his father, feelings he has disguised through the groundless assignation of blame to Claudius as a scapegoat. But in Innes's satirization, all this is compounded by a repressed memory: of how Hamlet once observed his father making love to a woman for whom he himself had an adolescent passion — and how this woman was then hastily married to Polonius and was thus, of course, none other than the mother of Ophelia! Innes, in going Ernest Jones one better, is thus in his own way doing the same job of rebuttal of unsound critical ideas that Stewart was doing in "straight" criticism at virtually the same time.[25]

The second *Hamlet* radio play, "The Mysterious Affair at Elsinore," is not really a play at all, but a "highly mannered talk," as Heppenstall called it, in which Innes, as a sort of don-detective, takes a look at the "scene of the crime" at the end of *Hamlet* — at who was killed and at the disposition of the evidence — and then, through the time-tested method of analyzing opportunity and motive (who most stood to gain from the deaths), solves the mystery. The culprit, Innes concludes, was Fortinbras: It was he who was in a position to orchestrate each killing and who would profit from having systematically eliminated all possible heirs to the Danish throne or anyone in a position to produce future heirs (including Rosencrantz and Guildenstern, whom, Innes "deduces," must be illegitimate sons of Claudius!).[26]

Also in this period, shortly after his return from Australia, Innes was initiated into the Detection Club of London. The club had been founded in 1932 by G. K. Chesterton and Dorothy L. Sayers and twenty-four of their colleagues as a forum for mutual amusement and with the idea of fostering and upholding standards of excellence in the genre. According to a recent book on Sayers, Chesterton and Sayers "are said to have written the election ceremony, which included the new members swearing on Erik the Skull that they would be faithful to the oaths of the Club. They promised to honor the King's English, to reveal clues, but not to depend on 'Divine Revelation, Feminine Intuition, Mumbo-Jumbo, Jiggery-Pokery, Coincidence or the Act of God' to solve their cases."[27] Innes approached his own initiation in a spirit of whimsey: "At my first appearance, I found that there was an initiation ceremony. Among other things, one took an oath not to do this and that: not, for instance, to write a story turning on identical twins. Being donnish and intellectually arrogant, I thought poorly of this; indeed, the next day I started *Night of Errors* [1947], a mystery novel turning on triplets. But the oath-taking didn't offend me."[28]

Neither at first did the presence of two symbolic objects on the table, the skull and a coil of hangman's rope. But these jesting emblems took on a different cast when the speaker of the evening, a barrister, told a story about the abysmal howling in a courtroom of a woman convicted of murder and sentenced to die. There had been a couple of incidents like this that always brought home to Innes what a nasty business the world of real crime was, and reinforced his sense that the appropriate approach for detective fiction was the construction of amusing fantasias, in which nothing *real* was let in, and the playing of witty variations on established conventions.

(Innes's association with the club, incidentally, was to be short-lived in any case because he could not, he says, really participate in the discussions, not having read the other authors' works — the same problem C. Day-Lewis experienced.)

Meantime, *Character and Motive* had secured Stewart his fellowship, and from 1949 until his retirement in 1973 he was a Student of Christ Church, Oxford, and from 1969 to 1973 a Reader in English Literature of Oxford University (a university lectureship in the British system being distinct from a college fellowship). The years 1950–62 form a convenient bloc for surveying the Innes/Stewart canon. This period saw a few major academic publications by Stewart, including an edition with introduction of Ovid's *Metamorphoses* (1955) and a monograph on James Joyce for the Writers and Their Work series published for the British Council and National Book League (1957).

These years also saw the commencement of a whole new literary endeavor for Stewart, the publication of "straight" fiction under his own name. The differences between the Innes fictions and the Stewart fictions are very real ones in the mind of the author himself, and he would prefer to keep them entirely distinct, although reviewers have been fond of pointing to resemblances. The one, he says, is a sort of light entertainment that he does not carry around with him: they are in his head only when he is at work on them, and they more or less come right out of the typewriter: "I never brooded over them as I was to brood over ordinary 'straight' novels later."[29] Nothing in that statement, incidentally, implies any necessary inferiority of the Innes novels to the Stewart novels; a writer's "pastorals" may in fact be more successful as art than his more ambitious productions. Indeed, the author has rather wistfully conceded in an interview that he supposes Innes is rather better at what *he* does than Stewart is at what *he* does.

Moreover, whereas it was perfectly respectable for an Oxford don to be (pseudonymously) the author of best-selling mysteries, the writing of "straight" fiction was a bit suspect: "There seems to be a feeling," he says, "that this is something a lecturer on Thomas Hardy and Henry James should keep clear of."[30] At any rate, Stewart says he never discussed any of his fiction with his Oxford colleagues, and that they seemed to respect the idea that he'd be a bit touchy about it.

Innes, incidentally, offers us a wonderfully comic "Cambridge version" of himself in *Appleby's Answer* (1973), in the person of one Professor Hussey, an authority on Greek epigraphy and given, "every decade or so, to uttering some deep mystery in the tradition of Douglas and Margaret Cole or Ronnie Knox." In a thinly disguised fictionalization of his own situation as a mystery-writing don, he has Hussey explain how he set his first mystery story at his old college: "My own first story was about a peculiarly ingenious murder in a Cambridge college. I know nothing whatever about such places. I had been no more than an undergraduate in one. And undergraduates, of course, know nothing. Nothing at all" (p. 38). The allusion is clearly to Innes's own first novel, whose American title, *Seven Suspects*, is echoed by Hussey's *The Seventeenth Suspect*. And then, like Innes, Hussey had eventually returned as a fellow to that same university, in great apprehension of discovery: "It was a most urbane society. Or so I judged for a while. Then I observed that there were frictions here and there. Subacute irritations. Irritations which could not, in honesty, be so described. Unspeakable passions . . . and unquenchable animosities! I lived for months in terror lest one of these phrenetic scholars should chance upon my book, and that comprehensive holocaust should succeed" (pp. 38–9). Of course, no such catastrophe ensued — for Hussey, or for Innes!

In the decade 1952–62, Stewart published four novels and a collection of short stories under his own name. These first Stewart fictions received a generally positive but somewhat mixed reception from the reviewers as highly literate, erudite, and donnish entertainments in a Jamesian manner. It was also noted that they had, not surprisingly, some of the characteristics of Innes's detective fiction. The point was summed up in a review by Samuel Hynes in the *New York Times* commenting on this group of stories as a whole:

"Mark Lambert's Supper," "The Guardians," and "A Use of Riches" are all intelligent, stylish novels; yet they have the essential qualities of the detective stories: they depend on melodramatic,

"twisty" plots rather than on character and emotion; they are sprin-
kled with allusions and quotations, and their origins are literary,
rather than human situations. They are more like novels by Henry
James than they are like life.   (7 May 1961, p. 3)

Other reviewers alluded favorably to the "Innesian" qualities percep-
tible in these Stewart fictions. For instance, about *A Use of Riches*
(1957), critic Walter Allen wrote that with its highly convoluted and
melodramatic plot, "It is as carefully and expertly plotted as any detective novel; Mr. Stewart continually surprises by his invention and ingenuity, and he never fumbles, never puts a foot wrong; and I think
he should be granted the same protection that he would have if he were
writing as Michael Innes" (*New Statesman*, 10 Aug 1957, p. 176). It
is evident that Innes had built up a large balance of good will that was
drawn upon in appreciation of Stewart's new venture. In fact, perhaps
the best-received Stewart work of these years was the short story collection, *The Man Who Wrote Detective Stories* (1959). The title story
concerns a writer who learns that the plot of his as yet unpublished
latest mystery story has been unaccountably appropriated to lethal effect by a real criminal (a true Innes obsession — see, for instance, *Stop
Press* [1939] and *Appleby's End* [1945]). As Boucher noted in his
review, this story is almost like a "Stewart-Innes collaboration" (*New
York Times Book Review*, 8 March 1959, p. 40). It offers a wonderful
fictional self-portrait of the author in the double character both of the
narrator and of the hapless man who wrote detective stories, and in
it he incorporates a number of autobiographical elements, in particular
a pair of instructive anecdotes that point up the inappropriateness of
attempting a "realistic" approach to detective fiction, anecdotes that
reappear in Innes's 1965 essay, "Death as a Game" (see epilogue).

Meanwhile, in this same decade, Innes continued his regular output of mysteries, beginning with one of his most successful thriller-
fantasias, *Operation Pax* (1951), and including a very well-received
straight thriller (Innes's "straightest" yarn, in fact), *The Man from the
Sea* (1955), and some ten other detective novels and two short-story
collections in what had by now become his characteristic manner: urbane, donnish, and rather fantastic variations on the traditional
English country-house mystery story.

The years 1963–71 mark a distinct next period for Stewart, because of the prodigious output of work under both the Stewart and

Innes names: these are, truly, his *anni mirabili*. A *Times Literary Supplement* reviewer had commented earlier that "The quite Trollopian productivity of Mr. J. I. M. Stewart commands our respect and gratitude. High-powered university teaching, high-fantastical thrillers, urbane, neo-Jacobean social comedies, lit. crit. for the Sundays — this industrious juggler can keep his eye on all these balls at once as they twinkle in the air above a pair of remarkably safe hands" (19 May 1961, p. 313). But then the years 1963–71 saw the amazing output of seven Innes mysteries, five J. I. M. Stewart novels and one short story collection, and a dozen scholarly publications, including Stewart's magnum opus, *Eight Modern Writers* (1963), published as the final volume of The Oxford History of English Literature, plus a monograph on Thomas Love Peacock (1963), full-length critical studies of Rudyard Kipling (1966), Joseph Conrad (1968), and Thomas Hardy (1971), a pamphlet on Shakespeare, and a number of editions, introductions, and critical articles. Stewart's refreshingly straightforward appraisals — intelligent, balanced, and erudite without being arcane — are a welcome antidote to the murky gnosticism of so much recent academic criticism that has been engaged, as Innes once put it, in giving English literature "the works." As Orville Prescott said of the Kipling volume, "Mr. Stewart is adept in performing one of the critic's most useful tasks — pointing out the less obvious merits, the nuances, and the true significances which hasty readers can easily overlook" (*Saturday Review*, 22 Oct. 1966, p. 58).

In the six volumes of fiction under the Stewart name — the "middle period" of the Stewart fictions — the author seems to have hit a comfortable stride and produced works almost uniformly consistent and satisfying in their sort: a mode of literary pastiche in a Jamesian manner. Of particular interest is the quite apparent interrelation between these extremely "literary" Stewart novels and the almost equally literary Innes mysteries, distinct though their author would prefer to keep them. A perceptive statement of this relationship appears in Richard Mayne's review of Stewart's *An Acre of Grass* (1965), in which he emphasizes the point, quite well taken, that the "mandarin prose" of both sets of novels is really but a continuation of the classic tradition in prose fiction which the Modernists had rebelled against. There has "obviously always been a novelist inside the writer of whodunits," Mayne wrote, "and the retort comes pat — isn't there also a whodunit writer inside the novelist"?

To say this, however, is only to restate the point that Stewart is
a traditional writer. Clues, climaxes, suspense, mystery and surprise are the tried ingredients of the classic novel. . . . Mandarin
prose may be lying down, but it isn't dead — Stewart himself, indeed, is a witness to what it can still achieve. Paradoxically, what
that is, I think, is a remarkable naturalness and honesty. The dons
and writers here are more self-consciously literary than those of
C. P. Snow; but . . . if their lives are artificially cloistered from
more boisterous concerns, they nevertheless admit an ultimate fine-
ness of perception, a patience and tolerance, that are valuable qualities, and less uncommon in Establishment figures than one might
suppose. (*New Statesman*, 20 August 1965, p. 206)

This period of Stewart's life and work concluded with his retirement in 1974. With his major scholarly work behind him, Stewart has
subsequently settled into a remarkably consistent pattern of productivity: from 1974 to the present he has maintained a pattern of publishing a pair of novels every year, one Stewart and one Innes, along with
the occasional scholarly article and a steady stream of book reviews.
This period has seen the publication of no less than fourteen works of
fiction by Stewart (eleven novels and three short-story collections) and
thirteen Innes volumes (twelve novels and one short-story collection).
The Innes works tend to be of a consistent length (the so-called
Simenon format of about two hundred pages) and tend to represent
amusing variations on the country-house theme (for example, *The
Open House* [1972], *Appleby's Other Story* [1974], *The Ampersand
Papers* [1978], *Sheiks and Adders* [1982]). In one new development,
Innes's long-standing interest in art finds expression in a series of
mysteries (four to date) that introduce a new series protagonist, the
academician-painter Charles Honeybath. The first three Honeybath
narratives are without Appleby, but the most recent, with which Innes professes to be quite pleased, brings the two together and is simply
and aptly titled *Appleby and Honeybath* (1983). The latest novel, *Carson's Conspiracy* (1984) is Innes's forty-fourth mystery novel and his
forty-seventh volume of detective fiction.

The Stewart novels of the past decade have, not surprisingly, continued to explore life from the vantage point of the senior common
room and high table. Beginning with *Mungo's Dream* (1973), a novel
of two young Scots who share rooms in their first year at Oxford,
Stewart has devoted a good part of the decade to the re-creation of the

Oxford experience, above all in his fictional magnum opus, the Oxford Quintet, collectively titled *A Staircase in Surrey* (the use of the place-name going all the way back to Innes's *Death at the President's Lodging* in 1936), published between 1974 and 1978. The five novels chronicle the experiences and fortunes of a large number of Oxford-affiliated individuals, but always at the center is the narrator, a Scot named Duncan Patullo, the focal point for many of the manifestly autobiographical elements in the quintet.

The Oxford Quintet incorporates many interesting, more or less autobiographical reflections of Patullo's boyhood in Edinburgh, including descriptions of his grammar school, summer vacations with highland relatives, the severely classical — and philistine — Edinburgh Academy and the counterpoint relief of the Scottish National Gallery (vignettes and locales that can instructively be compared with Stewart's reflections in his essay "An Edinburgh Boyhood") — as well, of course, as the main fare, the rich milieu of Oxford itself, as experienced by Patullo first as an undergraduate and then as a fellow. In the course of the five volumes some very memorable Oxford portraits are developed, some based on well-known figures such as Nevill Coghill and J. R. R. Tolkien. The crucial underlying feeling is an unabashed but almost ineffable "staircase sentimentality," the feeling that, after all, "we all belong to this place." As Patullo recollects about his first year at Oxford, "I had ended that Term in love with the place to an extent which might have been said to constitute a disease" (*The Gaudy*, p. 188).

All in all, the Quintet amounts to a unique literary celebration of Oxford life. Critics' reservations about the Oxford Quintet have, predictably, had to do with their perception of its "neo-Edwardian" subject matter and, once again, the "mandarin prose" and donnish manner — the sense that Stewart mirrors his society a little too closely, that he gives perhaps too flattering a portrait of the privileged milieu he is gently satirizing.[31] But the other side of this "snobbery" imputation is nicely expressed by a reviewer who commented that in these works Stewart is after all only offering "an educated, subtle discourse for readers whom the writer is courteous enough to suppose as educated and subtle as himself" (*New Statesman*, 13 June 1975, p. 783).

That is a thought that seems a fitting introduction to the man himself. Professor Stewart today continues to lead the quiet, industrious life of the assiduous writer at his modest home outside Want-

age on the Berkshire Downs near the Vale of White Horse. It is the
dream locale that he and his wife had set their hearts on and which
twenty years ago Michael Innes enabled them to purchase (the re-
muneration and housing arrangements that Oxford makes available
for a married don being "most unassuming," as Stewart put it); and
it is a locale familiar from many Appleby adventures. Since his retirement in 1974, and especially since the death of his wife in 1979,
Stewart seldom ventures far from Fawler Copse, not even to his beloved Oxford. In fact, Stewart reports, on a recent visit to Oxford, he
actually had to reapply for admission to the Bodleian Library (where
all his books and many of his manuscripts are deposited), even to the
taking of the famous oath not to light a flame or deface a book! But
administrative procedures have always amused him, as *A Staircase in
Surrey* amply attests. Of late he has been living with his youngest son,
Angus, himself a novelist, the two spending their days together
writing—though they do not, they say, interact over each other's current projects.

Forty years ago Howard Haycraft, having corresponded with
Michael Innes in the course of writing *Murder for Pleasure*, described
his long-distance impressions of the writer from Australia as follows:
"Photographs of 'Michael Innes' show a pleasant, bespectacled, thirty-
ish young Scot, not unlike one's mental picture of Margery Allingham's
Albert Campion,"[32] and he adds that Innes seemed "overly-modest"
about his productions. Over the years the book jackets have continued
to present essentially the same image, latterly showing Stewart writing
in his garden or posed with his dogs (his dogs and country walking have
been his favorite recreations). In person he gives the impression of a
small, comfortably rumpled man exuding an air of great good nature,
quiet confidence and humor; he strikes one, above all, as enormously
polite and unassuming, his dignity sitting easily with a wit that carries a hint of the elvish. He very much conveys in conversation the sense
of being the same narrator one has listened to, or rather conversed
with, through those scores of novels and short stories that make up one
of this century's major achievements in the art of sustained conversation
as well as fiction. One is minded to borrow the words Madame de
Sévigné exclaimed over Montaigne (and with which Stewart concluded
his own first published essay): "Ah, Charming man! What good company he is!"

2

Enter Appleby:
The First Innes Mysteries
and the State of the Art

Death at the President's Lodging
Hamlet, Revenge!
Lament for a Maker

"John Appleby came into being during a sea voyage from Liverpool to Adelaide. Ocean travel was a leisured affair in those days, and the route by the Cape of Good Hope took six weeks to cover. By that time I had completed a novel called *Death at the President's Lodging*."[1] The year was 1934 and J. I. M. Stewart, a recent graduate in honors from Oriel College and lecturer for four years at the University of Leeds, was on his way to assume his post as professor of English Literature at Adelaide University in South Australia.

Although intended to be "lightly offered and lightly received," Innes's contribution to detective fiction has proven to be a monumental endeavor and accomplishment, comprising a literary career spanning half a century and some forty-seven volumes. From the first, Innes was recognized in virtually every quarter as an important new entry in the mystery-writing field, acclaimed as a writer of erudition, wit, and command of the grand style. Opinion over the years has ranged widely in reviews of the steady stream of novels from the Innes pen. Everyone will continue to agree that Innes is witty and erudite—in a word, donnish—and that as a prose stylist he simply has no peer among writers of detective fiction. But not every reviewer will be amused by Innes's bookish, humorous, and sometimes bizarre approach to the detective story; Ralph Partridge of the *New Statesman* seems to have been consistently disappointed and even offended by his manner, accusing Innes of not taking his plots, or his audience, seriously. And, whereas for James Sandoe Innes will too often become "the club bore," for Julian Symons he is consistently "the finest of the Farceurs."[2]

The fact is that the term "detective fiction" has come to encompass some very diverse categories or genres of popular literature — including the thriller, the hard-boiled detective story, and the police procedural, as well as the "classic" or formal detective novel of manners — each of which has its strong and sometimes intolerant adherents. It has become a commonplace to note that readers partial to the hard-boiled story seldom have a taste for the refined pleasures of the English country-house weekend sort of story, and vice versa.[3]

Michael Innes and Inspector Appleby made their appearance at a particularly critical and formative period in the history of detective fiction. The twenties and thirties have been considered by most historians of the genre as its "Golden Age," witnessing much of the best work of such practitioners as Chesterton, Knox, Crofts, Christie, and Sayers. Innes's first work appeared at that critical moment when Dorothy Sayers had laid aside her pen as a mistress of mystery to turn to religious drama, theology, and Dante. Sayers's signal accomplishment had been to make the attempt to unite detective fiction with the "great tradition" of the novel of manners. As Michael Holquist has convincingly argued in a recent article, the detective fiction of this "Golden Age" represented something more than an important source of popular entertainment or a fashionable diversion for bishops, statesmen, and intellectuals. Holquist believes that it was literate detective fiction that helped keep alive the traditions of social realism and straightforward plotting that had always been the hallmark of the "great tradition" of the English novel, at a time when the mythic and psychoanalytic predilections of modernism were becoming dominant influences in "high" art and literature. "The same people who spent their days with Joyce were reading Agatha Christie at night."[4]

To be sure, the detective story had not always been a bearer of the novelistic "great tradition" — indeed, the idea of the novelistic detective story was specifically owing in large part to Dorothy Sayers's approach, or rather, to her revival of the approach of Wilkie Collins. Her proposal to (re-)wed detective fiction to the novel of manners was thus quite innovative insofar as in the early decades of the twentieth century, detective fiction, after its impressive literary beginnings in Poe, Collins, and Conan Doyle, had settled rather discouragingly into one of two well-worn ruts: that of the formulaic puzzle story or that of the pulp/journalistic adventure story or "novel of sensation." In such works, especially in the puzzle story, there had been little scope for development of character, setting, or any of the other traditional literary concerns.

It is important to realize, as George Grella has recently shown,[5] that the idea of the detective story as a puzzle to be solved by the reader has not at all been the traditional or usual one in the history of detective fiction. True, the acknowledged progenitors of the form, Poe and Doyle, created archetypes of the "Great Detective" in Dupin and Holmes, embodiments of the scientific, ratiocinative mind as a power able to combat and overmatch the criminal mind. But while Holmes's amazing deductions are certainly the heart of Doyle's stories, it is clear that the reader's interest in them cannot be in competing with Holmes at arriving at solutions: the reader can only passively admire Holmes's interpretation of clues that we are merely told about as they are brought forward.

Once the novelty of the amazing deductions in the manner of Dupin and Holmes — deductions held up for the reader's passive admiration — had worn off, it was clear that detective fiction needed other resources to hold reader interest. One obvious recourse was to let the reader in on the challenge and invite him to compete with the Great Detective in the interpretation of evidence and the solution of the crime. Hence the advent of the true puzzle story, a form that flourished in the twenties and thirties and was propagated most notably in the work of Agatha Christie and Ellery Queen. In such stories the elaboration of the puzzle and the solution is the main business, indeed often the whole business, and a chief appeal was meant to be the challenge of working out the solution on the basis of clues, still largely physical, dutifully set forth by the author.

In the interests of the competitive challenge of puzzle solution, this type of detective novel went in for charts, diagrams, timetables, and other apparatus for the reader to work with. As Grella points out, however, there is little evidence or testimony to show that many readers actually bothered trying to work out solutions on the basis of this provision of "evidence."[6] Nor is it clear how likely it is that a reader *could* often plausibly arrive at the "correct solution," for amid all the planted clues and red herrings the author's revelation of the "correct solution" is usually arbitrary after all.

In the early thirties, then, detective fiction, having achieved tremendous popularity, had nonetheless exhausted the possibilities of the mere ratiocinative tale or puzzle story, as Sayers and others recognized.[7] From that point the genre evolved in essentially two quite divergent directions: that of the detective novel of manners (or formal British detective novel) and that of the hard-boiled detective story and police procedural. Looking back to the example of Wilkie Collins, Sayers saw the possibility of blending detective fiction and the novel of manners. Surveying the world of real crime and mean streets, and glancing back to Hammett, Chandler looked to give murder back to those who were really good at it and to those really good at combating it. Other than their common concern with the theme of murder and the shared vehicle of prose fiction, these two "schools" have rather little in common; certainly the specific conventions, the general ethos and the literary expectations generated by the two approaches are vastly different.

To consider the Chandler school first, what the hard-boiled detective story, the police procedural, and the related form called the thriller, share in common is a vision of the world of crime in a historically or sociologically realistic vein — at least their pretense is to present a down-to-earth and circumstantial realism. The hard-boiled detectives, even when they no longer embody the calm scientific rationality of Holmes, nevertheless share with Holmes their psychological hardness and mastery of feeling, their "empirical vision," their capacity for marshaling facts and seeing clearly and distinctly — as well as their status as amateur/outsider in relation to the law-enforcement establishment. And while the police procedural works *within* that establishment, the portrayal of the cops' dogged persistence and painstaking gathering and sifting of evidence and testimony is recognizably in the same tradition. Moreover, even these official members of the law-enforcement establishment are commonly shown as sufficiently alienated and "fed up" to qualify as outsiders in their own right (for instance, Beck, of the Sjöwell/Wahloo series).

The ancestry of these hard-boiled forms, with their "empirical vision" — Sergeant Friday's "Just the facts, Ma'am" attitude — clearly goes back not only to Holmes and Dupin but to the more realistic criminal investigative memoirs of Vidocq and the Bow Street Runners, to the matter-of-fact low-life prose of Defoe, and to the tradition of rogue literature and criminal narratives as well — for before the detective was hero, it was the criminal who was the protagonist of crime fiction. Herein one can locate the source of the strong anti-hero bent in this whole hard-boiled tradition.

More or less this same background is shared by the related form of the thriller, extending from Buchan's *Thirty-Nine Steps* (1915) through the oeuvre of Alfred Hitchcock, and the James Bond stories, to the contemporary revival of the novel of international intrigue and espionage. As Ralph Harper argues in his recent study of thriller fiction, theirs is an existential world,[8] a world that, if no longer dignifiable as tragic, is at any rate ironic. The characteristic situation in these works is to place the protagonist, a more or less ordinary person, in suddenly exciting and sinister situations, especially when familiar and seemingly normal surroundings themselves prove sinister. These works thus traffic more in suspense, vicarious excitement, and anxiety or dread than in the solution of puzzles — one might say that in them life itself proves to be the puzzle.

These three related forms — the hard-boiled story, the police procedural, and the thriller — belong essentially to the tragic and ironic modes of fiction. They share a common ethos that sets them dramatically apart from the formal detective novel of manners, which belongs essentially to the comic mode. In the hard-boiled forms, the reader is confronted with an open-ended universe threateningly intruded upon from every direction. Society and things in general are seen as fundamentally in disorder; it is, in short, a dirty-minded world of "mean streets."

Reviewers took notice of the divergence of the two "schools" or approaches represented by Hammett and Sayers. As Rupert Hart-Davis put it in his review of *Hamlet, Revenge!*, Innes's second novel, in 1931:

All are agreed that the detective story is in a dilemma. Almost every possible plot and murder-method is exhausted, the old, leisurely gun-and-fingerprint problem will no longer do (no one has left a fingerprint in a detective story for years, except occasionally a faked one). Whence cometh help? On the one hand stands the mighty Miss Sayers (whom God preserve) and her latest novels "not without detective interest"; on the other, the snappy, quick-fire school of Dashiell Hammett. In one of these directions the craft will

probably develop, and the second is surely preferable. The trouble about Miss Sayers' method is that nowadays it takes Miss Sayers
to carry it off.   (*Spectator*, 30 July, 1937, p. 214)

Hart-Davis concedes however, that writers such as Nicholas Blake,
Margery Allingham, and now Michael Innes could pull it off.

However, after a few full-fledged attempts at this more ambitious
approach to detective fiction, notably in *Lament for a Maker* and *Stop
Press*, Innes decided that it didn't really work, as he explains in his 1965
essay, "Death as a Game": "Here is the main obstacle to achieving
what, following Miss Sayers, I've had a shot at often enough: blending
the detective story with 'straight' fiction, so as to achieve a distinct kind
with some literary substance. It doesn't work. As soon as I start
caring — or even just exploring in a disinterested way — the thing goes
wrong." In other words, a detective novel cannot be allowed to take
on the sense of reality that informs "straight" fiction: "Nothing *real*
must be allowed in. Let your guilt and misery, for instance, be real
and you crack the mold of the form." If it is a question of serious crime
fiction, Innes argues, then that is properly the work of Aeschylus,
Shakespeare, or Dostoevski — not the Detection Club.[9]

This is a powerful piece of self-criticism, and challenges the critic
to discern the meaningful boundaries of detective fiction. And whether
or not one is inclined to accept Innes's modest confession of inadequacy
about the level of literary art of his productions, it is important to
recognize that the tradition out of which their mysteries grow is not
so much that of Poe, Vidocq, Defoe, and the Newgate Callendar as
that of Collins, Dickens, and Fielding, that is, the great masters of
comedy of manners.[10]

The world of Sayers's or of Innes's novels is as fundamentally different in ethos from the world of the hard-boiled detective or the police
procedural as the world of Fielding is different from the world of
Defoe. In the comic vision one has a fundamentally ordered, innocent
world, recognized (or at least remembered) as well and happy, and
now threatened by some intrusion of evil which, however ghastly or
malevolent the shadow it casts, is known to be but an aberration that
the detective will expel so that what Charles Williams called The City
could resume its work and play. It is the pattern, say, of Shakespeare's
Merchant of Venice; however critical the threat, however violent the
crime, the story remains one of the social organism cleansing itself and

returning to festivity and celebration. It is H. Marion Crawford, playing Watson in the 1950s televised serial, saying at the end of a case: "The villain has been apprehended, the young couple are safely back together, and here we are, eating cold lobster and tomatoes—I have a magnificent sense of well-being, Holmes!"

The manners tradition is comic too in the more specific sense that it is built upon social satire, the portrayal of what Fielding in his preface to *Joseph Andrews* called the ridiculous, through exposure of affectation, whether of vanity or hypocrisy (Fielding's formula is remarkably apropos in any discussion of Innes). And there is straight humor as well, even the joke—for as Panek points out, the puzzle itself is a form of joke, the presentation of a totally unlikely situation or concatenation of circumstances that yet has a solution (compare Johnson's definition of metaphysical wit as residing in just such *discordia concors*). The detective's enigmatic or mystifying summation of relevant clues often has precisely this jokelike quality (see *Stop Press*, p. 344).

Over the years Innes has taken the detective novel in several directions, including the thriller, but predominantly he took it in the direction Sayers had indicated: the novel of manners applied to the world of fantastic crime in traditional British settings. One who comes to Innes with expectations generated out of Raymond Chandler or the 87th Precinct will naturally have difficulty understanding and appreciating what he is about. Innes's novels should be approached not as the puzzles, whodunits, or procedurals they were never intended to be, but rather as detective novels of manners in the comic and pastoral modes, offering images of an English society remembered and idealized rather than observed.

Death at the President's Lodging, 1936 (alternate title: *Seven Suspects*)

"A society remembered," and remembered as much in terms of literary convention as of life, is exactly what one finds in Innes's first novel, which presents a magnificent caricature of the milieu of the English university. The volume (which in the United States was given the tame title *Seven Suspects*, lest there be any misassociation with the American presidency) is an extraordinarily complex puzzle story of the sealed-room variety, set in what had become one of the favored settings of British detective fiction: the university quadrangle. As with other traditional settings such as the vicarage or the country manor, the quadrangle is chosen because the physical structure of the English university is ideally suited to the machinations of such stories, *and* because it is initially unlikely that violent crime will occur in such a setting. The whole ethos of the life of the cloistered university — the quiet pursuit of not very relevant learning in a disinterested spirit — is presumably inimical to the emergence of rampant greed, or sexual passion, or vindictive malice. As Innes says of dons in his headnote to the novel, with tongue firmly in cheek: "They do nothing aberrant; they do nothing rashly or in haste. Their conventional associations are with learning, unworldliness, absence of mind, and endearing and always innocent foible" (p. 5). But of course part of the fun as well as the shock is the revelation that these things indeed do flourish there. Just as one "rule" of successful detective fiction involves the initial *un*likelihood of anyone's guilt, so the complementary "rule" concerns the gradual revelation that any number of these people — dons, clergymen, or gentry — are likely suspects indeed. Such is precisely the case — with a vengeance — here.

The situation is this. On a murky November night the body of Josiah Umpleby, president of St. Anthony's College, transparently modeled on Oxford, is found in his study in extraordinary circumstances. As the narrator says at the outset, "The crime was at once intriguing and bizarre, efficient and theatrical" (p. 7) — a formula encountered frequently in Innes. The alarm is given by the president's butler and Titlow, one of the fellows of the college. Titlow had arrived for a habitual 11 P.M. visit to the president and just as he was being admitted by the butler the two heard a shot from the study; rushing in they found the sprawled body of Umpleby, his head swathed in a black academic gown, and strewn about the body a skull and litter of human bones, and grinning skulls scrawled in chalk over the fireplace.

The reader is immediately confronted with a classic "sealed-room" mystery, as the local investigator Dodd explains to Scotland Yard's Inspector Appleby, in an explanation studded with references to the conventions of detective fiction:

"Dr. Umpleby was shot dead at eleven o'clock last night. That's the first of several things that make his death something like the story books. You know the murdered squire's house in the middle of the snowstorm? And all the fancy changes rung on that — liners on the ocean, submarines, balloons in the air, locked rooms with never a chimney? St. Anthony's or any other college, you see, is something like that from half-past nine every night. Here's your submarine." As he spoke, Dodd took up the ground-plan and ran a large finger round the perimeter of the St. Anthony's buildings. "But in this college," he went on, "there's more to it than that." This time his finger ran round a lesser circuit. "In this college there's submarine *within* submarine. At half-past nine they shut off the college as a whole from the world. And then later, at ten-fifteen, they shut off one bit of the college from the rest. That is almost a pure story-book situation now, isn't it?"

These self-conscious references to detective fiction serve not only to put the reader on notice that reader and author are expected to share an awareness of the literary tradition, but more importantly they serve the purpose of verisimilitude. Such references forestall the reader's own objection that this is all "story-book" material, and help generate a willing suspension of disbelief because of the confidence they impart that *this* is nevertheless no mere story.[12] Innes will prove to be especially adept at this sort of self-referential comment. There is a great deal of it, for instance, in *Stop Press*. It is called "*autodeixis*" in the language of current structuralist literary criticism, the sense in which the subject of a work of art is really itself.

At any rate, the submarine-within-submarine situation of the Orchard Ground (as the fellow's quadrangle is called) immediately creates the awkward suspicion that the murderer was actually one of the fellows of the college, specifically one of those fellows in possession of a key, a suspicion reinforced when it is learned that the gown swathing the president's head belonged to one fellow and the pile of bones came from the anthropology collection of another. At first this seems enormously implausible as well as embarrassing. The dean, a figure reminiscent of Matthew Arnold, tries to impress on Appleby that, nothing could be less likely than that a shy scholar could be responsible for such a crime — the very irrationality of the display of bones must be a sort of bulwark against suspicion, unless of course a deliberate plant or bluff.

No sooner is Appleby introduced to the fellows at high table and in common room, than it is evident that the college is rife with every manner of animosity and suspicion. In fact, as the investigation progresses, it begins to look as if *all* the dons might be implicated; as one bewildered elderly professor, who has seen indications of the guilt of half a dozen of his colleagues, puts it in a gloriously alliterative comment to Appleby: "It is really disconcerting, Mr. Appleby, for a retiring scholar to find himself incarcerated in a college court with a congeries of criminal lunatics. . . . And since then I have waited . . . for what was most plainly a horrid conspiracy to unmask itself" (p. 250). To which Appleby, although aware of the veracity of all the incriminating evidence, startlingly replies with confidence, "There was no conspiracy."

Appleby's solution of this first of his recorded cases is based on an elaborate computation of movements and times. The original publisher, Gollancz, supplied the reader with a fold-out plan of the college as an aid, but to really appreciate the ingenuity of the problem and the solution the reader virtually needs to construct his own time charts as well. But it is not, ultimately, computations and physical sleuthing, but rather psychology that proves to be the heart of the matter.

Appleby is at this point a young man, an inspector of CID, Scotland Yard. He is a fortuitous choice to be called upon in this case because Appleby in this novel is said to have himself graduated from St. Anthony's College some eight years before (p. 101–although the evidence as to Appleby's origins and education "becomes a shade confused in some later chronicles," as Innes admits in his 1978 essay on Appleby), so he is eminently suited to deal with these dons on their own terms. Thus, while not one of the "newfangled" sort of policemen recruited from some university criminal-justice program, Appleby does possess in this early chronicle "a fairly notable power of orderly analysis," although "later on he is hazardously given to flashes of intuition, and to picking up clues on the strength of his mysteriously acquired familiarity with recondite artistic and literary matters."[13]

In the novel itself, Appleby's character and methods are effectively established through a contrast with the local inspector, with the appropriately stolid Saxon name, Dodd. The latter is "heavy, slow, simply bred," representing an England "fundamentally rural still," in which crime, when it occurs, was clear and brutal, calling for vigorous physical action more than subtle analysis. "Beside him, Appleby's personality seemed at first thin, part effaced by some long discipline of study, like a surgeon whose individuality has concentrated itself within the channels of a unique operative technique. . . . Nevertheless, there was something more in Appleby than the intensely taught product of a modern police college. A contemplative habit and a tentative mind, poise as well as force, reserve rather than wariness — these were the tokens perhaps of some underlying, more liberal education. It was a schooled but still free intelligence that was finally formidable in Appleby, just as it was something of tradition and of the soil that was finally formidable in Dodd" (pp. 10–11).

Thus the two complement each other perfectly in the Umpleby affair. Whereas Appleby (admitting to some weakness for mystery stories) was "half-prepared to accept the artificial, the strikingly *fictive* as normal," Dodd's native shrewdness, fed by Bunyan and the Bible, led him at once to recognize the artificiality of the crime's circumstances. They leave room for seemingly endless speculation: do they represent a true Gothic sensation, or something for some reason made to look like a Gothic sensation? was someone criminally insane, or simply trying to frame someone else, or even trying to frame a frame-up against himself in order to incriminate yet someone else?

In this bizarre situation Appleby is the archetypally observant detective, but always in a quiet sort of way; his favorite technique is that of "sitting back and watching and listening" (p. 132), an activity in which the reader can comfortably join him. Most distinctive, of course, is Appleby's startling range of unpredictable learning of a scholarly sort. In a notorious passage, Appleby notices something wrong with the bookcase in the murdered don's study:

> Here was yet a third revolving bookcase — and Dodd found himself confronted by the fourteen bulky volumes of the Argentorati Athenaeus.
> "The *Deipnosophists*," Appleby was murmuring; "Schweighaüser's edition . . . takes up a lot of room . . . Dindorf's compacter — and there he is." He pointed to the corner of the lower shelf where the same enormous miscellany stood compressed into the three compact volumes of the Leipsic edition. Dodd, somewhat nonplussed before this classical abracadabra, growled suspiciously: "These last three are upside down — is that what you mean?"
> "Well, that's a point. How many books do you reckon in this room — eight or nine thousand, perhaps? Just see if you can spot any others upside down. It's not a way scholars often put away their books."   (pp. 39–40)

Thus Appleby proves admirably unintimidated by the scholar's library—though the reader may realize that the recognition that three volumes were upside down did not require this display of bibliographic pyrotechnics.

Nevertheless, Appleby's literary proclivities do lead him in relevant directions and eventually the clue that guides him to the heart of the mystery is a literary one: it is a reference by Professor Titlow to an anecdote about Kant in De Quincey's "Murder Considered as One of the Fine Arts." "You would find that interesting," Titlow says, "if only because it deals with an academic attitude to murder. And if you turned it upside down it might even be illuminating" (p. 101). The clue enables Appleby to crack the case, and for the reader not industrious enough to track down the reference, Innes has Titlow give an account of it near the end: "Kant maintained that in no conceivable circumstance could it be justifiable to lie—not even to mislead an intending murderer as to the whereabouts of his victim. Standing there over Umpleby's body I seemed to see quite a different imperative. If the cunning of a murderer could only be defeated by a lie, then a lie must be told—or acted" (pp. 256–57).

Thus the inversion of Kant's imperative provides the explanation for the incredible succession of scenes witnessed by old Professor Curtis: Haveland with the gun, Titlow dragging a body into the Orchard Ground, Pownall dumping a body into the study, and Empson, amid the body and bones, monkeying with the bookcase. *All* but one (the actual murderer), each acting independently *on the converse of Kant's imperative*, each having reason to believe that a different one of his colleagues was guilty of murdering the president, and each believing that colleague too fiendishly clever ever to be caught, *was engaged in planting incriminating evidence on the man he believed actually to be guilty*. Thus, beginning with the murderer's attempt to frame one of his colleagues, who in turn suspects another colleague and attempts to incriminate *him*, what is created is a neat hermeneutical circle of mutual incriminations.

Suffice to say that in this version of the locked-room puzzle story, complexity is the keynote. Not surprisingly, reviewers differed as to its effectiveness. Isaak Anderson in the *New York Times* felt that the story was so complicated "that it irritates more than it entertains," and that the behavior of the dons "suggests that they would be more at home in an institution for the mentally afflicted than in academic cloisters" (17 Jan. 1937, p. 6). That echoed Ralph Partridge's judgment in the *New Statesman* that "Mr. Innes seems to think that the only task of a detective author is to hide his criminal from the reader at all costs, no matter what outrages to human nature that obligation may involve. In consequence his story soon becomes sticky, and then unbelievable, unless St. Anthony's is really the pseudonym of a lunatic asylum and the dons are the star patients" (10 Oct. 1936, p. 520). On the other hand, the *TLS* considered the book "the most important contribution to detective literature that has appeared for some time" (26 Sept. 1936, p. 767), and Nicholas Blake (mystery pseudonym of poet C. Day-Lewis) called it "the most brilliant first novel I have had the luck to read. It is perhaps too complicated to become a classic in this *genre*. But Mr. Innes commands such a battery of wit, subtlety, learning and psychological penetration that he blows almost all opposition clean out of the water" (*Spectator*, 30 Oct. 1936, p. 770).

What may be missing in some of the negative reviewers' comments is an appreciation of the comic and satiric intent of the narrative: what matters is that Innes's pictures of the dons at table and in their quarters is so on the mark in terms of what one likes to *think* one knows of such people that their believability survives the gross incredibleness of their actual behavior. This effect of verisimilitude is heightened through the device of using one of the fellows, Giles Gott, as informal amateur assistant to Appleby. Gott, himself under suspicion for a time, is himself, it turns out, a writer (pseudonymously) of mysteries. His chats with Appleby are not only helpful to the inspector; more important, because his mind runs to even more fantastic and ingenious situations than the plot actually yields up, he helps establish by contrast the "reality" of Innes's story — much as the wooden eloquence of the Player King and Queen in *Hamlet* serves to contrast the mere fictiveness of their play with the "reality" of Shakespeare's play. It is a technique Innes will use again and again; in this case, the effect is redoubled, because in a farcical subplot, a trio of Gott's students come up with their own even more sensational theory and attempted solution.

Innes's satirical intent is nicely set out in a headnote to the novel which, as has been noted, begins: "The senior members of Oxford and Cambridge colleges are undoubtedly among the most moral and level-headed of men. They do nothing aberrant; they do nothing rashly or in haste. Their conventional associations are with learning, unworldliness, absence of mind, and endearing and always innocent foible."

After this outrageously ironic declamation, Innes goes on to say, rather more straightforwardly, "They are, as Ben Jonson would have said, persons such as comedy would choose; it is much easier to give them a shove into the humorous than a twist into the melodramatic; they prove peculiarly restive to the slightly rummy psychology that most detective-stories require."

This is a sufficient indication that what the novel, murder mystery though it is, really will traffic in is not mean streets and malice but rather, as Fielding called it in his preface to *Joseph Andrews*, the ridiculous — affectation and vanity. And as with any satire, one would not be amiss to look out for the moral vision tucked in amid the comedy. Indeed, the fun made of St. Anthony's really works only because the narrative presumes a belief in the bona fide academic ideal to begin with. There is a reflection of this ideal, for instance, in Professor Titlow's distressed monologue, suddenly pitched at Appleby, about the crumbling of the "transcendental idea," about the growing flux and chaos of the times, *das Üntergang des Abendlandes* — although as always in Innes, when somebody starts spouting references to the decline of the west the reader knows he is marked out as either a knave or a fool. And yet, pastiche that it is out of Spengler and Yeats, the speech does remind us of what the dons, and Appleby — and Dodd, too, for that matter — all set store by, and what the reader too, if the novel is to work, must be presumed to set store by as well. In one suddenly somber passage there is a glimpse of Appleby's deep convictions on this score:

> The darkness, the silence, pregnant somehow with the spirit of the place, had brought him momentarily a strange bitterness — bitterness that he had come to these courts he knew as an instrument of retributive justice. And that mood had been succeeded by anger. He remembered touching the cold carved stone of an archway and feeling a permanence: something here before our time began; here while our time, as Titlow was to paint it, moved fearfully and gigantically to its close; to be here in other times than ours. He remembered a significance that the light over Surrey archway, shining steadily amid the darkness and vapour, had taken on. And he remembered how he had sworn to drive out the intrusive alien thing.   (p. 130)

The imagery could be that of the darkly brooding *Beowulf* poet; the passage is a brief and privileged glimpse of the remembered ideal for which Appleby works, and of the moral vision that informs Innes's detective fiction.

Hamlet, Revenge!, 1937

Innes's first novel was enormously complex and clever and, for its type — the locked-room puzzle — highly literate and erudite. But with his second novel, *Hamlet, Revenge!*, he took an enormous leap forward in literary sophistication: setting, character, atmosphere, and plot are all far richer, far more novelistic than in *Death at the President's Lodging*. Many critics continue to regard it as among his very best. From the beginning the book was hailed with enthusiasm; the *Times Literary Supplement* averred that *"Hamlet, Revenge!* confirms the fact that became clear in his first book, that Mr. Michael Innes is in a class by himself among writers of detective fiction" (3 July 1937, p. 496). It was the sheer literateness of the novel that struck virtually every reviewer and prompted immediate comparisons with Sayers. As Ralph Partridge put it, "There is an aroma of Miss Dorothy L. Sayers about Mr. Innes which many will find agreeable. Powerful, fluent, well-educated prose almost condescending, as it were, to act as vehicle for detection — that is the force at Mr. Innes' disposal" (*New Statesman*, 7 August 1937, p. 225).

But *Hamlet, Revenge!* is a literate novel not only in being beautifully written and skillfully crafted, but also in that the setting, the murder, and the solution are all couched in specifically literary terms. To begin with, the story concerns the murder of Polonius. That is, during a performance of *Hamlet* the character playing Polonius is killed behind the arras — and as it turns out, Shakespeare's play proves to have a good deal to do with the crime and its solution. The *Saturday Review* quite justly concluded that this was "Possibly the most literary mystery ever dished up. . . . Capitally worked out, beautifully written, and erudite no end" (28 August 1937, p. 20). It turns out to be no Wimsey-like affectation when midway through the novel Inspector Appleby repairs to study "the document in the case" that proves to be none other than Shakespeare's play itself (p. 183). Indeed, it would be most helpful and add no end of enjoyment if the reader approaching *Hamlet, Revenge!* also were freshly to reread *Hamlet*. And, to tell the truth, it would not hurt if the reader were to brush up on the currents of Shakespeare criticism in the early twentieth century as well. Still, for one who approaches the novel without such academic preparation, there will be no impairment or obviation of the fun, for Innes provides the dutifully attentive reader with all he needs to know of that sort of thing. As the *Boston Transcript* pointed out, "The reader of *Hamlet, Revenge!* may acquire vast knowledge about the Elizabethan theater, the various editions of *Hamlet* and similar plays" (28 August 1937, p. 4). As Appleby and his amateur competitor, Professor Giles Gott — who makes his reappearance here from *Death at the President's Lodging* — work jointly toward a solution of the crime, it turns out that they are guided by two fundamentally conflicting interpretations of the play *Hamlet* itself.

The occasion for the mystery is the mounting of a private theatrical at Scamnum Court, seat of the Duke of Horton (a noble household, with a notable art collection, which will reappear in several Innes novels). It is to be a production of *Hamlet* staged by noted Elizabethan scholar Giles Gott; the principals will be the noble family themselves, and their friends and associates, joined by one professional actor, Melville Clay, who plays the part of Hamlet. In the old courtly manner, this is to be an entertainment *by*, not for, Scamnum Court. The duke and duchess will play Claudius and Gertrude, their niece Elizabeth will play Ophelia, and her brother Noel Gylby (a student of Gott's) will be Laertes; Lord Chancellor Auldearn, an old friend of the duchess, will play Polonius. Various other parts and stage jobs are taken on by the other guests: Gervase Crispin, a kinsman of the duke and a powerful industrialist, and his paramour, Madame Merkalova, a former ballet dancer; Professor Malloch, another Elizabethan scholar; Richard Nave, a London medical specialist; Dr. Bunney, an American philologist and nuisance, who is tape-recording the production, as well as samples of everyone's speech patterns. It is altogether a splendid mix of nobility and gentry, novelists and actors and artists, journalists and pedants — perfect ingredients for a true comedy of manners. "No conversations," said Julian Symons, "so recondite or so witty as those carried on by the guests at Scamnum Court."[14] Or, as the reviewer in the *Spectator* put it: "Rather a lot of talk, perhaps, but mostly good talk" (30 July 1937, p. 214).

Moreover, the setting for such a comedy of manners, soon to be suddenly plunged into malice and suspicion, is here perfectly realized. Scamnum Court is not only the isolated country house conventionally dictated by the mechanics of detective fiction, it is also a symbolically significant microcosm, a pastoral ideal world like the Belmont of *The Merchant of Venice*. Set amid "the subtle rhythms of English down-land," Scamnum Court, if not "the very stateliest of the stately homes of England," is nonetheless "a big place; two counties away it has a sort of little brother in Blenheim Palace." But far from any imposing vulgarity, such as that condemned in Pope's *Epistle to Burlington*, its eighteenth-century mixture of fantasy and restraint reveals

> the chastening severity of a classically-minded age. . . . For what is this ordered immensity, this dry regularity of pilaster and parterre, but an assertion in material terms of a prime moral truth of the eighteenth century: that the grandeur of life consists in wealth subdued by decorum? . . . Scamnum unguarded and unspoiled, a symbol of order, security and the rule of law over this sleeping country-side.   (pp. 11–13)

Later in the novel, after the murder of the lord chancellor, as Appleby prowls through the house in chiaroscuric moonlight, he apprehends its spaces "now composed into order and proportion, now a vague and raw material for the architectonics of the imagination . . . less a human dwelling than a dream-symbol of centuries of rule, a fantasy created from the tribute of ten thousand cottages long perished from the land" (pp. 122–23). And this setting, so carefully and particularly described, proves to be more than just atmosphere: it has a great deal to do with more than one possible line of solution.

The plot adheres closely to the unity of time as well as place; the action occurs during the days immediately preceding and following the production of the Scamnum *Hamlet*. The rehearsal days, dominated by the bustle of theatrical activity and lively literary conversation, are gradually but irresistibly plunged into an atmosphere of apprehension by a series of threatening messages, all drawn from Elizabethan texts. The first comes by way of a crumpled paper tossed into the car carrying Professor Gott and Lord Auldearn through the gates of Scamnum court, bearing apposite words from *Macbeth*:

> The raven himself is hoarser
> That croaks the fatal entrance of Duncan
> Under my battlements.   (I.v.38–40)

The second arrives by post, a scrap of typescript, this time quoting from *Titus Andronicus*, Shakespeare's bloodiest play:

And in their ears tell them my dreadful name,
Revenge, which makes the foul offender quake.   (V.ii.39–40)

The third message (actually the first one sent) came as a telegram to
Gervase Crispin, the industrialist; it consisted of just two words, "*Hamlet, revenge!*" This time, as Elizabethan scholar Gott notes, "There's
a little more than mere knowledge of Shakespeare involved." But Gott
is far from being the only one of the Scamnum gathering in possession
of sufficient learning to identify the reference. The senile painter Cope
immediately pipes up, "In fact, it's 'Puzzle find the oyster-wife' — eh?"

> "Cope means," Gott explained, "that Crispin's message, 'Hamlet,
> revenge,' is not — as you may remember — actually from Shake-
> speare's play. It was probably a line in an earlier play, now lost,
> and is quoted as a joke in Lodge's *Wits Miserie* in 1596: there is a
> reference there to a ghost that cried miserably in the theatre, like
> an oyster-wife, 'Hamlet, revenge.' It doesn't follow that our joker
> has any special erudition, but he does seem to have browsed about
> in an antiquarian way."   (p. 36)

And Melville Clay, at first puzzled by Cope's nattering about the
oyster-wife, adds eagerly, "Of course! I'd quite forgotten. And there
are other references too. It was quite a familiar quip."

This academic abracadabra in fact proves to be of the greatest
relevance to the mystery, for the fourth message (delivered startlingly
in a high falsetto by way of Dr. Bunney's recording device) is: "I will
not cry Hamlet, revenge." This at first seems to be nothing but absurd
mystification, but near the end of the novel Gott supplies the information that the reader, only with unwonted bibliographic industrious-
ness, might have retrieved:

> My mind failed to go at once to the source of this message. And with
> a sort of obstinacy with which Professor Malloch, perhaps, will sym-
> pathise, I avoided looking it up. I didn't see the matter as significant
> and I wasn't going to be beaten over something I certainly knew.
> Actually, the phrase *I will not cry Hamlet Revenge* comes from
> Rowland's *The Night Raven.*

In other words, the sender of the original "*Hamlet, Revenge!*" message
realized he had not thereby with sufficient exactness indicated the

source of his quotation — which apparently was of such importance that the emended message was sent.

Meanwhile, however, a fifth message is delivered, by means of a gramophone recording, set to play at alarming volume in the middle of the night, the ominous words of Macbeth:

> Come, seeling night,
> Scarf up the tender eye of pitiful day,
> And with thy bloody and invisible hand
> Cancel and tear to pieces that great bond
> Which keeps me pale! Light thickens. . . .   (III.ii.46–50)

at which point the gramophone is discovered and switched off.

Appleby remains baffled — the general intent of sending threatening messages might be clear enough, but why so many messages, some dramatically effective, others seemingly rather labored or even lame? He is reduced to trying to calculate times and movements to trace the provenance of the messages. As this laborious process is going forward, however, Gott pounces upon the solution, so dramatically that when, late in the proceedings, a sixth and last message is delivered (by telephone and, disconcertingly, just as the last remaining available suspect is being interrogated), Gott successfully identifies the message *before* its contents are reported to him. Presumably the reader of the novel (and of this account) should be able to predict the message too! It is the line from *Hamlet*: "The croaking raven doth bellow for revenge" (III.ii.254).

How could Gott know this? True, all the messages have dealt with the theme of revenge and all drew upon Elizabethan texts — but the clinching principle of association was provided by the emendation of the original "*Hamlet, revenge!*" message by the otherwise mystifying, "I will *not* cry Hamlet revenge," an amplification intended to pinpoint the source, Rowland's *The Raven*. For that is the connecting link: all the messages save the *Titus Andronicus* quote (which itself suggests that the messages contain a key to the name of the sender) involve references to a raven (the recording of *Macbeth* was switched off a moment too soon; if the reader consults the text he will find a reference to a "crow" and a "rooky wood" immediately following). And "raven" is recognized by Gott as the clue that enables the mystery to be solved — and that enabled him to predict the contents of the final, most apposite raven quote of all.

The murder, as noted, takes place during the actual performance of the Scamnum *Hamlet*. Gott has mounted the play in the Elizabethan manner: a thrust stage has been constructed at one end of the long gallery of Scamnum Court and it is staged so that scene follows hard upon scene on this relatively bare platform without any rigmarole of curtains and house lights impeding the flow of action. As a concession to modern endurance (the aged dowager in the front row sleeps through much of it as it is), one intermission is granted, following the second act. By this point, it had become clear that Gott and his mostly amateur actors were in the process of achieving a rare theatrical triumph: a bona fide recreation of what was, according to the (then) "new historical school" of Shakespeare criticism, the original Elizabethan conception of Hamlet. Not the supersensitive melancholic conceived by the romantics — the delicate vessel too fragile for its task envisioned by Goethe — but the more "muscular" Hamlet conceived as a Renaissance prince facing with tremendously concentrated energy a great predicament:

> It was a *Hamlet* in which, through all the intellectual and poetical elaboration of the piece, a steady emphasis was given to the basic situation of wary conflict between usurper and rightful heir. The sense of desperate issues, of wits matched against wits in a life-and-death struggle, was to be perpetually present. The battle of mighty opposites — one side the crafty king and his equally crafty minister Polonius; on the other the single figure of the more formidably because more intellectually cunning prince — this was to be the heart of the Scamnum *Hamlet*. . . . The meditative Hamlet was revealed as only a facet of the total man; the Queen and Ophelia were pushed back; the play showed itself as turning predominantly from first to last on Statecraft.   (p. 65)

In short, "Here, in fact, was the Hamlet of the historical school come rather terrifyingly to life" (p. 76).[15]

These pages of the novel will hold a special delight for the literary reader, independent of but not unconnected with the detective element proper. At any rate, the performance arrives eventually at Act III, scene iv, the famous "closet scene," in which Hamlet confronts his mother in her bedroom, on the main stage space, as Polonius slips behind the arras, into the curtained rear stage.

The altercation between Hamlet and the Queen grew. The
Queen's cry rang out:
"*Help, help, ho!*"
From the rear stage came the echoing voice of Polonius:
"*Help, help!*"   (p. 77)

But Polonius's cry departs from the exact text ("What, ho! help, help,
help!"), and indeed in the next second a shot is heard; a matter of
seconds later, Hamlet — Melville Clay — rushes through to the recess;
a split second before, the prompter has rushed in from the side, and
a few seconds later Gervase Crispin and the duke push in from backstage. What they find is Polonius — Lord Auldearn — shot dead at point-
blank range. From this moment on, events are kept tolerably in order,
first by the duke and then by the police. First of all the great hall is
sealed; secondly, the audience is kept sealed off from the players: once
or twice the duke comes forward with general announcements and to
speak privately to the dowager in the front row; once Giles Gott comes
down to speak to a fireman at the door; and once Clay drops down
from the thrust stage to speak quietly to the dowager; and that is all.
Only the butler, with his coffee urn, goes in or out.

Hamlet, Revenge! proves to be yet another classic sealed-room
mystery — and, as in the case of *Death at the President's Lodging*, there
is again a submarine-within-submarine situation. To begin with, the
great hall itself is sealed off from the rest of Scamnum Court, and then
the playing area at one end of the hall effectively divides the audience
from the players. Here is where Gott's faithful rendering of an
Elizabethan stage — the Fortune, as Professor Malloch observes, though
he himself he says, would have favored the Swan, despite the inac-
curacies of the famous De Witt drawing — comes into play. At one
point, in what proves to be a most instructive lecture on the subject,
Gott's pupil, Noel Gylby (nephew of the duke) explains the peculiarities
of Elizabethan theaters, which derive from their origin as platforms
in inn yards. There is the thrust stage, surrounded on three sides by
the audience, and with a trapdoor to the area beneath the stage; an
upper stage against the back wall, and below that a recessed area called
the rear stage, with a curtain hung in front of it, and with a trapdoor
connecting it with the upper stage above (Gott's rear stage is actually
a small rectangle enclosed by curtains, one in front and a double row
at back and sides, creating a narrow curtained corridor round three

sides); behind and to the sides, the backstage and dressing areas. The whole setup is uncommonly conducive to the machinations of detective fiction — as publisher Timothy Tucker remarks to Gott, with reference to the latter's pseudonymous efforts in that direction (and to certain subliterary currents in that genre):

> But what strikes me is this. Here's a perfect material setting for a mystery: upper stage, rear stage, trap-doors and what not. Why not write it up, Gott, and we could issue it with a cut-out model of the whole thing — Banqueting Hall, Elizabethan stage, corpse and all? Toy-shops have the kind of thing: "Fold along the dotted line," you know. I dare say we could run to coloured cardboard and a bright scrap of curtain. Everybody would set up his own model and study the mystery from that.   (p. 54)

Of physical clues there are almost none: a heavy iron cross is found toppled near the body; the gun — without fingerprints — is found thrust into Yorick's skull; and a sensitive document carried by Lord Auldearn is discovered exactly where Auldearn, using the purloined letter principle, has concealed it: in his hand, doubling as a prop, the scroll carried by Polonius.

Once the police work of sorting out times and movements has been accomplished, the dimensions of the mystery are made clear. At the time of the shooting, Polonius was alone in the rear stage; out in front on the thrust stage were Hamlet (Clay) and Gertrude (the duchess). The other players were, of course, backstage and able to account for one another adequately, with a few exceptions. Above, on the upper stage, old Maxwell Cope was working on his painting of the Scamnum *Hamlet*. Off to the side but with a view of front and rear stage was the Hindu, Mr. Bose, the prompter. Two of the principles, Gervase Crispin and Madame Merkalova, had each gone off down one side of the little curtained corridor on either side of the rear stage to watch the action or what Mr. Bose refers to as "the suffering." Barring the matter of conspiracy, the suspects would seem to be confined to that small group — any one of whom, alternatively, might have been a witness to the murder.

One of them apparently has been — for the next day the body of the young Indian, Bose, is thrown across a threshold virtually under the nose of Inspector Appleby, and in the ensuing hours enough other

suspicious circumstances, old quarrels, and rampant jealousies surface
to throw almost everyone under the mantle of suspicion.

The immediate question, however, remains: why was Lord Auldearn killed and why in just this way — so dramatically and hazardously and in the context of a series of threatening messages? Two
motives suggest themselves: first, because of who he is and because of
the sensitive document he carries, Lord Auldearn may have been killed
for reasons of espionage; alternatively, and especially because of the
dramatic circumstances, he may have been killed as a matter of some
private, passionate concern. Certainly the former alternative seems incompatible with the dramatic and hazardous nature of the crime, and
in their friendly competitive sleuthing, Professor Gott naturally plumps
for the passional interpretation, while Appleby — operating under strictures emanating directly from the prime minister — must keep his eye
out for the national security angle.

From the beginning Gott believes "The shooting has to do with
the play. It's been thought out in the context of the play" (p. 108). And
in support of this Gott is able to suggest an ingenious practical reason
for the murderer's selection of the moment to shoot Auldearn: perhaps
Auldearn, having already lain down behind the arras preparatory to
being discovered stabbed, was actually shot from *above*, through the
trapdoor to the upper stage — but leaving the suggestion that he had
been shot from in front while still standing!

At any rate, Appleby, as well as Gott, returns again and again
to *Hamlet* itself for clues. Was the crime "the working of a mind
theatrically obsessed; a mind outlandishly absorbed, over and above
any practical motive for murder, in the contriving of an astonishing
effect . . . within the framework of the Scamnum *Hamlet* [?] And that
framework had been itself more simply melodramatic, apparently,
than modern *Hamlets* commonly are. The show of violence . . . and
then a show of violence within the show" (pp. 169–70)? Moreover, as
Appleby verifies, whenever anyone is asked to comment on *Hamlet*,
the point of departure and foremost association is always the theme
of revenge — *delayed revenge*. As Professor Malloch sums it up, Hamlet's motives may be described variously as the punishment of fratri-
cide, incest, or usurpation, but in character "it is a procrastina-
ted revenge. That is what has always been debated about *Hamlet*:
why the delay?" (p. 238). Is the manner of murder therefore a statement of some sort, at least in the murderer's own mind, of a delayed

revenge at last accomplished — or is it merely *contrived* to suggest just that?

Between these conflicting possibilities Appleby vacillates: compared to the local officer, determined to push ahead and get somewhere, Appleby, "very still and absorbed, seemed a personification of wary doubt" (p. 220). It is the type of mind familiar to Gott, but in other and less criminous contexts: "a lingering and speculative mind — a mind of which the true territory lay, possibly, elsewhere" (p. 215). But it is precisely in Appleby's scholarly intuitiveness that lies his strength as an investigator. One intuition that nags him throughout the investigation is that he is continually distracted — haunted — by the memory of the ballet he has attended just prior to being called onto the case, a performance of *Les Présages*: "what delighted him most in *Les Présages* was something essentially dramatic, the entrance of Fate. . . . On the great stage the common traffic of life was proceeding with an even, untroubled rhythm — and then Fate was *there*, his entrance unnoticed, his menace waiting to strike home" (p. 80).

Irrelevant as all that seems, it nonetheless becomes one of the threads that leads Giles Gott to his ingenious reconstruction of the crime and results in the arrest of Dr. Richard Nave. Gott's elucidation of his solution is a brilliant piece of sustained explication. It begins with his decipherment of the threatening messages: all had to do with rooks or ravens, the latter image pinpointed by the emended message, "I will *not* cry Hamlet revenge," from Rowland's *The Raven*. Gott, in short, recognizes that "raven" is simply an anagram for R. Nave; the messages are a signature to a crime of revenge. Second, there is Gott's emended explanation of the *structural* reason for the murder's occurrence at just the moment it did: not that Auldearn is prone, but that at that precise moment in the play the avenger — like the figure of Fate in *Les Présages* — is able to appear dramatically before his victim in the rear stage just as Polonius is *scheduled* to cry out for help! It is a fiendish stroke, giving the avenger a few seconds of utter triumph over his helpless victim.

One thing, however, has seemed fundamentally wrong with the crime according to Gott's dramatic sense of the thing. Why was Auldearn *shot* rather than stabbed, which would have allowed Polonius actually to be found appropriately slain behind the arras? Gott's explanation of this snag, and his related account of the *motive* of the crime, are his tour de force. These men had no personal quarrel between them; what mattered, explains Gott, was symbolism. To the rationalist and convinced atheist Nave, Auldearn, along with Scamnum Court, stood for everything reactionary, complacent, and establishmentarian. For this was a crime of *ideological* passion. As for the snag—Nave's original intent probably *was* to stab Auldearn, but the presence of the heavy iron cross as a prop gave him the idea of braining Auldearn with the very symbol of his superstition. But, suggests Gott, at the moment of raising the cross, *Nave discovered that Auldearn had Paget's disease*, an abnormal thickening of the skull, and so had to settle in a split-second change of plan for shooting him instead. . . !

So ends the "dénouement" section of the novel.

It must be confessed that Gott's interpretation is incorrect; as the reader must have guessed, the foregoing is all, of course, utter nonsense, a product of Giles Gott's wonderfully prolific imagination. All, that is, except for the brilliant elucidation of the structural reason governing the moment of the murder, and his decipherment of the anagram in the messages as a reference to Nave. But that, as Appleby realizes, was simply a plant concocted by the real murderer, whose identity appears only in the "epilogue" of the novel. The murder turns out to have been rather straightforwardly planned (with one hitch, which necessitated the murder of the prompter, Bose); the motive was the theft of Auldearn's secret document — statecraft after all — but the murderer did not need to steal the actual physical document at all and had only to read it quietly into Bunney's recording machine at the front of the stage, while pretending to speak to the aged dowager in her front seat after the murder, while she was, as usual, dozing!

If the solution, sketched here only in a very vague way, is somewhat anticlimactic, especially after the fireworks of Gott's spectacular theory, that may be made up for by a sudden change of pace as the final pages of the novel transform themselves into a gripping chase sequence. In the finale, Elizabeth, the young woman being courted by the shy Professor Gott, finds herself trapped at night by the murderer, with no apparent exit, in a garden corridor bounded by high, impenetrable hedges and a sequence of classical statuary on pedestals on either side of her. But as suddenly as Fate in *Les Présages is* there, so just as suddenly she is *not* there. Immediately the baffled murderer is apprehended in the garden, at the foot of a statue of Aphrodite, and as the dust settles

Again there was silence. And then the statue spoke from the darkness. "I should like to get dressed now," it said firmly.
Everyone jumped. Noel exclaimed, "Who on earth—"
"The Pandemian Venus," said Elizabeth mildly from her
pedestal.   (p. 271)

The empty pedestal, that is, from which the statue of a naked
Aphrodite had been removed by the Victorian sensibilities of a previous
tenant!

Thus does Innes's story, once again, in the pattern that will continue to dominate his detective fiction, resolve itself into fantasy and
humor, a combination not to the taste of every afficionado of detective
stories. Within such a convention, however, *Hamlet, Revenge!* may
be seen as a particularly clever variation on the country-house and
sealed-room types of story, and Innes's use of the literary setting of a
production of *Hamlet*, particularly of a *Hamlet* conceived according
to the then new strictures of the "historical school" of interpretation,
may be seen as a stroke of genius. For anyone who at all relishes literary
talk, the dialogue will be a source of constant delight. Nor is this all
a matter of the rather frivolous business of "quotation-spotting," for
the Shakespearian setting and allusions are structurally integral to the
mystery. As Anthony Boucher noted, "Since *Hamlet* is based upon the
device of the play-within-a-play, what could be more fitting than to
let *Hamlet* itself serve here as the play-within?"[16] In fact, Innes's
novel is structured in such a way as even to suggest a parallel to classic
drama: it consists of the four parts—prologue, development, dénouement, and epilogue—that correspond to the traditional dramatic
structure.

Finally, as in *Death at the President's Lodging*, Giles Gott, bibli-
ographer and pseudonymous author of fantastic detective fictions, continues to serve as the perfect foil for Appleby: the recurrent talk about
Gott's fictions, and his own superimaginative constructions on the case,
serve only to heighten the verisimilitude of Innes's own plot—as the
artificiality of the play-within-a-play in *Hamlet* enhances the realism
of the main plot. In one conversation between Gott and another literary guest the Coleridgean distinction between imagination and fancy
is brought up; perhaps it might be said that Gott's fancies help us to
believe fictively in Innes's imaginings (though Innes himself humbly
foreswears any reaching after anything so exalted as "imaginative

truth"). Similarly, Gott's absurdly melodramatic hypothesis of Nave's ideological hatred driving him to murder the lord chancellor with an iron cross is only a burlesque of the moral sensibility momentarily revealed on Appleby's part — his quiet outrage at this violation of order at the heart of England. *Hamlet, Revenge!* remains a novel worth reading and rereading for its literary qualities alone, even apart from its very clever detection elements.

Lament for a Maker, 1938

As *Hamlet* and the revenge motif provided the literary key for *Hamlet, Revenge!*, so *Macbeth* and the fifteenth-century Scottish poem "Lament for the Makarys [poets]" provide the dark guilt-ridden and death-obsessed background of Innes's most Scottish and most deeply-hued tale, *Lament for a Maker*. This story of a crazed and hated Scottish laird who is found hurled to his death at the foot of his snowbound ancient tower on a Christmas morning, has laid claim to being Innes's masterpiece. Every afficionado naturally has his or her own favorite work of a writer for frankly subjective reasons, but Melvyn Barnes is justified in saying about this book that it "is generally recognized as his supreme achievement," adding his own assessment that "This must surely rank as one of the most beautifully written detective novels of all time."[17] Almost all the original reviewers were dazzled by the book's literary brilliance. Kay Irvin called it "such an original piece of grisly fascination as we may seek, perhaps, only from an inventive, scholarly, witty and poetic mind," adding that in this most dramatic of his works "haunting atmosphere and stirring events and vivid characters are presented . . . in prose which it is a pleasure to read" (*NYTBR*, 28 Aug. 1938, p. 17). And in the *Spectator* Nicholas Blake said that "Innes gives us in this, his best book, a situation compounded of Aeschylus and Drury Lane melodrama — and gets away with it" (17 June 1938, p. 1118).

It is of interest that many years after the book's original publication, Erik Routley, still almost the only historian of the genre to have offered any extended commentary on Innes, reiterates these early judgments:

> Despite the long run of excellent stories he has produced since, I still think this was the profoundest plot he ever constructed. In

many ways it achieved things which Innes never came near
again. . . . The sheer beauty of the long narratives of Ewan Bell,
in faultless Scottish prose, the powerful evocation of the presbyte-
rian grimness of a Scottish castle, the quite distinguished communication of the narrator's integrity and moral agony, are all at a level
which the author doesn't seem to have wanted or tried to repeat.[18]

Indeed, it is precisely true that Innes did not seem to want or try
to repeat such an effort. Already noted are his comments in his 1965
"Death as a Game" essay to the effect that in his opinion the attempt
to combine the qualities of straight or serious fiction — work, that is,
in which one really *cares* about the characters — with the manipulations
required by detective fiction just doesn't work.

Whether it can work as a general principle or not, is beside the
point, but *Lament for a Maker* is clearly Innes's major effort in this
direction; it stands as something like his equivalent to Sayers's *The Nine
Tailors* in literary artistry and moral seriousness — without abandon-
ing his characteristic note of humor and touch of the fantastic. *Lament
for a Maker* has all the elements of a Gothic mood piece; in addition
to the heavily Scottish atmosphere of the laird's castle, reinforced by
the running literary allusions to *Macbeth* and Dunbar's medieval elegy,
"Lament for the Makarys," there is a powerful passionate subplot of
romance in the manner of *Wuthering Heights*. Altogether it is a highly
colored and richly textured story.

The first thing to be noticed about this novel is Innes's use of the
old device of multiple narrators borrowed from eighteenth- and nineteenth-century fiction and here specifically a tribute to Collins's *The
Moonstone*. The first of the narrators (who reappears briefly to provide
the conclusion), a village cobbler named Ewan Bell, establishes immediately the rich atmosphere of the book. Written in a fluent broad-
Scots dialect, and sustained for some eighty pages, Bell's narrative is a
brilliant stylistic tour de force. Right off, Ewan Bell tells about the
reported suicide of Ranald Guthrie, found dead at the foot of his tower
on a Christmas morning. The cobbler, who reveals himself as a man
at once traditional and liberal, and possessed of the driest wit and
wryest humor, gives us a rounded picture of the life and characters
of the Lowland village of Kinkeig, but focuses, of course, on the
enigmatic figure of the eccentric laird of Castle Erchany, Ranald
Guthrie.

From the time he returned to Scotland from Australia in 1894, as a young man and sole heir of Castle Erchany — having left behind a deceased older brother — Guthrie has lived as a radical recluse, and in so miserly a fashion that "Of all the dwellers in the glens about it was only of Ranald Guthrie you could honestly say that he was as mean as an Englishman" (p. 7). In fact, he was so near-going that he stalked his own and his tenants' fields checking the pockets of scarecrows for loose change, as Ewan Bell tells in more colorful dialect:

> Well, all Kinkeig knew how Guthrie was fair haunted by the bogles in the fields round about; fair haunted, that is, by the thought some feckless chiel might have left a bittock silver in the pooches when breeching and jacketing the sticks. An unco sight it was to see the laird striding his own parks from bogle to bogle, groping ghoul-like among the old clouts for those unlikely halfpennies.   (p. 14)

Much of the castle Guthrie has simply nailed shut, living alone in the drafty remainder, except for a ward, presumably his niece, and attended only by a single housemaid, a halfwit stable boy, and a villainous factotum. Over the years Guthrie has evicted most of his tenants and in general has acquired such an evil reputation among his neighbors that "indeed the opinion grew from that time in Kinkeig that Lucifer himself was enthroned at Castle Erchany" (p. 19). To our narrator, Ewan Bell, however, what Guthrie reveals is a tormented soul: "If you'd held the book of human nature long open before you you could see that he was the kind that is driven and tormented by some deep and single thing" (p. 18).

The other significant development in the Guthrie household concerns his ward, Christine. Brought up in the isolation of Erchany Castle, Bell says, "as she grew again and her maidenhood came to her and she saw the strangeness of her life, a Miranda islanded with a black-thoughted Prospero, she became a secret maid, and with a growing sorrowfulness, too, deep at the heart of her" (p. 55). But one midsummer day, on Ben Cailie, this Miranda has her first glimpse of a brave new world in the crofter lad, Neil Lindsay. She first sees him as he stands, unmoving, absorbed by a great outcrop of rock, "until his hand moved — sensitively, Christine knew with a knowledge that strangely moved her — over the weathered surface" (p. 61). She slips and falls, he raises her up and talks to her, "and talking so, eager and wary, as

if he would turn that sensitive and exploring touch he had from the
hard granite to the very contours of her mind" (pp. 62–3). Bell concludes his retelling of her story with words as definite as Guthrie's nail-
ing up of his gallery: "From that moment it was all over with Christine.
. . . When I asked her — perhaps in foolish words enough — 'And you
really want to marry him, Christine?' she looked at me almost mock-
ingly for a moment and just said 'I'm driven'" (pp. 63, 64).

And so it is that Neil Lindsay has become Christine's betrothed,
but because Guthrie, out of ancient bad blood between the families
and his own inflexible pride, has indignantly rejected the suit, the two
lovers must plan to elope.

Things stand so until one snowy winter day when Guthrie suddenly gives the curt order, "Open the house." He orders in stores of
provisions, even — unheard of — items of luxury and, oddest of all, a
collection of medical texts. As the climax of this activity, Guthrie axes
in the door of the gallery he nailed shut on his return from Australia
forty years before. The great door was sealed ostensibly to economize,
but so powerfully and deeply were the nails driven that "here surely
was some other passion, forty years past or forty years hidden, that
had yet left record of itself like a sculptor's passion, deep bitten into
the dark oak" (p. 25). And now he rampages before that door, "as it
might have been Satan raging before the portals warded by Sin and
Death," hacking at it "as a man might try to hack his way out of a
burning cottage." Innes gives an epic grandeur to the scene, heightened
by the Miltonic allusion and the powerful implied analogy between
the great oaken door — marked as though by a sculptor's passion — and
the ravaged soul of Guthrie himself.

In this newly, and violently, opened gallery Guthrie stalks by
night in a great passion and, seemingly, some fit of apprehension; he
glowers fearfully over a standing globe, muttering, "He will! It's in
the blood, and by the Great God he will!" To the servants, "it was right
fearsome to think there was something the laird himself was feared of"
(p. 30). Finally, as his housemaid reports, each night he paces the gallery
chanting verses "with a queer run of Scottish names to them and then
ever a bit of gibberish" — verses that prove to be from Dunbar's "Lament for the Makarys," his lament for all the brother poets death has
taken, each stanza ending with the Latin refrain, "*Timor mortis con-
turbat me.*"

Thus the situation stands, except for the coincidental arrival, on

the day before Christmas Eve, of an American cousin of the Guthrie
family and of an Oxford undergraduate (Noel Gylby, in fact, of
Hamlet, Revenge!) who has gotten lost in the snowstorm. Both are
forced to put up at Erchany Castle and thus are present on the fateful
night when Neil and Christine confront Guthrie and elope. The next
morning — Christmas morning — Guthrie's room is found ransacked,
his gold stolen, and he himself is discovered dead at the foot of his
tower.

The events of that night and of the subsequent days of investigation are told by a succession of other narrators: Noel Gylby, who keeps
an urgent, Pamela-like journal; Aljo Wedderburn, an attorney (Writer
to the Signet, to give him his proper Scottish title) appointed to represent Sybil, the American cousin; and Inspector Appleby himself — the
only time, outside of some short stories, where he serves as narrator.
The device of successive narrators, of course, allows for heightened
dramatization, especially in Noel's hour-by-hour journal, and for the
emergence of plausible but inevitably partial interpretations of events.
The popular version of events, as Wedderburn reports, is a full-fledged
Senecan Drama: "revenge, murder, mutilations and a ghost." For the
villagers' understanding is that Neil Lindsay has consummated the old
family feud by hurling Guthrie from his tower, stealing his gold and
his niece (or daughter, or mistress, as local rumor variously has it and
which, as rumor further would have it, are not "mutually exclusive
propositions") — and for good measure chopping off his fingers in requital for a comparable deed perpetrated by a Guthrie ancestor on a
Lindsay. (Actually the corpse shows no such mutilation, but several
villagers have reported seeing the ghost of Ranald Guthrie since the
murder, raising his mutilated hand to the moon.)

The chief witness to the fatal events of that night, Sybil Guthrie,
indeed saw — as she reluctantly admits — Guthrie lash Neil Lindsay into
a fury during their midnight confrontation in the tower, and a few
moments later saw Guthrie pushed from the battlements, although in
the darkness she could not really identify the assailant. Wedderburn,
however, is able to relieve those who fear for Neil Lindsay's guilt by
showing that Neil could not have been the one to push Guthrie: wit-
nesses saw the body fall just as Neil was seen coming down the tower
stairs. Therefore, he concludes, the whole thing must have been a case
of suicide by Guthrie, but contriving to make it *look* as though Lindsay
murdered him, stole his gold, and eloped with his niece. Thus Wedder-

burn seems to build an unshakable case elucidating that "rarest of human achievements, a truly diabolical crime" (p. 202).

But when the next narrator, Inspector Appleby, enters the case, he reopens the entire mystery. It was the niece, Christine, herself — although she must have been overwhelmingly relieved at the construction Wedderburn has been able to put upon events — who raised a subjective but wholly persuasive doubt: it was that her uncle, malevolent as he was, had a "finer mind" than to plan something so psychologically unconvincing as to make it look as though Neil Lindsay had not only killed him and eloped with her but had stolen his gold as well. That would be an entirely false note — and Appleby agrees.

Then, in a perfectly timed apparent non sequitur to all that has gone before, Appleby pronounces that the decisive clue is an enigmatic inscription on the flyleaf of one of the medical reference books Guthrie has recently acquired, a text by a Dr. Flinders of Australia; the inscription records that Flinders was born in 1893 (the year, remember, before Guthrie himself returned from Australia) — and received his medical degree just seven years later!

At this point, the reader might be inclined to agree with Wedderburn that this business of the inscription is all plain nonsense — but Appleby insists that, "On the contrary, it is the first glimpse of the truth" (p. 214). Along, that is, with the verses from Dunbar's "Lament for the Makarys" which had so obsessed Guthrie:

> Sen he has all my brether tane,
> He will nocht let me lif alane;
> Of force I mon his nyxt prey be;
> *Timor Mortis conturbat me.*
>
> Sen for the deth remeid is non,
> Best is that we for deth dispone
> After our deth that lif may we;
> *Timor Mortis conturbat me.*

As Appleby explains, in Guthrie's ironic and morbid interpretation, Dunbar's lament for his dead brother poets and consequent fear of death became for Guthrie a gripping fear of the brother he treacherously left for dead in Australia forty years before.

Of course, Ranald's brother Ian did not actually die; to the contrary, he has just made the visit to Castle Erchany so obviously dreaded by Ranald Guthrie.

At this point in the narrative, Ian's diary makes a fortuitous and dramatic appearance (through a *mus ex machina* — it's brought by a rat as a matter of fact), which gives us Ian's story, right up through the fateful night of December 24, the final entry written as Ian, imprisoned in the tower, waits for Ranald to kill him. The diary is a brilliant piece of thriller narration, full of authentic local color and detail, and told in Australian dialect. In it, Ian relates the melodramatic tale of his abandonment by Ranald in the Australian bush, his awakening in a state of total amnesia, his incredible survival trek through the outback and eventual rescue, and how he acquired the identity of one Richard Flinders — who is thus "born" in 1893, gets his degree seven years later, and goes on to become a surgeon and renowned medical researcher. Eventually Flinders recovered his memory and his identity as Ian Guthrie (triggered by a skirl of bagpipes heard one afternoon), upon which he announced his return to Erchany with some idea of making straight the old issue between himself and his brother. But there Ian committed a gross error in psychology: he intended to do no more than shock Ranald and, in a sort of reversal of the situation in *The Tempest*, bring about by his sudden arrival the reformation of his brother. What he failed to apprehend is that Ranald is the one who has the driving need to avenge *him*self on Ian — for a life of guilt and shame; moreover, Ranald cannot forgive his older brother for having achieved a life of success and social benefaction, in spite of losing every advantage of his heredity and even identity, whereas Ranald, with all these advantages, has achieved nothing. Ranald's crime is truly that of Cain, but with an especially diabolical twist: *Ranald Guthrie's crime was the murder of his brother Ian, but contrived to look like the murder of Ranald himself by Neil Lindsay!* (The theft of the gold, which seemed such a false note to Christine, simply turns out to be some dirty work on the side by Ranald's evil factotum.)

Appleby commands some impressive psychology in this analysis, even to seeing the ultimate satisfaction in this situation of the pathological miser's desire: in bringing off the murder of Ian as his own murder at the hands of the hated Lindsay, and subsequently living as Ian in retirement, Ranald Guthrie would be enjoying the fruits not only of his brother's pension, but his brother's reputation as well.

Actually, there are a number of startling turns of plot still to come in the final thirty or forty pages of the novel, as the narrative is picked up again by Appleby and a conclusion supplied by Ewan Bell. The matter of the ghost with the mutilated hand comes in again — and it proves to be a most palpable ghost; the taciturn local minister has a shocking bit of family history to relate; the true character of Neil Lindsay is revealed in a final tragic gesture; and when it's all over, the reader understands why John Appleby lets the real murderer go, aptly enough, scot free.

These final twists and turns can be left to the reader's own delectation. It is enough to reiterate that in this novel it is true, as several reviewers averred, that, magnificently written as it is, the extreme richness of characterization and atmosphere, the romantic *Wuthering Heights* subplot and the stylistic brilliance all rather overwhelm the detective interest, to the point that the latter may even be said to be frivolously handled. *Lament for a Maker* remains a strange, perhaps unique combination of entirely artistic storytelling — featuring one narrator (Ewan Bell) full of "integrity and moral agony"[19] and another (Ian Guthrie/Richard Flinders) whose story is full of the pathos of a failure to comprehend the depths of another's moral degeneration — with almost farcical melodrama featuring Learned Rats who scurry about with notes and diaries.

Thus one comes back to Innes's own assessment that the blending of the detective story with "straight" fiction "doesn't work," and asks whether he regarded his own *Lament for a Maker* as a case in point. Certainly, as Erik Routley observed, he never tried anything quite like it again. That is, anything like it in literary artistry and moral seriousness, because certainly he used many of the same plot ideas again, most notably in *The New Sonia Wayward* (1960) and *The "Gay Phoenix"* (1976) — the latter, in particular, is almost like a simplified, "popularized" version of *Lament for a Maker* for those readers for whom the Scottish novel is just too daunting. One may reserve judgment on the question of whether the detective novel can work as serious art, while at this point simply registering whole-hearted agreement with Routley that there must be many readers who, however long ago they first read *Lament for a Maker*, "have found it impossible to forget."[20]

3

The Chased Hero:
The Innes Thrillers

Flight-and-Pursuit Stories
The Journeying Boy
Thriller-Fantasias
Impersonation Tales

G. K. Chesterton once said in defense of detective fiction that it was "the only form of popular literature in which is expressed some sense of the poetry of modern life," by which he meant especially the atmosphere of the modern city,[1] and Jacques Barzun paid tribute to the contribution of detective fiction to our "understanding . . . of the silent life of things," an understanding in which "objects . . . are taken literally and seriously. They are scanned for what they imply, studied as signs of past action and dark purpose. This search for history in things is anything but trivial. It reflects the way our civilization thinks about law and evidence, nature and knowledge."[2] Chesterton and Barzun are speaking of the traditional detective novel and not the thriller, but in calling attention to the objectivism of the detective story, they are leading to a central point about the thriller as well.

Alain Robbe-Grillet argues that life itself is structured very like a detective story and that, modernist fiction having failed to come to terms with objective reality, it has remained for writers of detective fiction and the postmodernist innovators of the *nouveau roman* to do justice to that reality. In a typical detective story, he says, the reader

encounters exhibits and evidence, varying interpretations, contradic-
tory testimony, explanations and alibis — and so

> you have to keep coming back to the recorded evidence: the exact
> position of a piece of furniture . . . a word written in a message.
> The impression grows on you that nothing else is true. Whether they
> conceal or reveal a mystery these elements that defy all systems have
> only one serious, obvious quality — that of being there. And that
> is how it is with the world around us.[3]

A striking instance of Innes's own cognizance of this point —
conveyed in a typically wry and bemused way — occurs in the country-
house story *Death at the Chase* (1970). Young Bobby Appleby is a
prime witness to an enigmatic murder. At this point in his career Bobby
has aspirations as a budding antinovelist; what he goes in for is the *anti-
roman* school, *la nouvelle écriture*. During a conversation early in the
novel with his wife Judith, Sir John Appleby reports that his son "hasn't
given up hope of educating me" along these lines:

> Appleby picked up a book. "I've been told to read this, by a chap
> called Alain Robbe-Grillet. It's described as a novel, but a great
> deal of it seems to be just describing a house. The first paragraph
> is about a veranda. Listen. *Since its width is the same for the central
> portion as for the sides, the line of shadow cast by the column ex-
> tends precisely to the corner of the house; but it stops there, for only
> the veranda flagstones are reached by the sun. . . . At this moment
> the shadow of the outer edge of the roof coincides exactly with the
> right angle formed by the terrace and the two vertical surfaces of
> the corner of the house."* Appleby put down the book. "Odd, don't
> you think?"
> "It ought to appeal to you. It's by rather an observing kind of
> person." (p. 45)

Later on Bobby airs his own "professional reflections of this
nouvelle écriture" as he drives with two friends on what he regards
as a useless errand:

> They were off on a futile and absurd trip — he told himself as he
> drove out of the yard — but one wouldn't in so many words say so.
> What one would feed through one's typewriter would be not the

object in view, or even the thoughts and feelings of his two companions and himself. Only what was tangible and visible must be
treated as relevant. And perhaps what one could smell as
well. . . . But the main thing was the movement of the wheel
which set a faint light from the instrument panel caressing its two
spokes; this, and the quivering needles, and the perplexing flicker
near the accelerator which was in fact moonlight coming in over
his left shoulder, and his own two knees and his gloved hands.
(pp. 82–83)

Actually, both these apparently irrelevant little literary digressions
prove to be a significant key to the solution of the crime in *Death at
the Chase*. The absurd errand of Bobby's reflections was a seemingly
ridiculous attempt by a friend to woo himself into favor with an
estranged and eccentric but very wealthy relative to further a romance
he cannot afford. A midnight encounter with old Martyn Ashmore
seems to come off well enough — but suddenly it is learned that the old
man has himself become engaged to the young woman in question —
Robina Bunker. The next morning the rich uncle is found murdered,
lying in the cold ashes of his fireplace.

There seems to be no clue as to who could have perpetrated the
murder until Robbe-Grillet and "the silent life of things" come into
play. Appleby calls upon Bobby, in the latter's character as a novelist,
to think back upon the circumstances of that midnight encounter, to
use that discipline: "Get the tangible and visible universe right, and
everything else will shine through" (p. 169). And indeed it works, this
adult version of Kim's Game (the children's party game in which you
are shown a tray of objects for thirty seconds and then try to recall their
identity and disposition); Bobby does remember one discordant detail:
a bit of electric cord in the fireplace. In other words, there never was
a *real* fire in Ashmore's hearth, only an electric fire. The "evidence"
that the body was found lying in ashes and was therefore murdered
hours later was completely misleading: Ashmore was in fact killed only
a few moments after the midnight interview. A Robbe-Grilletian
solution — but in a way it is the paradigmatic detective story solution,
hinging upon the accurate perception and recall of a revealing small
detail.

It is precisely that "objectivism," the sense that "things are there,"
their surface "smooth, clear and intact," that drew post-modernists like

Robbe-Grillet and Borges to detective fiction as a model.[4] Of course
Robbe-Grillet's and Borges's "hermeneutical tales" are actually inverted
or *anti*-detective novels, for in them — as in Kafka — everything remains
*un*resolved. Theirs is a world not of Father Brown or Appleby, but of
K. (in Kafka's *The Trial*) or Mersault. Unlike the formal detective
novel, in which a general innocence is reaffirmed, the guilt and anxiety
remain, we all continue to feel implicated.

In these respects, the postmodernist story is actually closer in spirit
to the disillusioned hard-boiled detective story or to the anxiety-ridden
thriller than to the formal detective novel of manners. For in the
thriller, especially, one encounters not only the detective story's objectivism but also a world full of confusion, suspicion, anxiety and
dread — which is why Ralph Harper is able to make such a convincing
case for the thriller as an existentialist literary form.[5]

Most critics of detective fiction have tended to draw a sharp distinction between the hard-boiled forms, especially the thriller, and the
formal detective novel. Auden says he rarely enjoys thrillers,[6] and
Barzun deplores what he calls "'stories of anxiety,' which cater for the
contemporary wish to feel vaguely disturbed," adding, "I do not question the pleasure derived from this sort of self-abuse. I merely decline
to call it superior to another pleasure which is totally different."[7]

The detective story is essentially analytical and hermeneutic, the
plot constructed around the process of investigation and the plausible
acquisition of knowledge by the detective. The detective hero himself
may or may not be deeply involved in the immediate action. The detective novel is usually marked by a distinctive "backwards plotting,"
that is, it concerns the correct reconstruction of the crime or, as Champigny puts it, "what will have happened."[8]

The thriller, on the other hand, is premised on action, specifically
on the "fortuitous personal peril" of the protagonist. The aim of the
novel is sensational, that is, to recreate an unfolding tale of suspense
(forward plotting) so as to maximize the reader's vicarious involve-
ment. While in the detective story the eventual and painstakingly
achieved identification of the murderer is everything, in the thriller
it may hardly be an issue. Where the detective novel is analytical, the
thriller is situational.

The formal detective story is premised on a "closed" environment,
a microcosm with a limited cast of characters in isolation, with the
threat (rightly or wrongly) presumed to come from within. The story
begins with the idea of an idyllic, if eccentric, social order in a *hortus*

conclusus; then there appears a blight in the garden that must be identified and extirpated, after which everything returns to its reaffirmed
pastoral innocence. The thriller is premised on an "open" environment,
with the tenuous order of things radically broken in upon and discred-
ited, as in the existentialist novel. Apparently no one and no thing are
what they seem; the most familiar surroundings become sinister. The
world of the thriller is Kafkaesque, a world in which the protagonist
does not know where he stands in relation to anyone or anything.
Suspicion is common to both detective story and thriller, but in the
thriller suspicion and deceit are the lifeblood of the narrative, with
each turn of the plot representing one more intolerable turn of the
screw.

The dominant mood of the detective story is puzzlement, while
that of the thriller is anxiety and dread. In the precarious balance between the human love of order and the rage for chaos — both operative
in all escape literature — the former dominates in the detective novel,
the latter in the thriller. The thriller's re-creation of life on the edge,
where anything is possible, and portrayal of man on the run makes
this form of literature a natural if melodramatic mirror of contemporary life.

The thriller inevitably calls for a different sort of prose — hard,
lean, and "muscular" — rather than the amiable and donnish narrative
style associated with the Great English Tea-Break school, as the detective novel of manners has been termed.[9] The latter is the manner
with which Innes is preeminently identified, yet Innes is also a past
master of the fast-paced thriller in the Stevenson/Buchan tradition, except that Innes has placed his stamp on the form in creating an unlikely
hybrid — the comic thriller, or thriller-fantasia.

Three distinct categories of thriller fiction can be discerned in the
work of Michael Innes: the straight, Buchanesque flight-and-pursuit
chase narratives; the distinctively Innesian thriller-fantasias; and a
group of anxiety tales based primarily on impersonation.

Flight-and-Pursuit Stories

Dramatic chase sequences occur in many Innes tales after the detective
phase has been concluded (as in *An Awkward Lie* or *A Private View*),
and sometimes as a Hitchcockian opening scenario, (as in *Operation
Pax* or *From "London" Far*). In certain novels the chase is paramount

throughout, with little or no detective interest; it is for these that the term thriller is best reserved. These usually involve suggestions of international intrigue and cold-war plot — a crucial missing scientist or perhaps a missing scientific formula.

The setting of *Appleby Plays Chicken* (1957 — the American title, *Death on a Quiet Day*, seems in this case more in keeping with the British atmosphere) is an Oxford "reading party." A tutor and a small group of his students put up at a country pub for an intellectual holiday of study and stimulating talk amid peaceful pastoral surroundings and a variety of character types out of Isaak Walton — a hearty publican, a bluff military man, a retired clergyman of the sanguine, muscular-Christian variety, and a full complement of stout, tweedy, rural types. Far from being a claustrophic, sealed-room mystery, *Appleby Plays Chicken*, like other Buchanesque thrillers, builds on the conversely intriguing situation of murder in a wide-open setting conducive to agoraphobia.

The protagonist, a bright-eyed undergraduate named David Henchman, sets out one morning on a walk, suitably equipped with hiking boots, wind-cheater, a respectably old pipe, and Plato in his pocket. Soon he finds himself at Knack Tor, where a rocky eminence rises straight out of the moor. He sees a thin column of smoke issuing from the top of Knack Tor, and then hears a sharp report. When he attains the summit, he finds a man shot through the forehead — a gun clutched in his hand. From the Tor Henchman can survey the whole surrounding country but can see only one casual-looking hiker sauntering past the base of the Tor. The hiker is all rural respectability, "smelling of tweed and tobacco," wholly correct, down to the way his mustache is trimmed. As the two wary strangers attempt to feel each other out, it develops that this enormously innocent-seeming stroller is in fact nothing more than a hired killer.

The instant this realization snaps into place, the chase begins, and it is pure hare-and-hounds through the recesses of Thomas Hardy country. What has hitherto seemed innocent and safe as houses suddenly appears full of insecurity and menace. As soon as the chase is on, the remote English countryside with its Goldsmithian deserted villages, offers little in the way of protection or deterrence against a determined and undisguised manhunt. The familiar features of rural topography and industry present a variety of challenges to the ingenuity of pursuers and pursued. Moving from open field to disused cider mill to passing hay wain, the chase finally comes to an end by virtue of an encounter

with that most English of all rural institutions, a point-to-point, or steeple chase, and the harried student actually ends his adventure by
mounting a loose horse and taking the final hurdles.

A certain class-consciousness, typical of Innes, plays a significant
role in the narrative. While David is at first somewhat hostile to what
he regards as all the "pooka" talk from the country gentleman types
and even from Appleby himself, it is just because David can detect the
false notes in the conversation of the rural hiker that he is able to mark
him down as bogus and suspect. At the end, when David is able to
separate the genuine from the bogus, he comes out with his own,
"Rather a good show." The old forms and values perdure.

While reviewers lauded *Appleby Plays Chicken* as a straightforward lark of an adventure, and a departure from Innes's more usual
ultracomplicated and fantasticated mysteries, it should be noted that
earlier in his career Innes had produced two non-Appleby novels even
closer to the traditional thriller form, *The Secret Vanguard* and *The
Man from the Sea*.

The Secret Vanguard (1940) was Innes's sixth novel and his first
thriller, although thriller elements had been present in some of the
earlier productions such as *Lament for a Maker*. *The Secret Vanguard*
has a World War II/Nazi conspiracy context, specifically the nefarious
operations of a Fifth Column within Great Britain. It is a kind of
parable about good and evil cast in simple political terms: good (honor-
able, humanistic) nation against bad (dishonorable, inhumane) nation;
loyal countrymen vs. treacherous defectors and sell-outs; truth and
order vs. conspiracy and dissimulation. The most notable precedent
was the work of John Buchan, whose *Thirty-Nine Steps* in particular
established a deft use of local topography and atmosphere and a formula of chase (predicament/ingenious escape/worse predicament) that
became conventions of the form. Graham Greene has identified the
essence of the Buchanesque formula as the "dramatic value of adventure in familiar surroundings happening to unadventurous men."[10]

The Secret Vanguard is Innes's tribute to Buchan (as *Lament for
a Maker* was to Wilkie Collins), even to the use of the same Scottish
milieu. As Ralph Partridge put it in his *New Statesman* review: in this
novel "Innes' talent for pastiche serves him faithfully, even gloriously. . . . Every step of *The Thirty-Nine Steps* he treads again with the
punctiliousness of a don and the fidelity of a Scotsman" (19 Oct. 1940,
p. 392).

What ties together the disparate elements of this novel — murder,

kidnapping, armed pursuit across the Scottish moors — is that all of it
has "something to do with poetry." The espionage gang in question,
on the trail of a British scientific figure taking an unauthorized vacation
somewhere in the highlands, has adopted as its device for intercom-
munication the insertion of bogus code verses in passages of innocuous
authentic poetry. In an early scene the protagonist, a girl named Sheila
Grant, herself on vacation, has an enigmatic encounter in a railroad
compartment. Towards the end of the long journey, an extroverted
fellow passenger (whom she nicknames "Burge") tries to interest a
reserved, repressed-looking man (she dubs him "Pennyfeather") in the
subject of poetry by reciting lines from a rousing military ballad. "Pennyfeather" coldly retorts by reciting some Swinburne and declaring,
"That, now, *is* poetry."

Sheila immediately realizes that Pennyfeather's recital has included four lines *not* by Swinburne:

> Where the westerly spur of the furthermost mountain
> Hovers falcon-like over the heart of the bay,
> Past seven sad leagues and a last lonely fountain,
> A mile towards tomorrow the dead garden lay.

After 'Pennyfeather' has left, Sheila confides to Burge that those lines
have been made up. "If you happen to know about Swinburne, of
course they stick out a mile" (p. 51). Events now turn sinister and the
stranger on the train suddenly seems quite other than what he is. When
she gets off at her remote station and Burge bids her goodbye, he bows
and "there was a faint click in the darkness." It is the accepted signal
in the genre of a Nazi presence.

The ensuing chapters involve a classic Buchanesque chase through
the moors, in which Sheila and a fortuitously acquired male companion (Dick, a Princeton student in Europe to study Caravaggio) play
hare and hounds with a relentless enemy. The essential ethos of the
thriller is Sheila's instinctive sense that here is something that, without
analysis, "had to be resisted, had to be resisted personally, immediately, head on" (p. 93). Without that sense, there would be no thriller:
the protagonists would quietly slip away and call in the appropriate
authorities.

The artistry of the sort of chase sequence that ensues is essentially
dependent on the handling of topography, on what French critic
Gaston Bachelard has called the poetics of space. Its effectiveness

depends upon the writer's creation of a vivid sense of place — of the nature of the landscape, its physical features and its points of entry and exit, as though it were an elaborate imagined board game of "Dungeons and Dragons." It is, Sheila feels, the "game of games."

The first stage of the chase is presented here in just these terms, with a specific board space defined for us: Sheila is in treeless heather on moorland precisely bounded by a reticulation of roadways and railway tracks. In the heather she can hide well enough, but can only move on peril of easy observation even from a great distance, while the roads and trackbeds represent at once points of possible escape and points of possible entrapment. And so it goes, like a treacherous point-to-point, taking the protagonist from one precarious and untenable situation to another, in a relentless rhythm of danger and respite played out on the carefully defined topographical board.

In the most dramatic and sentimental turn, a blind fiddler guides Sheila through a pine forest and to a hidden lair called the Cave of the Wolf on a high precipice. When this venerable character, full of Scottish ballads and national lore, shares his peddlar's meal with her, the moment is sacramental: "'Lassie, lassie, will ye no come into the body of the kirk?' It was from the little cave behind that the blind man was calling her"; after laving his hands, he "handed Sheila a scrap of fine linen, folded and spotlessly clean. He rummaged again and set out a tin of oatcakes, a little kebbuck of cheese, a loaf of bread. His hands hovered over them — open, in a gesture of offering. 'The Lord provides,' he said. 'Lassie, what are ye for?'" (p. 162).

It is from the fiddler that Sheila is able to interpret the code contained in the bogus Swinburne lines as directions to a certain spot — the wind-cuffer hill of one of his songs being none other than the falcon-shaped mountain of the message — a cliff near a place called Castle Troy. Castle Troy proves to be the den of this story's iniquity, and in its environs Sheila and her friend finally encounter the missing scientist, Orchard, innocently enjoying his fishing vacation, unaware of the machinations that have been set in motion to ensnare him and his crucial formula.

By this time Appleby, then a young inspector, has made his appearance on the scene. But before the forces of law and order are able to put to rout the alien intrusive presence, there is one shock, one magnificent plot twist still to come. Appleby shows the scientist two photographs of Orchard himself, with a story that someone has been impersonating him. What Appleby really shows him are a positive and reverse image, and when Orchard immediately picks the positive image as the true picture, Appleby triumphantly identifies him as an imposter. Ordinarily a person sees himself *only* in a mirror and would therefore instinctively choose the reverse image over the positive one, while for an imposter, the reverse would be true.[11]

With that business accomplished, the final action of the novel is the siege of Troy and the rescue of the real Orchard. The villains' final bid for escape is to fly from the scene in a hydroplane, but Appleby foils this by signaling to an approaching police aircraft by "writing" on the water of the loch with a speedboat. *The Secret Vanguard* is also a political parable; a friend of Appleby named Hetherton, a curator at the British Museum, has the last word, sounding a note rather like that of Sherlock Holmes at the end of "His Last Bow":

> "You remember the last chapter of *Rasselas?*" he asked. "It is called a Conclusion in which nothing is Concluded. That is so with us. And you must neither of you think that because war is coming other things must go for good. The shadows are dark over Europe; so dark" — he smiled — "that Caravaggio himself might be baffled by them. We must wait, knowing that always there are torches which do not go out." (p. 286)

Unlike Appleby's message to the police aircraft, these words, one is intended to hope, are not writ on water.

Innes wrote a number of other thrillers in the forties, but in a whimsical manner. They are more thriller-fantasias or comic-thrillers than straight Buchanesque. But in 1955, in the setting of the Cold War, Innes produced his straightest thriller of all, *The Man from the Sea.* This was a real departure for Innes, far less fantastic and less humorous than readers had come to expect of him. It is a straightforward, evenly paced narrative with almost no digressive or parenthetical elements, conveyed in a prose that is correspondingly "lean" and "hard." Yet it remains highly, even intensely, literate. As Richard Lister wrote in *New Statesman*: "He is literate and doesn't, in the prevailing fashion, pretend to be the opposite; on the contrary, he uses this consciously as one of his main weapons" (19 February 1955, p. 256). Far from being an affectation, Lister argues, this is what constitutes Innes's "bait" for the intelligent reader. Innes is no Chandler here, nor even a Hemingway; rather, he strongly hints of Conrad.[12]

The opening scene is written in a kind of stark prose-poetry, an art that is all silhouettes, shadows, and glints of moonlight. The scene is a rocky Scottish beach at night. The protagonist, a twentyish Cambridge graduate named Cranston, is sprawled naked on the sand and waiting for the next phase of erotic hide-and-seek to be signaled by Lady Blair, the laird's wife, with whom he is having a Mrs. Robinson affair. Into this moonlit occasion enters — right from the sea — another, older man, himself nearly naked:

> The swimmer dropped his feet to the sea bed and started to wade ashore. . . . He lurched forward foot by foot. . . . On this unfrequented strip of Scottish coast in the small hours, the two confronted each other like wary savages.   (p. 2)

Instantly Cranston feels a sort of *situational* secret-sharer bond between them. He is an adolescent mixed up in his first "messy" affair — doubly messy not only because adulterous but because he is pursuing it on the rebound from his rejection by Lady Blair's daughter — and so for Cranston, "What had risen from the sea was some harsh male predicament to which he responded as a release" (p. 3). The man from the sea has emerged like a primeval alter-ego, a *doppelgänger* who confronts Cranston with the possibility of wholly fresh choices; he introduces the possibility of *aventure*, in the Arthurian sense of quest.

The man from the sea poses an immediate dilemma for Cranston: whether to commit himself to aiding the stranger or not. The decision must be immediate and decisive, for the man is being hotly pursued by armed and formidable adversaries. The stranger explains that he is John Day, an atomic scientist who had defected some five years ago. Having discovered that he has radiation poisoning (and this is evident), he has come home to die and to see his wife a final time. This is something Cranston can immediately comprehend. He too feels he has fatally and finally committed an irrevocable, definitive act.

Because Cranston feels "implicated" with the outlaw from the sea — implicated by his own sense of guilt over his romantic "mess" — he sees that in helping Day get to London he will be performing a pure, definitive act that will cleanse and clarify. Such is Cranston's self-analysis, but the narrator adds ironically, "Could any mind so clever as his own — so swiftly lucid as this admirable piece of self-analysis showed it to be — stand in any substantial danger?" (p. 77). And of course danger is exactly what there will be, for getting Day to London means evading both the foreign agents *and* the British authorities.

The chase sequence once again exploits the possibilities offered by highland topography: a siege in a quarry, another hounds-and-hare chase through treeless heather, and a deadly hide-and-seek in a pine forest, "like a game in some enormous colonnade." Once again it is an elaborate board game whose boundaries are precisely defined by road-ways and service tracks cut through the forest. Day's determination throughout is an inspiration to Cranston, "romantic idealist" that he is. At one moment in the pine forest Cranston sees a temporarily blinded Day, back to a tree, fighting bare-handed to the last, willing to die in relentless pursuit of his aim.

In light of this, it is crushing and devastating to find at the end that Day has been a liar all along, that he has not fought his way to London to make that final gesture to his wife — but merely to defect yet again, to another crowd, in hopes of getting one final better deal. At the end Conrad's Secret Sharer is proven to be Mr. Kurtz. That the powerful intelligence and noble determination Cranston observes in Day only lead to another sellout is wholly disillusioning.

Perhaps equally crushing is the rebuke delivered to Cranston by his bluff female cousin from Australia, who has shared in the adventure.

> "Taking on a thing like this by way of getting straight with your-self over some small hole-and-corner immorality. It's outrageous."
> . . . It had become clear to her that there was a sense in which her cousin Richard Cranston had been hypnotized by this man from the sea. Cunningly — she was sure it was was that — John Day had touched off in him something that was not so much simply romantic as positively atavic. (pp. 171–3)

Not only does she undermine Cranston's delusive sense of being on a heroic quest, but she in a sense undermines the whole thriller ethos, premised on that idea of wading into a criminal situation directly and on one's own. Her wholesome antipodean wisdom more or less writes the epitaph to Innes's venture into the "straight" thriller, for only a "romantic idealist" could be misled into taking with any degree of seriousness the idea of heroic individual crusade against the enemies of God and country. More suited to Innes's sensibilities is the exploita-tion of thriller plots and thriller emotions in a comic vein.

The Journeying Boy, 1949
(alternate title: The Case of the Journeying Boy)

The Journeying Boy is Innes's most elaborate and novelistic chase story, a work deft in its handling of narrative, especially with regard to pacing and shift in points of view and subtlety in characterization. With respect to its literary qualities and general structure — a chase, followed by a sequence at a sort of "castle perilous" — it is closest to Operation Pax and From "London" Far. Will Cuppy greeted the book ecstatically. He judged it "the best mystery story in years," with "writing that will knock you for a goal," and saw it as a work that obliterated any distinction between mystery novel and novel proper. "Too good to be true, but here it is" (NYHT Weekly Book Review, 17 April 1949, p. 12). Even Ralph Partridge, who generally begrudged any praise of Innes, was constrained to declare that here "Innes has surpassed himself" (New Statesman, 23 July 1949, p. 106). Only Jacques Barzun denigrated the book, calling it "A failing attempt to be funny in the manner of Edmund Crispin. The wild plot is full of improbabilities one is willing to swallow, but the long-winded analyses of feeling and action are intolerable almost from the start."[13] Innes regards it as his favorite among his novels, one he supposes might be his best.

A non-Appleby story, it is not primarily a story of detection, although in it there is intermittent detection of a rather procedural sort, presided over by the dour Inspector Cadover (who appears in A Private View and What Happened at Hazlewood).

The narrative begins with what seems to be the most innocent and mundane of occasions. A fiftyish, mild-mannered Mr. Thewless (whose name, ironically, means "without strength or virtue"), an obscure and moderately successful private tutor, is being interviewed for the job of taking on the fifteen-year-old son of a renowned scientist named Bernard Paxton. The tutor is to accompany the boy, acknowledged to be a "bit of a handful," on an educational vacation with relatives in Ireland. Paxton and his home are enormously imposing, almost intimidating. The house, to Thewless, is actually rather too grand, with its heavily carved Spanish woodwork, its collection of Chinese artifacts, and its prominently hung Velasquez painting of a young prince.

> Positive opulence was something which he found uncomfortably to jar with the spirit of the time. . . . Why in the world should a

really great man take the trouble to surround himself with so em-
phatic a material magnificence? . . . Mr. Thewless found himself
distrusting everything around him. He distrusted an eminent
physicist who lived like a grandee.   (pp. 6, 8)

The imposing Paxton in his role as widower and father of an only son
seems to Thewless hopelessly muddled and vulnerable.

The interview is cut short as Paxton ushers in and subsequently
hires another candidate, Captain Cox, a man as opposite in character
and philosophy to Thewless as one could imagine — a beefy young
military man whose education ideas run more to hunting and fishing
than to Latin and Greek.

Chapter 3 of the novel consists entirely of a collection of documents, of letters and cables, all of which need to be carefully attended
if the reader is to follow the rather complicated following sequence
of events. A key document is a telegram to Paxton announcing that
"SUDDEN DEATH RENDERS IT IMPOSSIBLE ACCEPT POST AS ARRANGED COX."
At the last minute Thewless is hired after all, and it is arranged that he
should meet his charge, whom he has not yet actually met, at Euston
Station for the trip to Ireland.

This rendezvous turns out quite disconcerting to the tutor, for the
boy, Humphrey Paxton, proves to be a "handful" in rather an alarming
way. He appears to be completely caught up in melodramatic juvenile
suspicions and paranoid fantasies, even to the point of subjecting his
tutor to elaborate tests to prove his identity. Mr. Thewless is left
wondering whether or not the boy is seriously neurotic.

For an explanation of Hump's quite real state of anxiety, the narrative intermittently shifts to a seemingly unrelated police investigation
of a murder in a West End movie theater earlier that same day. A
man's body was found in its seat after the crowd had filed out of the
matinee of a vulgarly sensational film called "The Plutonium Blonde";
apparently the man had been shot during the film's deafening atomic
explosion sequence, and then the body had been stripped of all identification, including clothing labels — a grisly business accomplished
under the guise of petting.

The crime and the circumstances are wholly depressing to
Cadover:

Fifty thousand people had died at Hiroshima, and at Bikini iron-
clads had been tossed in challenge to those other disintegrating

nuclei of the sun. The blood-red tide was loosed. And here it was
turned to hog's wash at five shillings the trough, and entertainment
tax extra. That some wretched Londoner had met a violent death
while taking his fill seemed a very unimportant circumstance. . . .
Mere anarchy was loosed upon the world — so what the hell did it
matter?   (p. 51)

A painstaking investigation proceeds and finally reveals that the murdered man is a Captain Cox, recently engaged to accompany Dr. Paxton's son as tutor on an Irish holiday.

What Cadover additionally discovers, however, is that Bernard
Paxton's butler and others in his household are part of an in-house plot
to kidnap the scientist's son and hold him in exchange for Paxton's
crucial secret formula as ransom. The Irish relatives are the master-
minds of this plot; the unfortunate Cox happened to *know* the Irish
relatives.

The murder plot had been to lure Cox (who did not know of the
telegram cancelling his job) into the movie theater with the aid of a
boy chosen and dressed to resemble Hump. But coincidentally the real
Hump himself went to that theater on this last morning before his trip
and happened to sit next to Cox and the boy impersonating him. What
Hump saw was the wholly alarming spectacle of his own double ac-
companying the man originally selected to be his tutor but supposed
to have been called away by a sudden death! The suspicions of the boy
sufficiently explains his "paranoia" upon joining Thewless at Euston
Station.

With that, Cadover and the English and Irish police are on the
move to rescue the threatened boy and the unheroic Mr. Thewless.
Neither Mr. Thewless, nor the reader at first, have any notion of the
affairs that the Cadover chapters only intermittently and in piecemeal
fashion develop over the first half of the narrative. Thewless (unlike
the reader) will lack any clear conception of the state of affairs almost
to the end — and one of the delights of the narrative is to follow his stub-
born refusal, in the face of mounting and alarming evidence to the contrary, to admit that anything untoward is happening.

At Euston Station then, Hump has arrived to meet a tutor he has
never met for a journey to Ireland to relatives he also has never met,
having just fled from the bizarre and ominous scene at the theater.
These circumstances cap what to Hump is a whole series of evidences
that he is the intended victim of some sort of plot. But by the adults

around him his suspicions have been taken as nothing but disturbingly persistent fantasizing, so that the boy has begun to be very close about it all. And as the main narrative follows the viewpoint of Mr. Thewless, the reader is as at sea as the befuddled tutor about how to take those paranoid manifestations Hump is unable to repress, and which only increase as the journey progresses.

This situation prevails for the next hundred pages or so, which constitute the flight-and-pursuit section of the narrative. It is clear to Thewless as the journey begins that the poor lad in his charge is in a haunted state, much like that of the "journeying boy" in Hardy's poem "Midnight on the Great Western." Things get Hitchcockian on the train; their compartment companions are an enigmatic bearded man wearing "pebbly glasses" and a Miss Marple-like lady named Miss Liberty who never quite seems to be what she appears and who has the unfortunate predisposition to share with Hump a mutual interest in the stories of "Sapper," with their constant premise of suspicion and mistrust. Because, she asks, "Who knows anything, really, about anybody else?" (p. 69).

When Thewless suddenly realizes that Hump and the man with the pebbly glasses are both gone from the compartment he becomes alarmed and commences to search the train. This passage proves to be a wonderfully surrealistic sequence, in which Thewless encounters dwarfs and giants and a compartment occupied by a Chinese lady, a bowler-hatted black, and a figure totally swathed in bandages.

Of course all this involves nothing more sinister than a circus troupe (the bandaged figure is the rubber man), and in fact Hump is soon located. Nevertheless, Hump says he has been knocked out and bound in a confined space, only to have been released again. He shows Thewless the welts on his wrists to prove it. Thewless concludes the boy must be the victim of some sort of adolescent stigmata. "Mr. Thewless decided therefore to go straight ahead, and to support the harassments of the coming day upon a resolutely buoyant, nervous tone." The narrator goes on to suggest that if at this point an inspector of the CID (Cadover for example) might have been of more immediate use to Hump than his owlish tutor, it is nonetheless true that no one "could have been any more conscientious according to his lights" (p. 136).

Things do not improve when they reach Belfast, which the narrator describes as ominous and dreary in the extreme:

Belfast, grimly utilitarian and shrouded in rain, was very little evocative of any gateway to the holiday spirit; it suggested rather a various detritus from the less appealing parts of Glasgow washed across the Irish Sea during the darker years of the nineteenth century. . . . The railway station spread before them a classical portico nicely painted to look like milk chocolate. On one side stood an immobile policeman of gigantic size proportionately armed with truncheon and revolver. On the other a placard, equally generously conceived, announced

LIFE IS SHORT
DEATH IS COMING
ETERNITY — WHERE?

And upon this brief glimpse of the cultural life of Belfast their train received them and they were presently hurtling west.   (pp. 136–137, 138)

But when their journey continues via narrow-gauge rail out of Northern Ireland and into The hinterland of "Mr. DeValera's philosophical republic," poetry soon overtakes prose and the narrative enters a world that is pastoral, large, innocent, and comic. And yet it is precisely here that the journey comes to a crashingly violent climax: the train is wrecked in a tunnel and in the confusion Thewless is separated from his charge. This is indeed a kidnap attempt (but by a rival gang, not the wicked Irish relatives). By the time Thewless has made his way to Killyboffin Hall, their destination — still almost unshakably composed and, against all reasonable expectation, still confident — he finds that Hump has already been delivered safely to his relatives, the Bolderwoods, by the enigmatic Miss Liberty.

Throughout these adventures and escapades Thewless has proven to be, in the words of Hump's cousin, Ivor Bolderwood, "a man who was almost irrationally determined to deny that the universe holds anything dangerous or surprising" (p. 160). And yet, slow or bewildered or irresolute though he was, therein lay his strength. Back in London Cadover and Bernard Paxton finally get the hang of the affair and realize the danger facing Hump and his tutor in Ireland. Cadover asks Paxton for his impressions of Thewless. "Would you say that he would be a good man in a tight place?" Paxton makes a nice distinction: "I don't know. I am rather inclined to think that it would depend on the

degree of tightness involved. In a *very* tight place I imagine that Thewless might be a very good man indeed" (p. 238).

And a very tight place it is. The Bolderwoods are actually the central villains of the piece and Killyboffin Hall the very center of their
tangled web. It is the final irony of the classic thriller that the longed-
for sanctuary proves to be the very heart of the peril. At first the
Bolderwood home is presented as a broadly comic rural Irish household, run by a desperately ineffectual squire and his colorless but efficient son, Ivor. The house is a drafty Georgian mansion with much
of its furnishings and statuary draped in protective sheets. Thewless
warily notes the atmospheric effects of Killyboffin Hall, "the genius of
the place for disconcerting suggestions of murmered colloquy, stealthy
movement, and all the imponderables commonly associated with edifices of much greater antiquity" (p. 182).

Mr. Thewless wakes in the night to the sensation that there are
"presences" in his room. When he stumbles into the corridor to find
Hump's room and assure himself that the boy is safe and sound, there
begins an epic Gothic adventure through the sighing and murmuring
moonlit corridors. Erik Routley has noted that it is "the longest passage
of straight narrative, without dialogue, covering a moment or two of
time, which I know of in the literature."[14] As this tidal flow of Innes's
most masterly prose reaches a crescendo, it is almost as though the author has found it literally intoxicating, for it achieves a degree of pur-
pleness that becomes wonderfully self-parodying, as when Thewless
realizes that the candlestick he is carrying, its flame having blown out,
can still be hurled as a missile: "Moreover, it occurred to him that his
candlestick, being of the massive and ornamental rather than of the
utilitarian or dormitory kind, was by no means rendered entirely useless to him by reason of the temporary desuetude of its primary function" (p. 201).[15]

Thewless and Hump emerge unscathed. These nocturnal presences were indeed kidnappers — not the Bolderwoods but the aforemen-
tioned rival gang. The unheroic Thewless, almost unwittingly, really
did scare them off with his candlestick. With dawn, all seems decep-
tively peaceful once again. Ivor takes Hump down to the coast to explore the system of caves at the foot of the sea cliff. The caves prove
to be the most frightening environment yet for Hump, not only because
they are actually precarious, even treacherous, but because of their
primal archetypal power, as in the following description of one womb-

like cavern in the cliff: "This time the aperture was larger, and gave upon an oval chamber, low-roofed, down the longer axis of which the light of Ivor's torch led the eye to two further openings, set close together, that led apparently to further cavities or passages. And of this place the form was at once unreasonably alarming and mysteriously compelling or attractive; it seemed to tug at the very roots of the mind" (p. 280). All of his worst suspicions, distrusts, and fears are fully justified; the caves are the site of an intended kidnapping plot. But before Ivor can spring *his* trap, the rival gang members spring theirs, and in the ensuing confusion Hump effects a blind escape through the pitch black, slippery tunnels to the refuge of a tiny side cavern with an aperture so narrow that only he can squeeze through. From this absolutely secure womblike fastness, the terrified youngster can still his panic and even, like some ancient Saxon defender, revile and mock his frustrated pursuers. That done, his bruised and exhausted body curls in on himself and "He lay in a posture of infancy, a thumb stolen to his mouth" (p. 292).

But, when Hump reemerges from the cave he has in a very real sense been reborn as a man—he has undergone a kind of baptism of fire and been confirmed. While he knows that he could return to that sanctuary again if need be, he knew he never would, that all that was over now; instead, he "walked rapidly forward and out of the cavern" (p. 306).

In the final sequence of the novel, Hump and Thewless finally confront their enemies openly. Ivor Bolderwood, with a drawn gun pointed straight at Thewless's heart, demands of Hump the secret formula from his father's laboratory, which the boy supposedly has on his person. Thewless heroically urges the boy to remain firm:

> You made a bad mistake, even if an honorable one. And I have made equally bad mistakes at every turn. If we are to be killed, my dear, dear lad, we must put up with it. These villains must on no account be told where the plan now is. (p. 319)

Hump, however, has no formula to turn over—earlier he had rectified his error by simply posting it to Downing Street! And now a number of things happen in rapid succession: Miss Liberty arrives to disarm the Bolderwoods (*she* has been the real Secret Service agent all along); the rival gang lays siege to the house; and the Bolderwoods bolt. By this time Cadover and the Irish police have finally arrived, but when after a pitched battle they lift the siege and enter the burning house, they find only one figure in it — the nearly asphyxiated body of Mr. Thewless lying in a corridor out of the windows of which a whole line of guns has been ranged. For after seeing Hump and Miss Liberty safely spirited out of the building disguised as Irish peasant women laden with wool Thewless has held the fort single-handedly in the manner of the lone legionnaire of *Beau Geste*. In a *very* tight place, a very good man, indeed!

For all its humor and melodrama, *The Journeying Boy* still provides a very clear and distinct image of the values that underlie the Innes thrillers, above all the sense that integrity, modesty, and honor remain the most formidable things in the human universe.

Thriller-Fantasias

Appleby on Ararat (1941) is in every way Innes's most exotic production and seemingly one of his most frivolous. The opening situation may be the most whimsical lost-at-sea episode ever written: a cruise ship in the South Pacific is torpedoed and an assorted group of characters one might expect to find in an English country-weekend story find themselves cast adrift in midocean on what had been the sun-deck bar, complete with swizzle sticks and olives. Each of the characters — including such stock types as the fuddy-duddy minister, the flighty socialite, the gruff military man, and the hearty colonial, as well as Inspector Appleby himself — gradually attains the furthest reaches of self-parody.

Then, once they are cast adrift on what they believe is an uninhabited island, Innes next offers an amusing pastiche out of *Robinson Crusoe* and *Swiss Family Robinson*. The group is subjected to the intimidation of native drums (the island is not uninhabited after all) and an attack seems imminent when a flaming spear is cast into their midst as they sit around their campfire at dinner. Appleby has the perfect British solution to the crisis. He leads them in a toast to His Majesty:

> He rose and held up his gourd.
> "Mrs. Kittery and gentlemen," he said, "the King!"
> They stood as if drilled. The toast was honoured. And now it was

the monstrous creatures before them who appeared transfixed, staring at the incomprehensible ritual. For seconds the thing held like a tableau. Then the naked figures yelled, turned and fled. And in the darkness beyond their cowardice precipitated a rout. (pp. 58–59)

Satire or no, this is straight imperial romancing.

A murder does occur for Appleby to deal with when one of their party is found dead on the beach. At first the possible list of suspects would seem rather small, but investigation proves that not only are there natives on the island but a pair of rather suspicious looking archaeologists investigating a long barrow, and a whole hotelful of absurd and disreputable types who have fled war-torn Europe to hide out in this remote corner and do a little treasure-seeking on the side. The bogus archaeologists prove to be Nazi agents and the mysterious "barrow" contains neither treasure nor artifacts, but rather a fuel stockpile for U-boats.

The last stage of these proceedings is a rousing, wartime adventure. Appleby gathers his little group together and recruits one or two others from the hotel group who are "well-affected to His Majesty the King," and they conduct a kind of siege in reverse, setting the torch to the lone hotel and making a strategic retreat to the sea. Together they "become a little microcosm of ordered national effort" and even the unlikeliest among them discovers the truth of the mystery that even in the direst peril, "so unsearchable is the human heart — that when one is oneself actively engaged there may even come certain rare moments to be classed among the Good Times" (p. 156). They not only make their getaway in a motor launch, but in a rousing epilogue manage to hitch themselves to a German sub and return to the harbor outside the sub's disguised fuel reservoir, and with a single grenade blow the whole operation to smithereens. Rule Britannia.

The whole story is really just a good "Phhht" right in der Fuhrer's face. Typical of some of the sentimental British posturing is Colonel Glover's last-minute reservations about whether the Nazis should be attacked except by uniformed forces of the crown: "Worrying, Appleby — dashed worrying. . . . Attacking force oughtn't to be in civilian clothes" (p. 169). Fortunately, someone finds a Naval Reserve uniform, so the attack can proceed in good form! The important thing about this comic incident is that this is, in Innes's fictional world, how the good people, and political systems, can be distinguished from the bad.

For the rest, the novel gives Innes rare scope for some richly exotic descriptive prose: a Conradesque storm at sea; a dawn that "came luridly to the island, as if Sin and Death had thrown back their doors and admitted some reflection of the eternal bonfire to the sky" (p. 127); a rubbery jungle landscape at twilight, with scarlet flowers growing, like opening wounds (p. 112). All in all, this novel is a rare confection from Innes, an exotic adventure with unusual ormulu not to be found elsewhere in the Innes corpus. It is an interesting digression from Appleby's usual haunts, but not something, one feels, that could have been much extended.[16]

The year after *Appleby on Ararat* Innes published yet another fantasticated wartime thriller, *The Daffodil Affair* (1942), a work that concerns itself with a nefarious plot to dominate the postwar world by cornering the market in psychic phenomena; this, plus a setting in a South American jungle puts the work firmly in the exotic vein of its immediate predecessor. Will Cuppy in the *New York Herald Tribune Books* judged the novel as perhaps "the best of all this author's uniformly first-class work" (4 Oct. 1942, p. 25). Kay Irvin struck a note of praise premised on a recognition of the book's success in a specific limited genre:

> This latest opus is scintillating, shrewd and fearlessly and hilariously highbrow. But where his *Lament for a Maker* was a brilliant mystery novel, this book, like *Appleby on Ararat*, tends toward intellectualized farce. In other words, the plot dances off into the domain of the whacky, while the author delights his readers by conjuring tricks with gay colored balls of tireless wit.   (*NYTBR*, 11 October 1942, p. 10)

The opening sequence of *The Daffodil Affair* finds Inspector Appleby and another Scotland Yard detective, the grimly diligent Hudspith, in wartorn London, each working on a different case. Hudspith is following an abducted half-wit girl when he learns that the girl, Lucy Rideout, is not really retarded at all, but a rare case of multiple-personality disorder. The abductor who would seek out just such a victim must be, to Hudspith's mind, the most blackly depraved criminal of all. Appleby is pursuing a case that seems wholly opposite in tenor:

the kidnapping of a horse from its stable at Harrogate. Appleby learns that the horse, Daffodil, is a prodigy, an apparently clairvoyant counting-horse like the legendary Clever Hans.

Before this multi-stranded prologue is over, other cases are introduced, all seemingly quite unrelated, but sharing the common note of the bizarre: a descendent of Hannah Metcalfe, the famous Haworth witch, has been abducted, along with her ancestor's witchy artifacts; and an entire Bloomsbury house has disappeared in the confusion following a bombing raid — it is number 53 Hawkes Square, a famous haunted house recorded to have been visited by Dr. Samuel Johnson himself.

Abruptly, and with no transition, part 2 opens on a ship crossing the South Atlantic with Appleby and Hudspith. The tracks of the abducted girls, horse, and haunted house have all led to somewhere in South America. There is clearly some sort of bizarre conspiratorial operation aimed at smuggling an assortment of freakish, weird, and paranormal wonders to some central location, but the *why* has so far eluded Appleby and Hudspith, though Hudspith clings with obsessive abhorrence to the unspeakable depravity theory. Many of the ship's passengers represent the side-show assortment the hypothetical operation deals in. There are even two suspicious characters called Wine and Boglehole who freely acknowledge that they have persuaded their *wünderkammer* personages to a sort of Hidden City in the Amazon where they run the world's largest establishment for psychical research. They invite Appleby and Hudspith to come with them, insisting on seeing them as "spies" of a rival psychical researcher.

Part 3 finds the detectives at the Happy Isles, a weird international village on a group of islands in a river deep in the jungle. The village boasts pagodas, highland crofts, Swiss chalets, Cape Cod bungalows, and Victorian London mansions all resurrected among the cobra-infested tree ferns and alligator-infested river waters.

The Mephistophelian Wine expounds on the grand plan that all this grotesquerie is in aid of. His idea is quite simply to take advantage of the *götterdammerung* occasioned by World War II in order to gain centralized control over a new world order through manipulation of the resurgent "spiritualism" certain to follow the collapse:

> Grant but the initial collapse on which this bad man was counting,
> and the spread of subrational beliefs would be very swift. Power

> would go to him who had the most and the likeliest instruments of
> superstition to hand. . . . The project, if he had read it aright, was
> extravagant beyond the compass of a story-teller's art. And yet it
> was not ungrounded in the present state of the world.   (p. 122)

A freakish Faust or Satan, Wine shows Appleby and Hudspith his
microcosm of "the Kingdoms of the World," and invites them to join
him. He argues that the crumbling of traditional belief, abetted by the
advance of science, will inevitably be replaced by forms of occultism
and spiritualism. In support of his vision of this historical necessity,
Wine brings into play Gibbon's image of the barefooted friars singing
vespers in the Temple of Jupiter in Rome, and Yeats's apocalyptic
prophecy: "But things fall apart. The centre cannot hold. Mere anarchy is loosed upon the world. And so we can begin again."

The symbol of this work will be the inverted lamp of H. G. Wells's
fable, "The Man Who Could Work Miracles" in which a man in a pub
orders a lamp to turn upsidedown and, incredibly, it does. Wine
declares that the inverted lamp will become their emblem: "One by
one what men have taken to be the true lamps are going out, and only
the topsy-turvy ones will give any light at all. But are they topsy-turvy,
after all? Or have we followed false lights for a thousand years or
more?" Wine concludes that "what the intellect rejects shall be our emblem: the inverted lamp" (p. 147).

Appleby remains unhypnotized by Wine's Mephistophelian argu-
ments (as does the pragmatic Hudspith); at bottom, he sees, it is all
based on a mad miscalculation: "It is true that times do come to an
end, but the thing happens far less frequently than people expect. . . .
Now things were uncomfortable enough, and for the first time since
the creation every continent and every sea were under fire. But in the
end of his time or his country, his language or his civilization or his
race, Appleby was not very disposed to believe" (p. 123). Wine and
Boglehole finally are undone by their own fatal inclination to believe
in their own mumbo-jumbo, and an attack by surrounding natives
combined with a rebellion from within ultimately put an end to the
Happy Isles experiment.

Meanwhile, Appleby and Hudspith — and Lucy Rideout — have
made their escape through the jungle on the back of Daffodil, until
they reach a Jesuit mission. It is appropriate that such an adventure
should close on a discussion with the urbane and intellectual repre-

sentative of that learned religious order for whom reason and religion comfortably coexist. That, and the return of Daffodil to Harrogate where the novel ends with a landau ride taken by two elderly ladies in defiance of Nazi aerial violence, marks the triumph of the West, and the British way, after all. Fundamentally, this is one of those "There'll always be an England" sort of stories.

One could hardly imagine a more fantastic "detective" novel. Innes gives a knowing wink in this regard, with the only direct reference to himself in any of his stories. In a conversation between Hudspith and Appleby just before the dénouement Hudspith comments,

> "Here is a perfect detective-story motive, and yet we're not in a detective story at all."
> "My dear man, you're talking like something in Pirandello. Go to sleep."
> "We're in a sort of hodge-podge of fantasy and harum-scarum adventure that isn't a proper detective story at all. We might be by Michael Innes." (p. 177)

Under all the *bizarrerie* there is a real political parable. *The Daffodil Affair* is constructed out of themes obviously of persistent concern to Innes, and they recur in a number of his works. The idea of the exploitation of the chaos of war-torn Europe, under the pretext of a sophistical Mephistophelian argument, is presented again in one of Innes's most powerful novels, the art-thriller *From "London" Far* (see chapter 5).

Impersonation Tales

In the thriller category is a group of Innes novels that are neither flight-and-pursuit adventures nor exotic thriller-fantasias, but are thrillers that might be called "anxiety tales." Each is a story of deception and imposture or impersonation; the anxiety in each case is that of the threat of disclosure. The intensity of the anxiety stems not merely from the criminality or impropriety of the impersonation and the sheer legal and other practical consequences of disclosure. Rather, the dread seems disproportionately greater than the fear of any such consequences, because it connects with a more fundamental psychic anxiety: the deep-rooted, existential fear of disclosure, of being found out or unmasked. The dominant mode of these stories may be said to be what Paul Riceour calls "the hermeneutics of suspicion" — or rather, the hermeneutics of being suspect.

A number of Innes thrillers hinge specifically on this impersonation theme. Four divide nicely into two pairs. *The New Sonia Wayward* (1960) and *The "Gay Phoenix"* (1976) involve deeply criminal cases of assumed identity of a next of kin — the plots are rather similar — in which the guilty protagonist suffers excruciating anxiety and ends up as a kind of psychic prisoner of his own deception. The other two, *A Change of Heir* (1966) and *Going It Alone* (1980), are essentially comic narratives, though with thriller elements involved, in which the impersonation is rather more of a lark or scam. All but *Going It Alone* concern, to one degree of guilt or another, protagonists who are villains, and may be compared with *Money from Holme* (chapter 5), in which the contemptible art swindler Cheel forces a sort of impersonation on another character. Impersonation and related devices, such as identical twins — which are, as Panek notes, essentially devices of farce[17] — are motifs Innes has used frequently over the years, but these four Simenon-length novellas, very straightforward and forwardly-plotted stories with little in the way of subplotting or extraneous incident or detection, belong clearly with the thrillers as stories of sensation rather than detection.

Most recently, *Carson's Conspiracy* (1984), plays an interesting variation on the impersonation theme: a businessman facing a shaky financial future and wishing to liquidate his assets without suspicion and decamp, concocts a bizarre scheme based upon his wife's delusion that they have a son. Carson pretends that the long-absent son has now returned from overseas, only to be immediately kidnapped; his urgent need for ransom money will be Carson's excuse for liquidating his funds.

Another work that plays upon the impersonation theme without focusing directly on the protagonist's anxiety about exposure is the cold-war thriller *Hare Sitting Up* (1959). The novel begins with an academic prelude of sorts when a man named Juniper, on his way back from a conference of headmasters of preparatory schools, is joined by a group of recent Oxford graduates who tumble into his railway compartment and treat him to an earful of animated talk about their lives and their sense of the future that lies before them. Or that does *not* lie before them, given the madness of nuclear arms buildup and government by "near-corpses" who have "neither wits in their heads nor compassion in their bowels" but who sit at negotiating tables with "jaws set like rat-traps" (pp. 9–10).

Additionally disturbing is the thought of people who would welcome annihilation; as a girl named Jean notes, "there are people obsessed with a violent pathological loathing of the whole human species. I have one in my own family, as a matter of fact. Imagine giving Jonathan Swift a hydrogen bomb" (p. 15). This leads another student to mention D. H. Lawrence and the character Birkin in *Women in Love* who "has this hating mankind in the guts neurosis pretty badly. . . . Humanity is a huge aggregate lie, and things would be better if every human being perished tomorrow. . . . No more people. Just uninterrupted grass, and a hare sitting up" (pp. 16–17). Juniper's realistic response to this misanthropic fantasy is that the hare and the grass would be unlikely to be spared. "Who cares?" Jean wonders. "Perhaps there are people with whom that sort of thing goes home. But — although, as it happens, I'm rather keen on birds — I'm not one of them. This strikes me as a human world, or nothing" (p. 17).

As with the undergraduate conversation in *A Family Affair*, the talk — in addition to being what Barzun and Taylor call an example of Innes's "best academic wit"[18] — does set up an important leitmotif that will reverberate through the ensuing plot. The next scene finds Juniper back at the prep school, Splaine Croft, where he is visited by Appleby — who at first appears, uncharacteristically, in disguise as a prospective parent — on what proves to be a terribly urgent mission. Juniper has an identical twin brother, a man whose field is highly sensitive biological research, and this man, Howard Juniper, has suddenly vanished. Will Miles Juniper take advantage of an old school trick and take Howard's place in the lab while the search for him goes on? In fact the situation is precisely the reverse of what has been presented: Howard and Miles are already in the habit of taking each other's place, and they had already done so at the start of the narrative: the "headmaster" Juniper on the train was in fact Howard Juniper the scientist. It is brother Miles the headmaster, posing as scientist Howard, who has mysteriously vanished. Appleby tumbles to this fairly quickly, but not before Howard Juniper pretends to be Miles pretending to be Howard — a perfect Innesian plot contortion! "It was a situation," Appleby smoothly explains, "that would tax the most accomplished of profes-

sional actors, I imagine." The remainder of the story is a farily straightforward comic thriller, as the hunt for the missing brother and what if
anything he might have taken from the lab goes on in an atmosphere of
intrigue and potential catastrophe. Here the plot gets closer to Hitchcock than to Buchan, full of false leads and red herrings as the search
leads into a series of unlikely quarters, all seemingly as innocent as
could be.

Appleby's search eventually takes him in the direction of bird-
watching centers, for that proves to have been an absorbing hobby for
both Junipers. The most avid and eccentric of keepers of bird-sanctu-
aries, a Lord Ailsworth, proves to be the center of suspicion. Appleby
attempts to penetrate Ailworth's remote sanctuary, and the proprietor's
battiness is such that it is almost impossible to tell whether his behavior
is indeed sinister or only harmlessly mad.

The novel ends with a well-told and exciting chase sequence, but
the real interest of the story lies in the allegory, which takes the reader
back to the opening conversation. Ailsworth is not any kind of foreign
agent, but rather a radical misanthrope, sick and obsessed (as his name
implies) with the idea of somehow using his beloved birds as a vehicle
for the extermination of the human race.

There was considerable disagreement among the original reviewers as to whether the political theme in *Hare Sitting Up* was handled
with wit and intelligence, or amounted only to undergraduate "philo-
sophic clichés" about nuclear armageddon. Perhaps, as with the matter
of the literary cliché about the twins, this is really a false issue. For one
thing, the students' clichés are in character. For another, when
Howard Juniper utters the dark truth about Ailsworth — that "a mad-
man and his fantasies should be so perfectly symbolical of the whole
drive of civilization today" (p. 183) — or when Judith Appleby exclaims,
"There oughtn't to be such a man. He oughtn't to have lent his abilities
to such madness" (p. 87), the reader may feel that some clichés bear
repeating. As Appleby himself says, "Quite so." It is the Appleby mot
that says it all when it just isn't possible, or necessary, to try to articu-
late in any other way something that between civilized people, is just
understood.

4

Bodley Harm: Murder in the Great Good Place

Oxford in Innes
Operation Pax
Redbrick Stories
Private Scholars and Public Schools

As W. H. Auden pointed out in "The Guilty Vicarage," the detective story requires first of all a closed and closely related society that is threatened primarily from within rather than from without and where all the members of the closed group are potentially suspect. And yet this society "must appear to be an innocent society in a state of grace," where there is no need of law until the murder precipitates a crisis. Ideally, Auden further notes, the characters in a detective story should be "eccentric (aesthetically interesting individuals) and good (instinctively ethical) — good, that is, either in appearance, later shown to be false, or in reality, first concealed by an appearance of bad."[1]

These shrewd observations lead neatly to an explanation of why the university is a favored setting for the classic detective novel:

> It is a sound instinct that has made so many detective story writers choose a college as a setting. The ruling passion of the ideal professor is the pursuit of knowledge for its own sake so that he is related to other human beings only indirectly through their common relation to the truth; and those passions, like lust and avarice

81

and envy, which relate individuals directly and may lead to murder
are, in his case, ideally excluded. If a murder occurs in a college,
therefore, it is a sign that some colleague is not only a bad man but
also a bad professor. Further, as the basic premise of academic life
is that truth is a universal and to be shared with all, the *gnosis* of
a concrete crime and the *gnosis* of abstract ideas nicely parallel and
parody each other.[2]

To dwell a little further on the several points he raises, first, there
is simply the physical consideration of the college as a useful variant
of the locked room — a standard starting point of much detective fiction. On this score alone, the English university, especially Oxford,
has distinct advantages because ever since the bloody town-and-gown
disorders of the middle ages, the individual colleges have been designed, precisely, as "gardens enclosed." Each college as a whole is
walled off from the town, with access confined to specific entrance
gates, with a security system of authorized keys and a porter at the
main gate and strictly enforced curfew hours. Each college is subdi-
vided into a system of quadrangles and the residential buildings into
separate "staircases," which rather effectively isolates each half dozen
or so individuals.

Next, atmospheric and thematic factors favor the choice of an
academic setting for a detective story. Two distinct but related motifs
come into play: innocence and the pursuit of knowledge. The university serves as a microcosm of an innocent or blameless society that suffers the unexpected and discordant intrusion of violence, either from
without or, even more disturbingly, from within. The novelist may
play off this assumed blamelessness of the academic milieu with great
seriousness, as Dorothy Sayers does in *Gaudy Night*, or with affectionate satirical amusement, as Innes always does — but whether serious
or comic, the fundamental belief in the Edenic innocence and integrity
of the university is assumed. This assumption is crucial to the effectiveness of the sudden revelation of the university as a horribly murderous place. In his review of *Death at the President's Lodging*, Nicholas Blake wrote:

> Dons and beaks, there is no doubt about it, make capital murderers.
> Fiction, crime-fiction in particular, has accustomed us to the highly
> spiced dishes of malice and uncharitableness served up at High
> Tables, to the steamy atmosphere of sedition and privy conspiracy

pervading Common Rooms. In actual fact, all the blood feloniously spilt in our academies of learning during the last hundred years would probably go into a medium-sized ewer. But that is unimportant. The tradition is the thing.   (*Spectator*, 30 October 1936, p. 770)

The university is viewed as a particularly apt setting for the mystery novel because it is an environment presumed to be entirely devoted to the disinterested pursuit of knowledge that can be treated either solemnly or whimsically — again, as by Sayers and Innes respectively. In her essay on the writing of *Gaudy Night* Sayers recalls the lecture she herself was invited to deliver at her college's gaudy on March 5, 1935: "I had to ask myself exactly what it was for which one had to thank a university education, and came to the conclusion that it was, before everything, that habit of intellectual integrity which is at once the foundation and the result of scholarship." This principle she sees as the intellectual foundation of her novel *Gaudy Night*:

> By choosing a plot that should exhibit intellectual integrity as the one great permanent value in an emotionally unstable world I should be saying the thing that, in a confused way, I had been wanting to say all my life. Finally, I should have found a universal theme which could be made integral both to the detective plot and to the "love interest" which I had, somehow or other, to unite with it. . . .
> The book is thus seen to be very tightly constructed, the plot and the theme being actually one thing, namely, that the same intellectual honesty that is essential to scholarship is essential also to the conduct of life.[3]

The detective impulse is, after all, only a special instance of the general pursuit of truth. Academic types are a natural consituency for this brand of fiction; as a recent article on the subject puts it, "Since the classic detective novel appeals to reason and intellect and since the university still sanctions intellectuals, we are not surprised to find professors writing and reading about the milieu they know best. The form is too attractive."[4] Marjorie Nicolson, a distinguished scholar of literature and science, and an avid mystery novel addict, expressed the point eloquently in her 1929 *Atlantic Monthly* essay, "The Professor and the Detective":

After all, what essential difference is there between the technique
of the detective tracking his quarry through Europe and that of the
historian tracking his fact, the philosopher his idea, down the great
ages?[5]

There are, she goes on to argue, only two methods — induction and
deduction — in pursuit of truth, whether in scholarship or detection.
"For, after all, scholars are, in the end, only the detectives of thoughts."

What has been said here about the affinities of detective fiction
and the university holds true as well for other versions of the Great
Good Place: the English public or prep school, the vicarage, and the
library. Innes offers several glimpses of the public school world, and
while no Innes mysteries center on the milieu of the vicarage, fum-
bling and well-intentioned vicars abound in his stories.

The library too, conceived fundamentally as a place of innocence,
order, and intellectual pursuit, lends itself well to the purposes of detective fiction, as Jane Filstrupp points out in her excellent article in the
Wilson Library Bulletin:

> Many attributes of the private library make it a suitable backdrop
> for classic detective novels. First, it embodies the quiet, dignity,
> and inscrutability, but not the tedium, of the tomb. It is also a fine
> place for the laying out of clues. In this moldy locale for routinized
> behavior, irregularities like a burned match or sliver of fingernail,
> even a book protruding on a shelf, catch the attentive eye. There
> reigns in the library a surface calm, through which violence tears
> with strident drama. . . . The library is a symbol for civilized soci-
> ety at a height of respectability. None of the libraries is depicted as
> a morally shabby place. They are islands of safety in detective fic-
> tion's disordered, unsafe world. Even if small or crowded or sop-
> orific, they are doing their service to society in a spirit of efficien-
> cy. The flash of murder on subdued canvas plunges the story into
> chaos and menaces our sanguinity about human nature. But the
> crisis ends with the reassertion of civilized values.[6]

Thus, Filstrupp argues, the sleuth in a library detection ought to
be the benign, even slightly befuddled type who "accepts the same values as the library's staff and users. . . . A vein of humor runs through
the novels of this group, about police and private eyes, people of action, being out of their element in the feminized and shadowy library
world."[7] Conversely, she notes, "the hard-boiled dick distrustful of
society is missing from library mysteries."

Raymond Chandler advocated precisely the converse, that the body should be taken out of the vicarage garden and put back in the streets.[8] The realistic approach has become increasingly the more typical one, especially since the forties, as Krouse and Peters point out:

> More typically, the contemporary academic mystery contains more longing for realism than rationalism, more bitterness than admiration, more cynicism than belief. Devastating attacks on academe by writers like Hull, Macdonald, and Parker sacrifice an aesthetic ideal for realism, or what in their disillusioned view appears to be realism. For most writers of academic detective novels the traditions of academe have been shaken to their foundations, and a return to "the innocent society in a state of grace" envisioned by Auden is impossible.[9]

Now if the academic ideal is fundamentally *dis*believed in, if one is radically skeptical or cynical about it, then the university setting cannot function in the traditional way in the detective story. If writer and reader are oriented to Chandlerian realism, then it is simply a different genre, a different sort of literary experience. In that case, as Auden would say, one is dealing with "not detective stories, but serious studies of a criminal milieu, the Great Wrong Place."[10] And that, as Innes believes, is matter properly for writers on the order of Aeschylus, Shakespeare, or Dostoevski.

Thus, for Sayers — as for Knox, Blake, Crispin, or Innes — when the academic ideal is violated, either by the ridiculousness of the dons or by malice from without or within, it is precisely *as* the violation of an ideal that it comes, rather than as any sort of revelation or intimation that the ideal itself is false. In explaining the plot conception behind *Gaudy Night*, she emphasizes that of the two possible approaches to an Oxfordian crime she is not interested in exploiting the potential evil of the ideal perverted — "intellect starved of emotion" — but rather the evil that stems from antagonism to the ideal: "emotion uncontrolled by intellect . . . emotion revenging itself upon the intellect for some injury wrought by the intellect upon the emotions."[11]

Whether it be the university, the public school, the vicarage, or the library, as Auden argues, in the classic or formal detective novel there is a single coherent mythic topos: "In the detective story, as in its mirror image, the Quest for the Grail, maps (the ritual of space) and timetables (the ritual of time) are desirable. Nature should reflect

its human inhabitants, i.e., it should be the Great Good Place; for the
more Eden-like it is, the greater the contradiction of murder."[12]

Oxford in Innes

For Michael Innes the Great Good Place is, was, and always will be
Oxford University. Margaret Yorke has demonstrated that Oxford has
many more detective fiction connections than does Cambridge: more
stories are set in Oxford, more detectives are Oxford-connected, and
so too are more detective writers. It is even true that more detective
writers *live* near Oxford: "It cannot be coincidence that eight writing
members of the Crime Writers Association live within fifteen miles of
the centre of Oxford and only two live as close to Cambridge."[13] Why
should this be? For anyone familiar with both universities, there is no
mystery. Cambridge boasts a Chair in Criminology, but Cambridge,
"strong on science, deals with criminological facts whereas our subject here is crime in fantasy." Cambridge is wide and tranquil, surrounded by "flat fenland exposed to cobweb-dispersing winds"; the ancient university town has a modern, suburban feel. At Cambridge "the
eye is led ever upwards and one is aware, always, of the sky." However, the "heavens are not conspicuous above Oxford, where the climate is prone to fog and the atmosphere induces introspection." Oxford is centrally located, a great industrial center. The gray stones and
"dreaming spires" of the university and its colleges are tucked into the
bustling city, behind great formidable walls and amid wonderfully
winding streets and alleys in a medieval fashion. Everything on the
score of mystery tilts toward the dark blue of Oxford rather than the
light blue of Cambridge.

Innes knows Oxford inside and out, first from his experience as
an undergraduate and then as don for twenty-five years. He has written with great familiarity and poignancy about Oxford in the J. I. M.
Stewart magnum opus, the Oxford Quintet called *A Staircase in Surrey*. But he has also introduced an Oxfordian note quite often in the
Innes mysteries as well. In them there is no dark satiric vision of university life. In Innes one encounters only a Chestertonian whimsicality.
Neither Innes, nor Appleby, nor any of Innes's donnish protagonists
ever conveys the sense that he feels the validity of his deepest com-
mitments and values is seriously threatened or called into question.
As Krouse and Peters testify in their article on murder in academe:

"Innes's vision of academe has remained essentially intact"; his academic novels reveal his "essential reverence for university tradition and innocence. He takes it for granted that his professors' learning is vast, their integrity almost unchallengeable, and their flaws not serious enough to discredit their calling."[14] Innes's approach is always one of good-natured and high-spirited humor.

The keynote is struck right from the beginning in the tongue-in-cheek headnote to *Death at the President's Lodging*, his first words in print as Michael Innes: "The senior members of Oxford and Cambridge colleges are undoubtedly among the most moral and level-headed of men. They do nothing aberrant; they do nothing rashly or in haste. Their conventional associations are with learning, unworldliness, absence of mind, and endearing and always innocent foible. They are, as Ben Jonson would have said, persons such as comedy would choose" (p. 6). But while Innes's satrical portraits of dons are broad to the point of lunacy, it is always clear that there is a bona fide academic ideal, even in places like St. Anthony's. It is apparent in Professor Titlow's distressed monologue about the crumbling of that ideal, his sense of the misdirection of scholarship in a secular society lacking a "transcendent idea" (p. 98).

In one quiet moment, through Appleby, one sees a glimpse of the deeper moral vision infusing Innes's idea of the university; reflecting upon "the spirit of the place," Appleby

> remembered touching the cold carved stone of an archway and feeling a permanence: something here before our time began; here while our time, as Titlow was to paint it, moved fearfully and gigantically to its close; to be here in other times than ours.   (p. 130)

In the rhythm of these remarks a version of the liturgical *saecula saeculorum* is recognizable. Appleby's reflections conclude on a strong, emblematic note: "He remembered a significance that the light over Surrey archway, shining steadily amid the darkness and the vapour, had taken on. And he remembered how he had sworn to drive out the intrusive alien thing. . . . " In this passage there is no question that the university is clearly the Great Good Place and the detective the comedic hero who will guard its precincts.

St. Anthony's is but the thinnest of disguises for Oxford, despite the elaborate humorous disclaimer in the novel's headnote, in which he locates his fictional college at Bletchley, a place of small comfort to scholars midway between Oxford and Cambridge. Reviewers and critics have as often as not forgotten or dropped the fiction and openly located the scene of this novel as Oxford. In fact, Innes does so as well in his essays, "Death as a Game" and "John Appleby," while elsewhere, in *A Family Affair*, Appleby himself casually mentions to the master of his son's college at Oxford, Balliol, that, "Such as it has been, you see, my career as a copper began in a college just across the High. The affair of poor President Umpleby" (p. 21). And later still, in the recent *Sheiks and Adders*, Appleby openly refers to his first case as an Oxford affair (pp. 134–35).

Thus, Innes started off his career with a thoroughly Oxonian mystery, and Oxford has, in a sense, never been out of his novels ever since. Innes novels actually set at Oxford, in whole or in part, include *Death at the President's Lodging, Operation Pax, Stop Press, A Family Affair*, and *Appleby Plays Chicken* (the latter a group of Oxford undergraduates on holiday with their tutor).

Although the Oxford connection is presented at a slight remove in *Appleby Plays Chicken*, a marvelous opening paragraph provides an unparallelled description of the "reading party," an Oxford institution at which a group of undergraduates repair with their tutor for an intellectual holiday in some quiet country place:

> In the morning the young men pore over their texts, carefully underlining every third or fourth sentence, or pausing to copy whole paragraphs into bulging notebooks. Their tutor, who knows these to be virtually useless labours, is invisible in his room; he is writing a book which he knows to be virtually useless, too. In the evening the young men debate, argue, quarrel. . . . Their tutor, who regards this as the valuable part of the day's work, smokes a pipe, drinks burgundy (activities expected of him) and expertly sees to it that the hubbub goes on till midnight.   (p. 5)

The Oxford element here consists primarily in the collegiate conversations with which this novel opens. Their talk, which is appropriately sophomoric, both literary and a bit pretentious, focuses on the subject of freedom and courage, and the American adolescent game of "playing chicken" — which they try out with ludicrous rather than disastrous consequences.

In this novel, instead of Oxford and its dons, one has an alternative vision of the Great Good Place — an archetypal country pub (the George, of course) and a cast of characters all smelling of tobacco and

tweed. Among them is a retired clergyman, Dr. Faircloth, the very
type of the muscular Christian. He talks enthusiastically of barrows
and dolmens and seems quite conversant with the "set" books of university study. At an open window, "smothering his face with lather" he
calls a hearty good morning to one of the students who is setting off
for a solitary tramp. Faircloth sniffs and gulps the air, "rather as if
testing it before allowing the waiter to pour out a glass all round," and
declaims: "A fine day, solitude, and the *Republic* in your pocket: it's
not a bad definition of happiness." This of course requires the student
to try very hard not to grind his teeth too loudly. Clearly, retired clergymen of ample means who are "able to greet life with glad cries while
shaving" are among life's most "adept profaners of mysteries" (p. 20).
The atmosphere, in short, is wonderfully "collegiate," and conveyed
appropriately from a brash undergraduate's point of view.

The action in *A Family Affair* (1969) begins with a gathering of
undergraduates — this time at Oxford itself, and at Bobby Appleby's
own college.[15] The narrator recalls how in Bobby's father's time Oxford students had been divided roughly into aesthetes, hearties, and
the unobtrusive "sub-men." Now the aesthetes have pretty well disappeared, replaced by the reading men, or intellectuals, and the hearties have become rather diminished and defensive in their belief that "an
honourable number of boats should be propelled up and down the river,
and that fifteens and elevens ought to be fielded as required" (p. 6).

Sir John Appleby is their elderly guest of honor at the gathering.
The scene is a tour de force of witty and mannered conversation among
a group of spirited undergraduates who are fond of affecting "a great
air of elderly ease" and who begin their evening's round of port, dispensed "with gravity," with a toast to Church and King (Appleby
presumes that the group "must attribute to themselves some vaguely
Jacobite persuasion"). They call themselves the Patriarchs. If the reader
is reminded by this of Tennyson, Hallam, and the Cambridge group
called The Apostles, so too is Appleby père, as he reflects that Bobby
and his friends seem as though "they might have been contemporaries
of Tennyson's or Thackeray's (only that would be at Cambridge) con-
scientiously entertaining themselves at what used to be called a wine"
(p. 8). Whether many students actually converse in the young, lordly
manner of the Patriarchs is immaterial — such Oxbridgians have the
reality of literary convention if not of sociological fact.

Conversation begins with great formal deliberateness on the chosen
topic of the evening, practical jokes: the etymology of the term (why

practical?); their origin (the first nightfall in Eden? the Flood?); practical jokes in literature ("Talking of the Flood," somebody said, rather belatedly. "There's a practical joke about it in Chaucer. The first recorded practical joke. It's *The Reeve's Tale*, isn't it?" "*The Miller's Tale*, you ignoramus."). The talk moves on to related topics: learned forgeries as scholarly jokes; college "rags" in Edwardian days. Nor is this a pointless prologue, for the subject of jokes and rags leads round at last to the story of an art theft of many years before, one that had been carried out, it appeared at the time, as an elaborate rag.

But this Oxonian prologue not only introduces the subject of the series of ingenious joke-like art thefts that will constitute the detective problem, it also prepares us nicely for the novel's dénouement. For after the investigation has run its course and the perpetrators of the thefts have been identified, they are lured into being caught redhanded by a trap laid for them at Oxford which takes the form of yet another extravagant collegiate rag.[16]

Another novel with a strong, intermittent Oxford element is *Stop Press*, a country-house story set primarily in a manor house deep in the southwestern rural womb of England. There is a strong Oxford connection as well; the house party that is the occasion of the unfolding of the mystery has its fair complement, among various other stock comic types, of Oxford dons and undergraduates. The preciousness of the conversation of the academic types is mimicked by the narrator, particularly in his amusing series of descriptions of Oxford. The first, representing the opening pages of part 1, is a more or less seriously intended portrait of the city on a November evening, an Arnoldian description awash in modulated sentiment and gentle melancholy:

> It was a November evening in Oxford and the air was stagnant, raw, and insidiously chill. . . . The sky, a sheet of lead rapidly oxidizing, was fading through glaucous tones to cinerous; lights were furred about their edges; in the glittering twilight Gothic and Tudor, Palladian and Venetian melted into an architecture of dreams. And the hovering vapours, as if taking heart of darkness, glided in increasing concentration by walls and butresses — like the first inheritors of the place, robed and cowled, returning to take possession with the night.   (p. 13)

Further along, the narrator offers a more whimsical view of Oxford as familiarly seen on arrival or departure from the viewpoint of a railroad journey, a wonderfully facetious piece of purple prose:

Oxford — adorable dreamer, cuckoo-echoing, bell-swarmed, lark-
charmed, rook-racked, river-rounded — Oxford shivered, lurched,
disintegrated into the fluidity of parallax. . . . Thus does the god-
dess, loosening her zone to the tempo of the Great Western Railway Company's locomotive, reveal herself to the novice in all her
naked loveliness; thus does she gather her garments about her at
the unparadising hour.   (p. 29)

But even this facetiousness is outdone later in the novel, as one
of the Oxford dons, Gerald Winter, effectively twits a crass publisher
named Wedge with an outrageously absurd exaggeration of the sort
of picturesque description the book begins with — but which the publisher guilelessly takes as an instance of Winter's masterful powers of
prose: "I sometimes think that Cambridge would have made a different man of me," says Winter. "All that warm brick — I should have
mellowed like a peach against a wall. . . . Consider the grisaille mo-
notony of Oxford. Cinerous colleges, ashen churches, and nowadays
a number of miscellaneous ecclesiastical edifices which are precisely
the colour of mud. A Gothic sprawling from slate through neutral to
dun; watered by glaucous rills, haunted by leaden vapours, and can-
opied by livid, lowering, low-toned clouds. When I look over the city
I sometimes feel I could take it up and squeeze it till it gushed red like
a fig at the fissure." Wedge is impressed; "Have you ever thought,"
he asks, "of writing these impressions down?" (pp. 193–94).
    The Oxford dons in their Common Room — a frequent enough
subject for Innes's satire — are at their most bizarre in this story, as their
conversation meanders with maddening inconsequence around the virtues of the port served at table, the subject of a notorious codex, the
mystery of the Spider (all are as surprisingly conversant with detective fiction as they are with the latest issues of the *Review of Classical
Archaeology*) and, interspersed with the rest, all manner of highly personal spites and nastinesses. The epitome of this common-room absurdity is something known as Dr. Groper's System. Groper was a
nineteenth-century master of the college who had decreed that dining arrangements in hall should involve a constant system of rotation
among places at a large table for general conversation and innocent
mirth, a medium-sized table for three for sustained, fruitful discussion, and a solitary table for profound introspection over one's port.
The orderly progression of the system was rendered less predictable
by the introduction of occasional guests:

This last provision . . . makes the calculations a little complicated;
it was instituted by Dr Groper as likely to maintain the standard
of mathematical study in the college. . . . It was one of the hor-
rors of Dr Groper's system that one never knew from evening to
evening with whom one must consort.   (p. 22)

The portrait of Dr. Groper, his hand gesturing toward an open page
of his *Commentary on Newton's Principia* and beside him an orrery,
presides complacently over the scarcely less elaborate motions and
gyrations he himself had set in motion and imposed on generations of
scholars. It is true that the system had once been challenged, but upon
the discovery that its terms were contained in an endowment of the
college wine-cellar contingent upon its due performance, it was never
challenged again!

Operation Pax, 1951
(alternate title: *The Paper Thunderbolt*)

In 1951, after his years spent in Leeds, Adelaide, and Belfast, and when
he had only recently returned to Oxford as a don, Innes produced his
preeminent academic tale, an Oxford mystery that transcends both the
locked-room puzzle approach of *Death at the President's Lodging* and
the farceur approach of the redbrick stories discussed later: the magnificently crafted thriller *Operation Pax*. Basil Davenport commented,
"In all his books Michael Innes has been pushing back the boundaries
of the detective story — into tragedy, into farce, into satire, and above
all into fantasia. This time he has broken through them altogether"
(*NYTBR*, 11 Nov. 1951, p. 26). Reviewers pointed to the "Hitchcockian" qualities of this highly suspenseful story[17] — not often applicable
to Innes's mysteries because of their high degree of whimsicality and
bookishness and general absence of the sinister. The rich network of
literary allusions (what the *Saturday Review* called a "morass of ses-
quipedalian whimsey" [22 Dec. 1951, p. 38]) is made integral to the
plot itself; as reviewer Partridge drily remarked, "English literature
never lets you down, remember" (*New Statesman*, 3 Nov. 1951, p. 42).
    Operation Pax is a good instance of how a really first-rate novel
can get lost, as it were, through being classified as just another detective story. There was at least one effort to bring this book to the attention of a wider readership. Harry Bauer, Director of Libraries at

the University of Washington, Seattle, in his column "Seasoned to Taste" in the *Wilson Library Bulletin* (vol. 31, June 1957, p. 756) hailed the excellence of the book while speculating that lack of appropriate recognition may have stemmed in part from its titles, both the "indifferent" British title (*Operation Pax*) and the "grossly inadequate" American title (*The Paper Thunderbolt*). "Some such title as 'Bodley Injury,'" he suggested, "would have won the attention of librarians far and wide, and as a droll substitute, would have been quite appropriate since the dénouement of *Operation Pax* occurs in the Bodleian Library."

The situation (although neither the reader nor any of the several protagonists get any clear sense of it till about two-thirds of the way through the book) is as follows. Entirely inadvertently, a rabbity three-quid petty swindler named Albert Routh stumbles into the operations of a gang of scientific criminals in a country manor outside Oxford near a Cotswold town called Milton Porcorum. It is a bogus sanitarium in which unspeakable experiments are carried out upon a variety of helpless victims, including alcoholics and political refugees, as well as various animals, all aimed at destroying the capacity for aggression (hence the title, "Operation Pax"); it is an interesting anticipation of the theme explored in Anthony Burgess's *A Clockwork Orange*. Such a drug is really a means effectively to control people, and this antiaggression formula — known as Formula Ten — would naturally have potentially disastrous consequences in the hands of an enemy power.

In the initial chase sequence, the disreputable Routh, in a panicky flight from a failed attempt to pass a small bad check, first gets himself ignominiously beaten up by a woman he attempts to molest in a country lane, and then finds himself to have blundered into the hands of the people who run the bogus sanitarium. Routh is a marvelous study in the pathology of self-pity and the smoldering, snarling resentment of a man who has been bullied by everyone from his father and the children he grew up with, to his teachers and the police. And now, worst of all, even the woman he tries to mug bullies him — after she brings him down with some swift maneuver, she orders him to rub his face in the mud and gravel. But a while later, his recovery of self-conceit is even more ignominious; noticing that the scratches are inconsiderable, he gloats to himself, "Wily Routh. He hadn't rubbed his face in the gravel half as hard as he'd pretended." "Routh," incidentally is another of those wonderfully ironic emblematic names so often found in Innes, "routh" in Scottish signifying wealth or plenty, while "ruth" of course means compassion (and also remorse — applicable without irony).

In the sanitarium Routh at first tries to carry off a bold bluff to save his neck from the really frightening gang that's got hold of him. But as he is about to be neatly and summarily dispatched, as reviewer Edgar Acken aptly paraphrased the scene, Routh "flew into one of those rages of which only cowards are capable" (*N. Y. Herald Tribune Book Review*, 9 Dec. 1951, p. 20), and, with the unexpected aid of a cat, kills his tormentor and escapes — with Formula Ten to boot.

Thus far part 1 of the novel, titled "Routh in an Infernal Region" and bearing an apt epigraph from *Paradise Lost*: " . . . involv'd / in this perfidious fraud." Part 2, "Routh in Flight," again bears an apropos headnote from the same source: "Who would not, finding way, break loose from Hell, / Though thither doomed?" And doomed Routh seems to be, as one of the most inventive and relentless flight-and-pursuit sequences ever penned unfolds throughout the ensuing hundred pages or so. This chase takes Routh from one impossible predicament to the next, each hopeless situation succeeded by an equally fantastic last-second reprieve or exit, only to be followed by the next, even more discouraging predicament, in a continual turning of the ratchet.

Innes takes Routh through a bewildering variety of locales, by means of all sorts of ingenious transportation, in a showcase of thriller topography. It begins in the labyrinthine corridors and grounds of the sanitarium; when Routh tumbles for refuge into a vehicle of some sort in a shed, it turns out to be a helicopter; after a spectacular crash landing of the chopper, Routh is off on his motorbike, only to be pursued by his enemies in a powerful car; a colorful truck stop provides an atmospheric interlude and a brief moment of proletarian camaraderie for Routh; then another road chase ends in a pursuit on foot through a bit of forest, ending with Routh tumbling into a tiny cottage; just as his enemies are trying to force a window, *the cottage slides away* — it turns out that it is a prefabricated house being transported on a flatbed truck! And so it goes, from pillar to post, finally taking Routh to Oxford, where the pursuit continues on a city bus and Routh poses as a telephone lineman and then crashes a neighborhood children's theatrical to scramble into a costume.

Thus the narrative leads on into part 3, "Routh and Others in Oxford," where, aptly enough, the Miltonic tag switches to *Paradise*

Regained: "Turrets and Terrases, and Glittering Spires" — for this city of dreaming spires, as Matthew Arnold called it, is manifestly meant to be understood as the Great Good Place.

The opening pages of part 3 are a leisurely evocation of Oxford as seen from the point of view of a rotund and ponderous don and Oxford character, Professor Bultitude, as he emerges from his college: "Mr. Bultitude stepped out of the main gateway of Bede's and looked about him in mild surprise" (p. 68). The prose of this section has some affinities with that of James Joyce where Mr. Leopold Bloom is introduced in *Ulysses*, but there is an even more specific literary echo, the conclusion of Keats's sonnet on "Chapman's Homer":

> Or like stout Cortez when with eagle eyes
> He star'd at the Pacific — and all his men
> Look'd at each other with a mild surmise —
> Silent, upon a peak in Darien.

As a little acknowledgment that the reader has correctly tumbled to the allusion, Innes provides a more specific reference a few pages on: "Like stout Cortez in the poem, Bultitude had now toiled to an eminence from which he could survey, on his right, the illimitable Pacific of Walton Street" — the thread of allusion to Keats's paeon to bookish adventure being most appropriate to this Bodley tale. This sudden change of venue to Oxford is occasioned by the fact that Routh's escape from Milton Porcorum has brought him to Gloucester Green, Oxford's bus depot — and also by the fact that more than one Oxford-connected person has disappeared in the vicinity of Milton Manor, notably a refugee woman engaged to an Austrian research fellow, and an undergraduate who happens both to be the nephew of an Oxford don and fiancé of another Oxford student who is none other than Jane Appleby, sister of Assistant Commissioner John Appleby.

The second half of the novel is a richly comedic and evocative Oxonian tale. In the fullest sense Oxford is a *character* in this novel, and high table and common room at Bede's is as full of affectionate ridicule as one has come to expect from Innes. Particularly effective is the portrait of the harried Austrian fellow, trying so hard to be proper in good English fashion, and perpetually failing, largely through the very earnestness of his exertions. In one moment he abruptly becomes a character of authentic human weight when Appleby appeals directly to him for aid, making the strongest appeal that, he knows, can be made: "I appeal to you, sir, as a scholar — as a scholar and a humanist" (p. 116).

At bottom this novel, with its Miltonic leitmotif, is conceived as a moral allegory in terms of the use and abuse of knowledge, the same issue that concerned Sayers in *Gaudy Night*. And as in that novel, it is a library that serves as the chief emblem of that allegorical struggle, in this case, the greatest library in the world. That the Bodleian Library should be the scene of such a moral confrontation is made humorously apt in a remark made to Appleby by Professor Bultitude: "How very interesting. It is true that highly criminal proceedings are frequently conducted there — but on what must be termed, conventionally, the intellectual plane" (p. 221). There are in fact two great Bodley scenes in *Operation Pax*: part 4, "Bodley by Day" and the sixth and concluding section, "Bodley by Night." The former centers on a scene in the Upper Reading Room that is a real stroke of *fantaisie*, a thriller episode in which Routh is finally run to earth by his relentless pursuers, an action that unfolds in accordance with the perfect decorum required of all users of that august institution.

Innes carefully explains the economy of the Bodleian at the outset, for the benefit of readers unfamiliar with it and for the delight of those who are. Rank undergraduates pursue their studies in the several department libraries that provide judiciously selected books "in what, to their large innocence, appears inexhaustible abundance." At the other end of the hierarchy of Oxford learning, "those in whom extreme fulness of years and exceptional depths of erudition" are conjoined, inhabit the venerable carrells of Duke Humphrey's Library and the Selden End, places so venerable, the narrator tells us, as to have generated "not only a peculiar aura but also an indescribable smell," adding that "As long as this smell endures Oxford will endure too" (p. 144). And for those occupying a middle station in this hierarchy, there is the Upper Reading Room.

It is to this Upper Reading Room that Jane Appleby, Somerville student, distressed — and embarrassed — at having "mislaid her young man," has repaired for intellectual solace, or rather, more accurately, for atmosphere, "for the smell of old leather and vellum and wood that permeated the approaches to the place. . . . She came, in short — an unconfessed tourist disguised as a scholar of Somerville" (p. 145). Near her a gray-haired woman is taking notes from a book the size of a postage stamp, and old Dr. Undertone, ninety-six, dozes over volumes of seventeenth- and eighteenth-century homiletic literature.

Into this orderly and somewhat somnolent world enters the hunted man, Routh, and for all his sordid shabbiness he does not, really, look all that out of the way: "He was shabby, but scholars can be shabbier than anybody else in the world. He was grubby, but that is not absolutely unknown among the learned" (p. 147). And even though, harrassed as he is, he has the appearance of one "whose mind is bent with maniacal concentration upon the solution of some single, urgent and ever-present problem," neither is this "uncommon among those who pursue the historical Homer or the origins of the Sabellian heresy, or who are hounded by urgent conundrums concerning the comparative phonology of the dialects of the upper Irrawaddy." The fugitive picks up enough sense of the place to pretend to browse, and even that is inconspicuous, even if detected as subterfuge, "For it frequently happens that scholars, seized suddenly as they are walking past by some irresistibly enticing train of speculation, and being brought to an abrupt halt thereby, avoid (what would be odious to them) the appearance of any singularity of conduct by going through just this conventional inspection of whatever shelves are nearest to hand" (p. 148). At this point a donnish-looking figure enters whom the reader knows to be Routh's ruthless pursuer. Immediately Routh thrusts his scrap of paper (Formula Ten) in between the leaves of one of the books stacked on the desk of the dozing Dr. Undertone, and moves off across the room. What Jane Appleby is then witness to, as she peers over the top of a book, must be one of the strangest scenes ever to transpire in the Bodleian. But once again, the reader unfamiliar with the disposition of things in the Bod must first be put in the picture about the central feature of the Upper Reading Room: a double row of low bookcases containing the monumental manuscript catalogue of the Bodleian Library. "To move round these massive islands is to circumambulate a brief record of the entire intellectual and imaginative achievement of the race. And this is what the two men — pursuer and pursued — were doing now. They were playing a sort of hide-and-seek round this monumental guide to human knowledge" (p. 150).

It is not a question of any overt chase; indeed, both make some show of doing what the other users are doing — lugging out a volume here and there by its leathern loop and consulting its pages. "Nevertheless their actual preoccupation was clear. The one was concerned

to edge up and the other was concerned to edge away. This went on
for some time. It was like some crazy sequence in a dream. . . . Watching the two of them at their covert manoeuvring around the catalogue
was like watching some ingenious toy. Or it was like watching a child
forcing one piece of magnetised metal jerkily across a table by nosing
towards it the answering pole of another" (p. 151). But abruptly Dr.
Undertone awakes with a start, the Bodley Librarian enters on his
wonted rounds, and when Jane next looks about, the two men have
gone. Shortly afterward, however, Jane does witness the final capture
of the hunted man and learns he has been taken by ambulance to the
vicinity of Milton Porcorum.

What ensues in part 5 of the novel, "Nemesis at Milton Manor,"
is a return to the thriller component, as the disparate forces set in motion thus far independently converge on the nefarious sanitarium: Jane
Appleby and a clever young dropout now working as a cabbie in Oxford; a group of children, a sort of Baker Street Irregulars, whose path
the pursuit of Routh in North Oxford has crossed; a Laurel and Hardy
pair of dons, the portly Bultitude and his cranelike friend, Dr. Our-
glass, uncle of the missing undergraduate who is engaged to Jane; and
of course Inspector Appleby himself. There's all sorts of exciting action in these pages, fantastic happenings that, as Ralph Partridge said,
"will rouse no resentment, once you can swallow the free use of fire-
arms in the English landscape" (*New Statesman*, Nov. 3, 1951, p. 42).
And hair-raising as the struggle is at Milton Manor (note, incidently,
the epigraph, from *Comus* this time: "And they, so perfect is their
misery, / Not once perceive their foul disfigurement"), Jane Appleby's
pickup hero, the young man with the Smollet-like name of Roger Remnant, is finally correct in his initial estimate that the whole operation,
once penetrated, would prove to be a paper tiger: "It will be paper-
thin. We just have to put a fist through it and it goes. Just remember
that we approach the job in the light of that knowledge" (p. 182).

At any rate the infernal palace does go up in flames, although the
ultimate villain evades capture and identification, and meanwhile the
ominous Formula Ten must still be recovered and kept from nefarious
use. The trouble is that the mysterious archvillain, along with Jane Appleby, her Roger Remnant, Professor Bultitude, and even Inspector
Appleby *all* know where to look for it: between the pages of some book
in the Bodleian Library!

In this ultimate version of the needle in the haystack, Jane and

Roger do have a starting point of sorts: the paper has been slipped into one of the books Dr. Undertone was reading the day before. These
have now been returned to the stacks. The obvious recourse is to consult Dr. Undertone himself. But the superannuated scholar has in-
conveniently died overnight! Their only clue is Undertone's field of
study, Pastoral and Homiletic Theology. He studies sermons. Roger
brightens with a naive hope:

> "And have a lot been published? I don't think I've ever seen any."
> Jane laughed a little desperately. "Far more of them than of any-
> thing else in the whole world." (p. 252)

Fortunately, however, they find a sort of memorandum on Undertone's desk, a list of books headed with the superscript *Perlegi* — "I
have read through. . . . " In other words, he kept a kind of daily diary
of his researches. Armed with these titles and their case marks (itself
a dauntingly byzantine code, they realize, for anyone but a Bodley
book-runner), Jane and Roger set off on a nocturnal adventure. Roger
is familiar with one aspect of the Bodleian: "It's a principle of Oxford
roof-climbing," he explains, "that there is no natural feature known
to climbers of which there is not a pretty fair artificial equivalent in
the buildings of this city. . . . Do you know about the Mendip caves?
. . . Well, like everything else in the world, the fissures that take you
down there have their equivalent here in Oxford" (p. 257). It is a sort
of vent that leads from Radcliffe Square down to the vast underground
stacks of the Bodleian. Like Aeneas at the mouth of the Avernus, they
take the plunge.

Jane and Roger land in a blank Stygian darkness; a torch reveals
that they are in a vast subterranean cavern, perched on some middle
level of a system of openwork catwalks of cast iron, connected by ver-
tical ladders, spiral staircases and a criss-crossing of supporting girders,
and ranks upon ranks of books as far as the light can penetrate below
or above or around them. It is as claustrophobic as a submarine — "it
was like something, Jane thought, by Piranesi — a dream-architecture
cunningly devised to suggest at once the search and the impotence of
the human mind" (p. 261). It is also depressing, as Remnant testifies:

> "I've never before been made so powerfully aware of life's utter
> futility. All those chaps scribbling away, persuaded that fame and

immortality were just round the corner. And now nobody so much
as remembers their existence, except this old fellow — what do you
call him? — Bodley's Librarian. It's the sort of thing that makes one
look round for a drink. Sorry to be such a barbarian."
      "You're not terribly singular. A great library made Dr. Johnson
feel much the same."   (p. 261)

Nevertheless, armed with their shelfmarks, they do eventually hit
upon the appropriate cases of obscure homiletic tracts and finally the
volume with the crucial scrap of paper — but at this point the various
other forces of order and disorder have similarly converged on the
Bodleian and what ensues is a final surrealistic chase through and
among the sliding book racks and catwalks, until the villain plunges
to his death, tripped up by the very volume he had been attempting
to make off with: "He fell sheer — and into a great darkness that now
flooded up over Jane. But for a second yet her inward eye could see
him — plunging down through a million books, rank upon rank of
books, armies of unalterable law" (p. 267). The title of the fatal volume
that tripped him up? *A Thunderbolt of Wrath against Stiff-Necked and
Impenitent Sinners*.

Appropriately, as order is restored in the final pages, the presiding
figure is Bodley's Librarian, "an elderly man with a high, domed
forehead, quite bald, on which were symmetrically disposed several
tiers of spectacles" (p. 152). He confesses to Roger, "My dear boy, I
first entered Bodley that way myself. It was what first drew my interest to the Library. So it is very possible, you see, that one day this
room will be your own" (p. 268). He even puts the romantic subplot
in order, giving Roger the same injunction that Dame Nature gives to
the courtly Eagle in Chaucer's *The Parlement of Fowles*, to put his
love to the test by going away — "The other side of the world. For a
year."

An amusing footnote may be added here. Innes tells the story of
how the real Bodley librarian, when he read the novel, was so disturbed by the notion of a secret underground access to the stacks, that
he immediately got out of bed that night to check Radcliffe Square for
such a "Mendip Cave" aperture. The librarian subsequently attempted
to revenge himself by inviting Innes to autograph the Bodley's copy
of *Operation Pax*; Innes says he was quick-witted enough to decline —
realizing that the librarian's intent was to entrap Innes into defacing

a Bodley book and thereupon bar his any future access to the collection![18] And that's about as Oxonian a tale as you can get.

Redbrick Stories

Two other Innes academic novels, *The Weight of the Evidence* (1943) and *Old Hall, New Hall* (1956), have the interesting distinction of being laid in "redbrick" settings, that is, in provincial universities. As Innes drew on his Oxford experiences in the novels discussed earlier, so in these he draws upon his tenure at Leeds (1930–35), the prototype for the fictional University of Nesfield in *The Weight of the Evidence*. Erik Routley noted that the latter is "probably the first detective story located in a 'redbrick' university,"[19] and Christopher Pym, in his review of *Old Hall, New Hall* made sport of this Innes venture into middle-class academe: "Look where Lucky Jim's landed! Slap in the middle of one of those Oxford-Companion-to-English-Literature *Times*-crossword-puzzle crime stories — written about Redbrick, but by Greystone" (*Spectator*, 23 March 1956, p. 196).

In these redbrick fables, Innes turns his eye and his style to a somewhat more naturalistic realism than commonly encountered in his writing; he even puts on a turn of paratactic Hemingway-esque prose at one point, as he describes Appleby's reflections on the midland city of Nesfield: "You could see from here the city spread in a sort of drab sparkle in the darkness, and you could see a pool of darkness which was a park, and you could see the station and hard bright lights in the shunting yards beyond the station" (*Weight*, p. 51). It is odd, Appleby reflects ironically, "that the mind when tired churns out such flawless modern prose"! And later in the story Appleby finds himself at a very Midlands-style station buffet for breakfast, with its long horseshoe counter, its cauldrons of tripe and sausages, clatter of pots and jocose conversation. Another investigative lead takes him out to the suburbs, where the grimy spire of Nesfield Cathedral shares the skyline with municipal gasometers and lines of uniform row houses and yellow-brick conveniences for ladies and gents — all in all, a "compost of the banal and the bizarre" (p. 71).

Naturally, the image of the university and the students in such a place is a far cry from the Oxford of the Patriarchs in *A Family Affair*. Here, as the school shuts down for the day, instead of languid sherry parties, all is hustle and bustle: women with pails and brooms gather, doors slam, students flock home to pore over textbooks or to take in a movie as "sweetness and light were over for the day" (p. 47). Similarly, Innes's depiction of Old Hall, a Georgian mansion purchased and made over into a regional university by local industrial benefactors, presents a set of social and architectural incongruities: "The rather grandly bleak Georgian facades of Old Hall possessed, in their barely controlled disrepair, the rubbed abraded appearance of something done on canvas to an improbably stupendous scale. The sprawl of army huts, Nissen and Spider, on the one flank, and the raw brick boxes housing laboratories and workshops on the other, didn't look like anything that a responsible human being would pitch down beside an eighteenth-century mansion in a seventeenth-century park" (*Old Hall*, p. 9). Amid the trees and the benches and the gravel walks, all familiar enough in a university setting, one sees such novelties as signposts with mysterious inscriptions like "Women's Union" or "Strength of Materials" (p. 17).

Instead of a common room and high table, there is a refectory, located in "some sort of hangar that might have been reared to accommodate the last of the big dirigibles," where you shove your soup and stew past a till. Changing of classes is marked by an hourly bell, "an electric bell of almost incredible shrillness, guaranteed to dominate any uproar — and even (which was its principal function) to stop the most self-absorbed lecturer dead in the middle of a sentence." Registration for a new term is the Pig Market, where each department sets up a trestle table with tidy piles of syllabuses and entrance forms to peddle to any likely enrollees. Clouts's line on all this — Colin Clout is the young protagonist of *Old Hall, New Hall*, an aspiring novelist returning to his alma mater to seek a teaching position — is to view the scene not in terms of "redbrick realism," but rather with the eyes of Kafka:

> What Kafka, of course, would "do" — Clout remembered to put the magical word between its inverted commas — was the bewilderment: the ambiguities and the false casts and the *culs-de-sac*. Nobody would be quite sure whether anybody else was a student or a professor; and there would be intermittent doubt about the place being a university at all, and not, say, a maternity hospital or the municipal abattoir. (p. 45)

In fact, his current bright idea is for an antinovel to be called *The Examination*, in which the protagonist, C., is either giving or taking an examination, but is not sure which.

The dons in such a place Innes characterizes as "most of them genuine, if low-grade scholars, their persons distinguished by marmalade stains, missing buttons, improvised shoe laces, and their minds directed upon distant and impalpable things" (*Old Hall*, p. 24). They are, however, vaguely aware of existing in a sort of academic Siberia, and cruelly bereft of the comforting Oxbridgian rituals and amenities. Innes drily sums up the milieu from a don's point of view in a passage in *The Weight of the Evidence*:

> The provincial universities of England, although often abundantly medieval in point of architectural inconvenience, have little of the organization characteristic of traditional places of learning. The staff — a word which at Oxford or Cambridge might be used or persons employed in a hotel — is not accommodated in spacious common rooms and cosy suites. Sometimes it is provided with a cellar in which the extravagant may drink coffee-essence at eleven o'clock; sometimes there is also an attic with chairs, where meetings may be held; a midday meal is obtainable by those who will grab from a counter with one hand and from a cutlery basket with the other. . . . But although they cannot bring with them from Oxford and Cambridge the immemorial organization of a learned community, they can and often do bring the somewhat attenuated charities which such societies produce. (pp. 5–6)

A consequence of this environment is that these dons tend to be even more extravagantly pedantic and eccentric than Innes's Oxford dons. Nursing professional frustrations and wounded vanity, they adopt attitudes in the manner of Clout's old mentor and nemesis, Professor Gingrass of Old Hall, who cultivates a blend of the comic and ironic modes intimating that he, "like the Shakespearian Tragic Hero, was a being mysteriously but definitively superior to his environment" and whose smile in one's presence conveys "his sense that your mere continued existence was part of the high comedy of things."

Eccentricity easily slides into the sinister. At Nesfield, where the mystery is that a Professor Pluckrose has been found in the courtyard crushed to death under a meteorite, Appleby finds that no one mourns the dead don; either they make learned puns on his name, or devise weird theories about Galilean experiments or a "Sisyphus Complex."

Not surprisingly, the plots of these two novels are extremely fanciful. That of *The Weight of the Evidence* is particularly wacky. In attempting to solve the problem of how Pluckrose ended up beneath a meteor, Appleby has to follow up a mad-hatter collection of seemingly pointless leads — Professor Tavender's false beard, Timmy Church's bigamy, the skeleton in the dark room, and so forth. It is an Innes specialty to concoct an outrageously inconsequential chain of references and then tie them all together logically. Most, of course, are red herrings, but in the end it all makes a crazy, Alice-in-Wonderland kind of sense.[20]

The plot of *Old Hall, New Hall*, on the other hand, ties together its academic subplot with a traditional country-house mystery involving (much in the manner of *Christmas at Candleshoe*) two rival branches of an old family, buried treasure, and an old family journal that contains the key to the mystery. Colin Clout has returned to Old Hall fresh from Oxford as an aspiring avant-garde novelist seeking a faculty post — but all he is offered by Gingrass, the egregious chairman, is an absurd appointment as Shuffelbotham Student, a grant named after an important mercantile benefactor of the school, and supporting biographical research on eminent local dignitaries.

Clout's task, perhaps more Kafka-esque than his sophomoric anti-novel idea, is to research the life of the eccentric Sir Joscelyn Jory, an early nineteenth-century proprietor of Old Hall, whose descendants are now the Jorys of New Hall. Sir Joscelyn's thing was to do in a collecting way what Sir Thomas Browne had done in a meditative and philosophical way: he amassed funerary monuments, and on such a large scale that he even began to build a giant mausoleum that was to become a museum of funerary objects. It turns out that Joscelyn Jory had a brother who was also a collector, but what Edward collected was at once more simple and more singular — he collected women.

The family papers in question — a journal kept by the Jorys' priggish sister — indicate that the brothers ended their respective collecting careers with a gentlemen's agreement to trade their greatest finds: Joscelyn's of a mummy and treasure of a Caucasian queen, and Edward's of a Greek girl so magnificent that to Joscelyn she represents "the only true felicity he could now conceive." Sophie's journal indignantly records Edward's ribald talk about his find:

> She wasn't yet, he said, fit for the company of ladies. He must first take soap and water to her, and then we should see. To this Edward added something further in bad French. I caught the words tetons and fesses. This grossness I was unprepared to suffer. I bade Edward good-night. (p. 136)

The journal records how both treasures were abandoned in haste as the brothers had to flee angry pursuers. And so now, back in the present, this account precipitates a frenzied rival search for the buried Caucasian treasure on the grounds of what is now Old Hall campus. Eventually the treasure does turn up (hidden in a trunk labeled "Bound sermons / Bibles / Religious Tracts, etc." — the perfect hiding place!). But the big surprise is that Edward's treasure, the fabulous Greek girl, turns up too — not the skeleton of some poor abused Greek peasant lass but an absolute prize from Greek antiquity, the Aphrodite Entumbia — a statue and not a girl at all! This Aphrodite has been hidden where she could have been seen all the time (the purloined letter principle again) — as just another of the many indifferent classical garden ornaments disposed about the grounds of Old Hall.

This final twist brings in several of Innes's favorite themes at once: the confusion between a person and a statue, and the confusion between a great art work and a mere ornament. *What*, these confusions seem to ask, *does one really see?* Why does the masterpiece go unrecognized? Is it simply that for the most part one sees only what one expects to see? Moreover, the sophisticated antinovelist Clout has been forceably reminded of a few basic, hard-hitting facts of life about reality vs. romantic illusion or wish fulfillment and about the persistent force of some simple primitive fascinations as the sure foundation of any good story:

> It was the quite distinct excitement of the hunter. Buried treasure — it came to him — must be one of those deeply emotive notions that can really get you. There was probably an interesting subject of research in it — indeed, the fascination of research itself was related to it . . . buried treasure as an archetypal image. (p. 183)

It is something Michael Innes could have told Colin Clouts all about.

Private Scholars and Public Schools

Innes uses what may be called the academic connection frequently in his works, and not just in the university novels. There are academic protagonists in country-house stories such as *Hamlet, Revenge!* (Giles Gott) or *Stop Press* (Gerald Winter), or in thrillers such as *From "London" Far* (Meredith) or *The Journeying Boy* (Thewless). Or, at the other end of the scale, there is the absurd, vague, or tedious don or American professor in a sort of satirical cameo role — every Innes house party seems to have one — or even, in ultimate betrayal of the proper nature of things, in an actual villainous role, as in *A Family Affair* or *The Ampersand Papers*. And then there is that distinctively British type, the private scholar, featured prominently in *The Long Farewell*.

Not a university novel, but one focusing instead on that related world of the amateur scholar, *The Long Farewell* (1958) involves some of Innes's favorite themes, notably forgery and the lure of valuable literary remains. The central character in *The Long Farewell* — central even though he is killed early in the story — is Lewis Packford, a portly, Leslie Hotson–like amateur scholar (Hotson, a chief contributor to Shakespeare documentary studies, was not himself an academic, but a civil servant working in the Public Records Office in London) who specializes in springing research discoveries on the scholarly world with maximum surprise and unpleasantness. Packford is one of Innes's more memorable characterizations, a man "whose scholarship is unperplexed by any literary appreciation of his subject," as the *TLS* review nicely put it (11 April 1958, p. 193). Rather, he is one of those scholars who simply *digs*, and by dint of persistence and having a nose for it, is able to come up with scraps of hard documentary evidence concerning important literary figures and questions.

Packford appears in part 1 of the novel — "Prologue in Italy" (the four parts of the novel call attention to the analogy with classical drama) — in the course of an evening social call paid by the vacationing Appleby to his old but rather distant acquaintance at the latter's rented villa above Lake Garda. Then follow twenty-five pages of some of Innes's finest and most relaxed donnish prose as Appleby's and Packford's conversation meanders pleasantly about the topics of Italy, the Mediterranean, fine art, good living and, of course, the mellow pleasures and vague discontents of the life of a solitary amateur scholar of independent means. Appleby's professional instinct tells him that

Lewis Packford is on to something, something, naturally, to do with Elizabethan literature, and probably to do with the subject of Shakespeare and Italy. Appleby is able to make a good guess that it probably concerns some new documentary evidence shedding light on the frequently conjectured but never proven sojourn of Shakespeare in Italy. Despite Packford's disingenuous disclaimers that speculation about Shakespeare's private life is just inconsequential "Crackpot stuff, like saying he must really have been Lord Tomnoddy, since otherwise he couldn't have made all those references to hunting and hawking and heraldry," it is clear to Appleby that Packford is on to something precisely of that order. "To present himself before the learned with what he had called mere cobweb triumphantly transmuted to perdurable steel; to flourish before their noses, it might be, the dramatist's very hotel-bill on the Grand Canal: that would be precisely Packford's cup of tea" (p. 21).

Their talk then shifts to the subject of literary forgeries and finally drifts off to the matter of the psychology of scholarship itself, and to a somewhat embarrassing line of self-revelation offered by Packford:

> "But then my sort's a bit mad, too, wouldn't you say? Why do I mole away after obscure events, of no large human interest — of no genuine intellectual interest at all — back in the seventeenth century?"
>
> Packford had paused, almost as if puzzled at hearing himself turn serious again. "You know," he went on, "the plain man's answer: that I've found a tolerably harmless way of keeping myself out of the pub. Of the pub and — well — other things in that general area. But the devil of it is, you know, that it may let a chap down. A chap may feel he's been missing things." (p. 23)

Thus their conversation ends a bit awkwardly and abruptly, but the evening's talk has proved to be full of hints and nuances that in fact turn out to have all manner of relevance to the mystery to follow. This is the last that Appleby or the reader sees of Lewis Packford. He is later found shot dead in his study back at his English estate, Urchins, on the eve of a grand literary gathering that he was to host. Beside his body are found a pistol and a note in his own hand reading, "Farewell, a long farewell." Appleby, told of the circumstances, immediately recognizes the note as a scrap of quotation from Shakespeare: "Farewell, a long farewell, to all my greatness" (*Hen VIII*. III. ii, 352).

The assumption, of course, is that it is a case of suicide, perhaps the last act of a weary, disillusioned, and lonely scholar. The assumption is heightened — but the interpretation disturbed — by the discovery at the inquest that Packford had indeed had a secret life: he was secretly married; he was, in fact, doubly married, to two wives ignorant of each other's existence! So as things stand, it seems fairly evident that Packford has unaccountably gotten himself into a hopeless muddle and has chosen to take a clean way out.

When Appleby enters the case, there are clearly two leads to follow up, one dealing with Packford's secret bigamous domestic life, the other with the mysterious Shakespearian discovery hinted at earlier. According to Room, Packford's solicitor, what he found and was about to publish was a copy of the Italian novella, Cintio's *Ecatommiti*, the only known source for *Othello*, with marginalia in Shakespeare's own hand! This revelation puts the case in a new light altogether, and attention thus shifts from Packford's bedroom to his library. The quiet scholarly puzzle that ensues naturally brings out the don in Appleby as he potters about the house and engages in various and sundry literary chats with Packford's scholarly friends.

After various rather farcical comings and goings in Packford's library, with everyone trying to put a hand on the missing Cintio, and a second murder — of Room, the solicitor — Appleby is able to propose his solution, which is woven out of his recollections of the seemingly casual meanderings of Packford's conversation that last night in Italy. It was Room who purveyed the purported Shakespeare holograph to Packford — nothing, of course, but a spectacularly good forgery by Room himself, done as much for the pleasure of setting the complacent Packford up for professional ridicule as for the prospect of financial gain. It was Packford's eventual discovery of the forgery that led to his murder — and it was the expert forger Room who wrote the "suicide" note out of Shakespeare and who made sure the matter of the two wives came to light to muddy the waters.

Meanwhile another principal in the case has beaten Appleby to the solution and executed summary justice on Room — and then tidied matters up by committing suicide. Reviewer Ralph Partridge connected this last device of plot resolution to recent changes in the English Capital Punishment law: "No longer can our authors who wish to keep abreast of the times dismiss their murderers summarily to the gallows in the last chapter. Yet . . . (d)ie they must; and since the state unobligingly backs out, suicide must be called to the rescue" (*New States-man*, 3 May 1958, p. 576).

All in all, *The Long Farewell* is a very traditional British mystery — so traditional as almost to constitute in some ways a parody. What distinguishes the novel and makes it something more than that is its genuine literary quality. As the reader may have noticed, the leitmotif here is *Othello*, not only with reference to the elusive copy of the *Ecatommiti* and all the talk about Shakespeare, but in the very structure of the novel itself: its traditional four-part dramatic divisions (prologue, development, dénouement, and epilogue); the theme of domestic tragedy in the plot, with its interweaving of threads of suspicion and jealousy, both of a professional and a romantic nature; and not least in the idea of the murderer dispensing justice against himself at the end. All of this is underlined by the constant use of Shakespeare quotations, especially from *Othello*, throughout the narrative.[21]

Naturally a story like *The Long Farewell* will have special appeal to academic readers, whether students, dons, or amateur literati. But it is a mistake to think of the novel as esoteric. As Innes himself avers, his mysteries are not scholarly productions; rather they put on a scholarly turn. It takes great learning to bring it off, but ultimately everything the reader needs to know is provided by the narrative itself. With reference to another Innes novel with a different sort of academic connection, *Hare Sitting Up*, Anthony Boucher said: "Academic virtues and popular appeal are not so mutually exclusive as some writers and critics like to think" (*NYTBR*, 11 Oct. 1959, p. 30).

Hare Sitting Up, along with *Appleby's Answer* and especially *An Awkward Lie*, introduces us to yet another variant of the Great Good Place in the Innes mysteries: the milieu of the English public school, or what in America would be called the private or prep school. Here are the same elements for detective fiction as in the university setting, but with a somewhat different flavor. Once again there is the enclosed garden effect, both in a physical and social respect, an environment ostensibly devoted single-mindedly to truth-seeking, and, of course, the usual array of academic types — although as a whole the beaks (teachers) are a rummier lot even than the university dons.

The fact is that the school setting raises additional possibilities: sharpened satire, for one, based on the rather dismal lot of the tutors, who tend to be seen as and see themselves as a somewhat disgruntled crew, stuck in something of a professional backwater; the aura of innocence and precociousness, for another, more poignant in the school pupils than in the university undergraduates. All this allows for a good bit of out-and-out comedy, but also lends a hint or threat of villainy of a darker shade. There is always the hint of the truly sinister in detective fiction laid in school settings, as in Michael Gilbert's *The Body of a Girl* (1972). One thing Innes does not do, however, is to use the public-school setting, as some writers have, for any really gruesome murder stories or as the occasion for realistic black satire about brutality within the schools.

Appleby's Answer (1973), in Captain Bulkington's Kandahar, presents a picture of a wholly bogus school setup, a "crammers' academy" in which failed public schoolboys are supposedly given another shot at qualifying for university. In fact, so bogus is this establishment that Bulkington has only two pupils in residence, a pair of louts over whom he exercises brutal control by holding over their heads a bit of fornication with a village girl whom Bulkington himself has put up to the job. In one absurd sequence, Bulkington (whom his two unwilling charges refer to, unaffectionately, as the Old Bulgar) shows John and Judith Appleby round the school, arranging for the same two boys to play the role of a multiplicity of students in different classes to give the impression of a full enrollment. Kandahar, in short, represents a total burlesque of the public-school idea.

Hare Sitting Up (1959) offers a more meaningful transition from the world of the university to the world of the public school. This novel begins with an Oxfordian moment as a man named Juniper, on his way back from a conference of headmasters at the university, falls in with a group of undergraduates on the train and is engaged by them in some timely conversation about the hopes of young people in a nuclear age. The next scene finds the weary schoolmaster back at the prep school, Splaine Croft, one of those sheltered places where parents send their children mainly because they themselves or another relative have been to it, and where what transpires is not so much education as a kind of contained chaos: "Splaine Croft was a dismal place without boys: a slightly vulgar Edwardian country house degraded into a derelict barracks. But when the boys were there, you didn't notice how the once handsome appointments had been kicked to bits — or you didn't notice, provided you had a taste for boys mucking around" (p. 23).

Later, in the most Hitchcockian episode of the novel, when there has been reason to suspect foul play at the school, Judith Appleby is sent as a prospective parent to scout the buildings and grounds for any possible clues or evidences of the missing Juniper. In a literary way, the main fruit of the episode is a bit of Innes nostalgia; through her, he offers us his remembrances of such a place: "Hanging in the hall there would be a certificate praising the drains. And the headmaster's study would be protected by a supernumerary green-baize door, to muffle the howling when the headmaster's pupils were being caned. . . . Yes, Judith said to herself firmly, I have been here before. I can smell the disinfectant. I can slip on the tiles. I can extract, from the pitch-pine paneling of the interior, small gouts of resinous substance that can be satisfactorily rolled between finger and thumb. And that is sometimes the only resource through long weary hours" (pp. 63–4). They are Judith's reflections, but they can readily be compared to J. I. M. Stewart's own recollections in his essay, "An Edinburgh Boyhood," as well as to Bobby Appleby's in *An Awkward Lie.*

Innes's main excursion into the world of the public school is *An Awkward Lie* (1971) and, appropriately enough for this exercise in nostalgia, the protagonist is young Bobby Appleby, son of the retired commissioner, graduate of Overcombe prep school and Oxford, and now a promising "antinovelist." This is a tale whose plot develops into a thriller of boyish exuberance and fanciful melodrama, including at the end the appearance of a veritable crowd of Baker Street Irregulars, and to top it off *An Awkward Lie* represents one of Innes's relatively rare excursions into romance. In these respects, one of the nearest books to it in spirit is *Appleby Plays Chicken.*

The opening situation is quintessential British detective story, to the point of parody; in the words of Newgate Callendar, "There is something wonderfully comforting about an old-fashioned mystery that starts off with a body in a golf bunker" (*NYTBR*, 9 May 1971, p. 40). It is Bobby Appleby, "(successful scrum-half retired, and author of that notable anti-novel *The Lumber Room*)" (p. 9), who comes upon the body early one morning as he follows his golf ball into a bunker on the first hole. As a sort of literary joke, but appropriate to the opening narrative point of view — Bobby's — the first couple of pages are written in a style parodying the French New Novel — as Hanna Charney has shrewdly observed.[22] There is meticulous factual description of the disposition of everything in the scene, along with something approximating a stream of consciousness running alongside. After this highly literary opening salvo has been discharged, events move swift-

ly. Bobby studies the situation and senses vaguely that he should recognize the victim, horribly shot up though he is. A strange girl appears — a smashing girl, so far as Bobby is concerned. They talk the
situation over and Bobby goes off to call the police while the girl keeps
watch. But when Bobby and the police arrive back at the scene there
is no body, no girl, only Bobby's ball resting in the center of an un-
disturbed bunker. As constable Howard says, in perhaps Innes's most
outrageously contrived pun, "Mr. Appleby, you seem to be in rather
an awkward lie" (p. 23)!

Naturally the situation *is* awkward, disappearing evidence always
is, but also naturally enough, Appleby senior is wholly disposed to
believe in the exact truth of what his son has reported. The point of
placing the body on a golf course must have been to assure that it *would
be found*, but in a bunker so as not to be found *too soon*; and the point
of spiriting it away again must have been because it had been found
by the *wrong person* — perhaps by someone who, through unforeseen
ill chance, was in a position to identify it? This is as far as Appleby
senior is able to go — but it is right on the mark, with only the details
needing to be filled in. The rest of the narrative, more or less, has to
do with action, adventure, and romance.

While Appleby senior is quietly speculating in his garden, Bobby
rushes off with youthful impetuosity to take matters into his own
hands, acting on what would seem to be the wholly misguided sense
that the mysterious and ravishing girl — far from being a sinister accomplice to the crime — stands in some desparate need of chivalrous
rescue herself. Thus, motivated by a sort of Perseus complex as well
as to vindicate the truth of what he has reported, Bobby quietly takes
himself off to Overcombe, his old prep school; his one lead in the matter is a vague notion that the body in the bunker may have belonged
to none other than his old Latin instructor, Nauze (pronounced "Nose,"
and therefore "Bloody Nauze" to all the boys).

Overcombe is the scene of much of the narrative. It represents
Innes's most sustained description of the prep school environment, and
a brilliant job of writing he makes of it. For a time the mystery is
almost forgotten in the wash of nostalgia of Bobby's return to his alma
mater. Bobby first encounters the ridiculous headmaster, Dr. Gulliver,
whose name is redolent not only of the interaction of big people and
little people but of the seventeenth-century byword for a dupe. Gulliver, in fact, is an impossible humbug, parading a shopworn sixth-

form classical learning that Bobby cannot resist ragging, first feigning a cobwebby ignorance and then matching Gulliver's tired Latin tag lines with dollops of real Latin that leave the headmaster floundering. More than Gulliver's overbearing pretension to immense learning ("and it had never occurred to anybody to reflect that unfathomable erudition is neither necessary nor customary in the proprietor . . . of a private school" — p. 43), is the headmaster's "chronic senseless agitation":

> It was this — or rather it was the schizoid pairing of this with his answering air of a scholar's deeply meditative habit — that gave Dr Gulliver his peculiarly bizarre note. Indeed (Bobby now saw), it was doubtless from this nervous peculiarity of the Doctor that Overcombe as a school derived its special quality of craziness. The thing didn't, so far as his recollection went, at all disturb the pupils. Amost all small boys are mad.   (p. 45)

The whole paragraph, going on in this vein, is a beautiful example of Innes's novelistic handling of point of view, giving the layers of Bobby's consciousness of the situation, but not quite directly, for it is all quietly mediated by the gently ironic voice of the real narrator, as the final sentence reveals: "It was at about thirteen (Mr Robert Appleby, brilliantly paradoxical novelist, reflected) that the individual is condemned to enter what the poet Yeats calls the stupidity of one's middle years."

The pompous absurdity of Gulliver is supplemented by Bobby's encounters with the various other teachers. For instance, there is the kindly and rather pathetic-seeming old art instructor, Hartsilver, whom Bobby is inclined to pity — and even fear, upon "finding that he and old Hartsilver had been the same sort of person all the time. And perhaps (despite the gratifying acclaim bestowed by Sunday newspapers upon Robert Appleby, promising author of *The Lumber Room*) — perhaps he was himself going to be as thoroughly unsuccessful as this old creature, lingering out his broken career in a crazy school" (p. 55). Then there are the anonymous middle-aged types who "looked highly intelligent, and must therefore belong to that class of persons who drift into humble employment through some sheer inability to manage their own lives" (p. 52). And on the other hand, there are the graceless young turks on the staff, whose smarminess Bobby despises. Finally, of course,

there are the boys themselves, precocious, savage, merciless, and delicate, by turns; among them, Bobby "felt a sudden envy of those writers — Joyce Cary, Forrest Reid, Richard Hughes, William Golding —
who could really 'do' children. There hardly existed a richer, more
marvellous world" (p. 53).

It all adds up to an enormous — and, to Bobby's modernist mind,
unwholesome — wave of nostalgia, a flowing *recherche du temps perdu*:

> Football-boots smothered in dried clay lay where they had been
> kicked into corners a term ago, their long, muddied laces writhing
> around them. Stamp-albums; primitive musical instruments; des-
> iccated goldfish in abandoned bowls; rejected pin-ups of male per-
> sons celebrated in one or another athletic world; the crumpled
> wrappings of Munchies, Crunchies, Scrumpties, Mintoes, Chock-
> oes, Maltoes and the like; boring letters from aunts; mildly minia-
> turized tennis-rackets and cricket-bats; all these silted up the in-
> terstices of these chambers devoted to the pursuit of learning.   (pp.
> 46–47)

These are the kind of direct, unmediated sensory recollections that
J. I. M. Stewart himself, in his article, "An Edinburgh Boyhood," says
that, in going back to visit his old school, "I could hardly bear."[23]
Moreover, these images that assail him at Overcombe also conjure up
for Bobby his memories of Oxford: "the whole thing starting again,
but with new sorts of relics creeping in: the menus of dining clubs, for
example, or of banquets given by the affluent to celebrate their ma-
jority. It all reeked of privilege, Bobby would tell himself." (p. 61).
Such doubts are undoubtedly natural enough to a young intellectual
in class-conscious British society, and indeed they reflect a charge of
elitism and even snobbery that has from time to time been leveled
against the novels of Michael Innes and J. I. M. Stewart. But despite
that sense of the elitism of it all, the passage continues, "Bobby, who
was an extremely honest young man, had to tell himself that, if God
were to let him choose, he wouldn't want to have had a day of it different. Very obscurely, it had accumulated some sort of debt, and not
one which you at all discharged by becoming an agreeably esteemed
tiro novelist."

Bobby is abruptly stunned to discover the mysterious girl from
the golf course, who proves to be one of the newer staff members at
the school. But when she denies any glimmer of recognition of either

Bobby or the incident, his own confidence is shaken, as he experiences that familiar Hitchcockian sensation of disorientation and mistrust of his own senses. The upshot of it all, for Bobby, is that "Overcombe had become, incredible as it seemed, a sinister place" (p. 71). And in fact Bobby does discover from an overheard conversation in a pub that everyone has apparently been lying to him, that Bloody Nauze indeed left Overcombe but came back recently, and that he and Hartsilver and the mysterious girl, Susan, were quite thick with one another. And beyond that, as though straight out of Kipling, or rather Ian Fleming, it also appears that there are mysterious foreigners (chunky and crew-cutted), and even helicopters, lurking about the school.

Helpful as Bobby's peripatetic cogitations are, however, it is only due to the fact that the girl, Susan, eventually breaks down and reluctantly explains the whole situation to Bobby that there is any enlightenment. Everything is rather opposite to what it seems. The obscure Nauze is in fact a master cryptographer; eventually he was captured and brainwashed, then rescued and cured, then recaptured and killed by hired agents who had left his body to be found in the bunker as verification of their success. But Susan trailed them and stole the body — thus creating Bobby's awkward situation — in order to thwart and confuse the enemy. Subsequently she and the seemingly ineffectual Hartsilver heroically undertook to continue Nauze's work. But by the time all this is explained, the action has again outstripped Bobby's grasp of things — for now Hartsilver is captured and presumably being tortured.

The climax of the novel is a kind of parody of chivalric romance in which Bobby and Susan (whose courtship has also now proceeded apace), along with the boys of Overcombe, storm the headquarters of the enemy agents, which Bobby has correctly reckoned to be in the Great Smithy, a megalithic chamber tomb, and one of the prehistoric monuments he was contemplating on one of his pensive strolls.

This rousing Kipling- or Stevenson-esque ending is supplemented by the flowering of the romance element, with similar overtones of adolescent literary associations. Indeed, Innes cleverly links the two elements together through the concept of danger, used both in its common adventure-story sense and in its sense derived from the literature of courtly love. During their supper at a pub just before the great assault, Bobby introduces the subject of courtly love, or *l'amour courtois*, and danger, explaining:

"When one was that sort of lover, one thought of oneself as within one's lady's *danger*. It was a relationship, really, between a vassal and his lord. Within the code, the lady's the lord, of course, and the lover's the vassal. The Lord (or mistress) can require the vassal (or lover) to do his stuff — to be modestly competent, for example, in that rough house."

"Yes?"

"In requital, the vassal (or lover) is entitled to enjoy the favour of his lord (or mistress). And the reciprocal relationship between the two is called *danger*. See?"

"Do see. *Danger* is definitely on."

The head-swimming business assailed Bobby Appleby again.

"Pray God," he said, "I'm not too madly drunk on you to drive this bloody car." (pp. 143–44)

Bobby's romantic vow to Susan, nicely cognizant of Hardy and modern realistic sensibility, is that he will be faithful to her and that "'You'll never again have anything that isn't nice.' Bobby stared at her — the dream girl, who must have nothing but truth. 'Except from crass casualty and blind fate'" (p. 134).

All, of course, turns out well in the end — except that the Great Smithy itself suffers violent destruction. "A most deplorable thing," as Dr. Gulliver says. "A great loss to English archaeology."

5

Salons and Satire:
"The Voonderble Vorlt of Art"

The Art Gallery Scene
From "London" Far
Honeybath

> We are looking at an English rural landscape on a summer af-
> ternoon. . . . The Englishness is unchallengeable, the rurality un-
> flawed, and the whole effect a landscape in the fullest sense of the
> word.

The reader might think he is embarked on a particularly unrestrained
passage from Nikolaus Pevsner's *The Englishness of English Art*, were
he not aware that these are the opening words of Innes's *Christmas
at Candleshoe* (1953). Of course, Innes's novels are full of descriptions
of Palladian English country houses and parks, for they are one of his
favorite settings, but what is remarkable is not only the novelist's loving attention to architectual detail, but the *painterly* eye with which
the scene is delineated:

> Delimiting the foreground, beyond a broad expanse of lawn, is
> a low and unassuming stone wall. Our eye lingers upon it, and we
> wonder why. Well, diagonally upon it falls another line — that of
> a small clear river flowing away into the middle distance. And it
> so happens that, in the picture-space we are contemplating, the one
> line cuts the other in a ratio which artists call golden section.
> Moreover the diagonal line of the river is balanced by an answer-
> ing diagonal in the long slope of an adjacent hill, and we are fur-

117

ther aware that to left and right, just comfortably within our pe-
ripheral vision, grove nods to grove and wood advances upon wood
as in the sinuous symmetry of some sophisticated dance. . . . We
are studying a work of art.   (p. 7)

The narrator's perception is fed by echoes of Pope and recollections
of the luminous Claude Lorraine, the savage Rosa and learned Poussin — itself a learned allusion to lines by the eighteenth-century poet
James Thompson: "Whate'er Lorrain light-touched with softening
Hue, / Or savage Rosa dashed, or learned Poussin drew." And were it
not for the sky and the actually moving clouds, one might think that
one is looking at nothing more out of the way than a good canvas by
Richard Wilson made ingeniously stereoscopic.

   This rather extraordinary passage is not simply an instance of
Innes's "deuced odd way" of commencing some of his mysteries, but
it emphasizes the essentially painterly eye and hand he persistently
brings to his work. For it is one thing to notice that Innes frequently
uses art and picture galleries as subject matter for his plots, and another
to note that his stylistic approach tends always to be "painterly."

   In the J. I. M. Stewart essay "An Edinburgh Boyhood," Innes
recalls how from the somewhat chilly philistine rigors of his boyhood
school, the Edinburgh Academy — a steady round of Greek and Latin
exercises and "disagreeably muddy games" — he was wont to take refuge in the sunnier halls of the Scottish National Gallery. As Sir Osbert
Sitwell said he gained his education during holidays from Eton College, Stewart notes, "I reflect that I got a modicum of mine" in those
rooms of "Italian light on Scottish walls."[1] Thus the Scottish National
Gallery was "salvation and glory. It alone nourished in me," he says,
"a simple sensuousness — aestheticism, if it must be called that — which
found little encouragement elsewhere in the Modern Athens." Here
then was a school for Innes's artistry that should always be kept in
mind.

   Great paintings are a sort of code for Innes, an emblem for the
whole idea of civilization itself. That is, great paintings both symbolize
the history of culture in the West, and at the same time represent actual irreplaceable and sometimes priceless treasures of that heritage.
Specific instances of the use of art and the art world as subject matter
in the novels are very numerous indeed, especially in the stories set in
country houses, each of which always has its own great picture gallery.

In a great many Innes novels there are brief digressive allusions to paintings and connoisseurship, sometimes without any particular relevance to the mystery at hand, such as the gratuitous little discourse on the Dutch painter Cuyp delivered by one of the characters in *Appleby's Other Story* (p. 116). But more commonly, connoisseurship, particularly Appleby's, has the ultimately practical value of discriminating between the genuine and the bogus, or between the really valuable and the relatively worthless, or even between the appropriate and the inappropriate in the display of art. In *The Case of the Journeying Boy* the modest tutor Thewless is made uneasy by a scientist's palatial home — the "distrusted and eminent physicist who lived like a grandee" (p. 8). At one point in the curious adventure of *The Open House* Appleby realizes that what looks like the attempted theft of a painting must really have had some other object in view, because he knows — and he knows that professional thieves would know — that the painting is of wholly indifferent quality and questionable value (pp. 74–5).

The primary instance of a case hinging on connoisseurship is — not surprisingly — the aptly titled *A Connoisseur's Case* (1962), a country-house mystery about the murder of a long-absent but recently returned household servant and the theft of the model boat the man has been carrying. The criminal situation that proves to account for the apparently senseless murder and theft is a massive scheme devised by the baronet's disinherited brother and the baronet's butler involving nothing less than the theft, piece by piece, of the mansion's finest and most valuable antique furniture, and the replacement of each piece by a forged replica. When Appleby sums up the case he names it himself "a connoisseur's case." The first connoisseur was the unfortunate former servant of the house, murdered because he was himself a craftsman (as the model boat demonstrated) and thus in a position to discern the fraud. It's the reason he was killed, and the reason the murderer took away the little barge: "It must come back into nobody's head that Crabtree had been the craftsman he was," Appleby explains (p. 187). The second connoisseur was Judith Appleby herself; after a visit to the mansion she reported that the place seemed a bit of a muddle to her: "Half a dozen rather good eighteenth-century paintings and a really fine range of the water-colourists. But two or three modish modern things he's obviously been told indicate enlightened patronage today. Some superb French pieces, but even more ultra-shiny, high-grade reproduction antique" (p. 127). The baronet himself, an ingenue, had no such percipience to prevent being practiced upon in this way, nor is he embarrassed by the fact — "Do you take me for a furniture dealer?" he huffs. Questioned as to whether such a scheme could make economic sense, Appleby assures him how easy and profitable it would be to market, say, a gentleman's social table by Hepplewhite.

> "Or a Gothic cabinet by Chippendale," Judith said. "Or a Louis XVI semainier, or a French provincial commode before about 1750, or a set of quartetto tables, or a Grecian squab, or a couple of Herculaneums, or some girandoles by Matthias Lock, or even a garden seat by William Halfpenny — "
> "My Wife studies these things," Appleby interrupted rather hastily.   (p. 188)

One never can tell what sort of knowledge may come in handy in the course of an investigation, but, as one reviewer drily remarked in another connection, it's a safe bet that English literature — and art history — will never let you down!

The fact is that throughout his long and prolific career, Innes has continued to exploit the many different possibilities provided by the art world for detective fiction, from straight art theft, through faking, forgery, and copying (all carefully distinguished, incidentally), to overpainting and various other art swindles. Quite a number of these come into play all at once, for example, in *Appleby's Other Story* (1974), a roundly conventional locked-room, body-in-the-library, country-house mystery. It is not a narrative where the art element is strongly marked throughout, yet the art motif *is* crucial to the situation and dénouement. It is simply the case that a conspiring baronet — hard up for cash as baronets so frequently are in these fictions — has perpetrated with the aid of his secretary and his butler a fake theft of his own art as an insurance swindle, that he then surreptitiously sells the allegedly stolen art to covert collectors and then, in a third level of criminal activity, uses the proceeds to buy illegally exported Russian icons disguised by overpainting as second-rate portraits. And this is only the "other story," inasmuch as Appleby's immediate concern is with the murder of this thieving baronet in his study.

It should be noted that art objects also frequently play a wholly different role in Innes, that is, not merely as financially valuable objects and targets of theft, but as occasions for perceptual confusion, particularly the mistaking of a person for a statue or a painting, and vice versa. It will be remembered that the nocturnal chase in the formal gardens of Scamnum Court at the conclusion of *Hamlet, Revenge!* involved the *belle fantaisie* of the heroine Elizabeth hiding from her pursuers by stripping naked and posing on an empty garden pedestal as the Pandemian Venus. An exactly similar conception underlies the complicated dénouement of *What Happened at Hazelwood* (1946), an ambitious, Edwardian-style domestic melodrama. When the tangled machinations of the fatal night in that novel are unraveled, one learns that the coy heroine and narrator Nicolette, the slain baronet's wife, has devised an elaborate scheme intended to get herself out from under his thumb, but that the overly ingenious plan has fatally miscarried. Prompted by the memory of an old whiskey ad in which an ancestor steps right out of a family portrait to hand a drink, Nicolette has thought up a clever confrontation scene with her husband designed to be a convincing bluff of a scheme to murder him — her real intention being to frighten him into giving her her freedom. Her plan is to hide in the study, a room notoriously stocked with scandalous nudes alternating with the family portraits; on the fatal occasion, playing a variant on the old adage that naked is the best disguise, she will pose as a Caravaggio Venus:

> I could be a Venus — of sorts. Look at Caravaggio's goddess above the mantelpiece. The picture stands recessed behind those Grinling Gibbons pillars and in its own heavy chiaroscuro. I had only to get up there with the help of the high-backed chair, take the required pose, and I would virtually have vanished from this ill-lit room. (p. 232)

She can then step out of the picture when the baronet is supposedly alone in his study and bluff him with the threat of an insoluble murder.

Unfortunately, the prurient vicar, whom Nicolette has duped into appearing below the study window to spy on a presumed instance of the baronet's infamous amours (a red herring intended by Nicolette merely to confuse the scene), actually pokes his head in the window just as Nicolette is stepping out of her frame to confront her startled husband. The scene is reminiscent of Gilbert and Sullivan's *Ruddigore* (which actually serves as Inspector Cadover's clue), but the poor vicar sees it in another light entirely. He believes himself to be witnessing

a veritable Faustian manifestation — one of the lustful baronet's lewd
paintings brought fantastically to life.

> What he saw seemed to confirm him in certain fantastic notions
> to which he was subject. Sir George Simney, he believed, had sold
> his soul to the Devil, and the Devil could summon him what recon-
> dite pleasures he wished for. At this very moment the thing was
> happening, and Caravaggio's libidinous image of Venus was be-
> ing brought to life to subserve Sir George's lust.   (p. 234)

And recalling, perhaps, that Luther had dispatched the devil with an
inkpot, the good vicar hurls the nearest weighty object at this succubus,
but accidentally strikes and kills the baronet, while the latter is in the
act of gaping in surprise at the vision confronting him!

Fantastic as the plot is, Innes does play by the rules. Nicolette's
device is not without preparation — a good bit of attention is focused
earlier in the novel on the infamous room with its voluptuous paintings. The novel's second narrator — Inspector Cadover's young assistant,
Harold — is much struck throughout the tale with Nicolette's charms
and tends to portray her in mildly erotic, painterly terms. "I must say,
my dear Dad," he writes in his chronicle, "that I would like to have
seen her when she came out of that bath-room in a towel — a regular
Venus, she must have been" (p. 98). So the solution is not, at least,
abruptly arbitrary.

The idea of pictures or statues being confused with living persons
seems an endlessly fascinating jest for Innes. It occurs again in *Appleby's End, From "London" Far,* and *Old Hall, New Hall.* In the latter, the confusion between a real woman and an art work is perpetrated through a profusion of double entendres in an old family
document. Such confusions suggest the old Platonic conundrum of
where reality lies in such matters: if a picture is but a representative
of a real object, is the real object but an image of some higher reality?
Or, more appositely, what, ontologically speaking, is the relationship
of an excellent copy to an original painting — is the former not *really*
a Raphael, for instance? If the copy is so excellent that only a scientific expertise or a scrap of circumstantial evidence can distinguish it
from the original, how does that, aesthetically speaking, put the copy
at any disadvantage? As the pedantic librarian Archdeacon says in
Christmas at Candleshoe, "we are all forgeries":

Brown himself [the family dog] is but a counterfeit, a feeble copy
of the real Brown — whom we should find, you know, only in the
kennels of Heaven. And were Titian — or shall we say the late Sir
Edwin Landseer? — to execute a painting of our Brown, what would
this be but a copy of a copy, a shadow of a shadow? Now, suppose
further that a forger gets to work on Landseer's painting. His work
will be at but one further remove from the real Brown — the shadow, we may say, of a shadow's shadow. There is here a field for
abundant speculation.   (p. 115)

At any rate, a copy, unknown to be a copy, may be treasured and enjoyed for years and no one the wiser — and yet the original, as soon as
authenticated, makes that formerly beloved object immediately worthless and instead becomes itself the object of the passion to possess.

One can see here all the opportunities this presents for the meta-
physically inclined mystery writer. First of all there are pictures as
treasured symbols of Western civilization and as fabulously valuable
physical objects in themselves; secondly, one thinks of pictures as objects frequently found in out-of-the-way country houses, objects rather
easily stolen and transported, easily forged and copied, easily disguised
through overpainting or pentimento (another favorite Innes theme
with strong psychological overtones, a sort of variant on the impersonation theme).

Christmas at Candleshoe (1953) and *Old Hall, New Hall* (1956) —
published only three years apart — share so many motifs, plot elements,
and structural devices that clearly they must have sprung from the
same imaginative impulse. Both deal with two rival branches of an
ancient family, two rival country seats, a disputed family treasure, and
old family papers that contain unexpected revelations in the matter
of the dispute and prove to be the crucial documents in the case. In
both stories the boyish obsession with hidden treasure is paralleled with
the more sophisticated but similar adult fascination with lost masterpieces of art.

Christmas at Candleshoe concerns a dispute between two country houses, each the seat of one of the two branches of a very old family,
estranged for centuries. The older and originally more distinguished
branch, the Candleshoes, is now virtually destitute and reduced to one
feeble and dotty old lady who simply does not acknowledge that any
age has succeeded upon the feudal; Candleshoe Manor itself is spectacularly derelict. The more recent branch ("up-starts" who go back

only to the seventeenth century) are the Spendloves of Benison Court, presided over by the Marquis of Scattergood. The Spendloves, however, have recently come up short for cash and it has occurred to Lord Scattergood that he might sell off a couple of his old paintings and lay down some new stock (as he might with his wine cellar). Looking over the "stuff" on his walls, two Titians flanked by a pair of Velasquez portraits, he decides to hang on to the latter as "a superb evocation of the aristocratic idea." But as for the Titians, although "deuced colorful" and mildly indecent, he has never really kindled to them — even as a boy, "he had been unable to imagine himself in any amatory engagement with females of this species turning the scale at anything like the figure to be posited of these sprawling monsters" (p. 104) — so they will go on the block.

But now comes the hitch. The critic hired to give an expertise pronounces the Benison Titians copies. When it is recalled that the Titians were sent to Candleshoe Manor for safekeeping during the war, it becomes clear that the originals must have remained there ever since. Why such an unlikely theft should have been perpetrated by an elderly lady and her private chaplain is explained when an old family document is brought forward. It is an eighteenth-century journal that tells the story of two young rakish cousins, a Spendlove and a Candleshoe, who make the Grand Tour of Italy and upon returning set up a "Temple of Solomon" for their further studies, especially "the observation of heavenly bodies," particularly the "motions of Venus." Of course it is nothing but a *bagnio*, suitably furnished with some uncommonly lascivious paintings acquired during their travels. After the parents broke up this spirited operation, the paintings were divided between the families, but as the journal makes clear, while the Candleshoes seemed clearly to be the proper owners of the Titians, it was the Spendloves who retained possession of them. So it seems that the Candleshoes simply took the recent opportunity to repossess them.

Meanwhile an entirely distinct but related drama begins to unfold at Candleshoe Manor. Here the antique Miss Candleshoe and her chaplain are served by an elvish group of local children who are convinced that a great secret treasure lies hidden somewhere in the house and who are also convinced that some formidable enemy is laying plans to besiege the mansion. Far from being a mere childish fantasy, it turns out that there is indeed a professional gang gathering its forces around the isolated house, their object the valuable paintings they know are disposed and hidden about the place.

At the climax of this country-house art thriller, the two threads come together. The Spendloves descend upon Candleshoe Manor about the matter of the missing Titians at the moment the professional art thieves begin to lay siege to the house. The assault of the gang brings the two feuding households together, and a bizarre pitched battle, waged with authentic feudal weapons, takes place in Candleshoe's Long Gallery, fulfilling every adventure fantasy ever nursed by the children who serve Miss Candleshoe. The battle ends when the attackers are finally hoist by their own petard; the floor caves in and the great marble monument to Admiral Candleshoe by the Jacobean sculptor Gerard Christmas is broken open, revealing not the hidden treasure the children had anticipated but a heap of faded canvases. After the thieves are routed and the dust settles, the general disappointment over the treasure is dramatically dispelled when Lord Spendlove's art expert, waving his arms in what seems to be a combination of mystical exaltation and agony, tells the assembled group that what has emerged from the "Christmas box" is the greatest work by the greatest artist in the history of European art — a hitherto unknown Giorgione that is "worth more than any other painting in the world." Thus the rivalry between the two families comes to an ironic close, with Candleshoe once again in the ascendency, its Giorgione clearly outranking the Spendloves' returned Titians.

In this "fantastic little taradiddle," as James Sandoe called the book (*NYHTBR*, 1 Nov. 1953, p. 120), Innes has woven a melodrama around immensely valuable art works, not simply or even primarily in terms of their monetary, but rather their emblematic, value. They are the hallmarks of civilization, transcending all loyalties of nation or profession or even class — and they are in the custody, it seems, of just the right people, despite all the apparent hazards to which these privately owned treasures are subjected. In *A Private View* the Duke of Horton becomes particularly perturbed over the theft of a Vermeer from his gallery — insofar as this grand old Olympian ever gets perturbed — not so much because of any personal financial or even aesthetic loss, as because of his sense of *stewardship* of the thing: "Upbringing, you know. I was taught that we simply held all those things in trust. Not for the nation. My father disapproved of nations, whether his own or any other. But for civilization in general. So in losing the Vermeer I feel that I've fallen down, rather, on the job" (p. 53). The Duke redeems himself at the end and the Vermeer is recovered. For the sentimental premise of that melodrama, as of *Christmas at Can-*

dleshoe, is precisely that the archaic rural values and staunch character of the "stones-in-the-rain," as Innes likes to call these people, are the best defense of these cultural emblems against external threat, whether by international conspiracy or professional criminals, because it *is* all a matter of values and character, after all.

Christmas at Candleshoe has the distinction of being the one Innes story to become a motion picture, the 1978 Walt Disney film *Candleshoe* starring David Niven, Helen Hayes, and Jodie Foster as an American tomboy brought to live in England who takes the place of the novel's enigmatic local lad. Michael Innes reports that in one of his very rare excursions to a movie house in recent years he did see the film and enjoyed it, though the screenplay by David Swift and Rosemary Anne Sisson bears little relation to the novel.

The Art Gallery Scene

In addition to the country-house novels involving an art-related element Innes has also produced, in a vein strongly marked by social satire, a series of novels specifically dealing with the professional art world. For three of these novels — *A Private View* (1952), *Money from Holme* (1964), and *A Family Affair* (1969) — he invented Hildebert Braunkopf, an egregious art dealer and proprietor of the Da Vinci Gallery, whose fractured English and mid-European accent produced a characteristic tag line, "the voonderble vorlt of art." These novels, along with the closely related *Silence Observed* — a London art thriller that dispenses with Braunkopf — all grow out of the more or less realistically rendered setting of the London art galleries and the business of art dealing, art swindling, and art thieving. Braunkopf exists somewhere between dealing and swindling, and usually outside the overtly criminal and Appleby treats him with a sort of contemptuous yet affable familiarity. He is a useful contact with the fringes of the real art underworld, which has become Appleby's specialty at the CID; while Appleby's wife, Judith, herself a sculptor, is a regular visitor to and sometime patron of the Da Vinci Gallery.

Innes's descriptions of the operations of the Da Vinci can be very amusing. As a man with a nose for what sells in art, Braunkopf unabashedly prostitutes himself to every tide of taste, while always maintaining his pose of wounded dignity in the face of Appleby's twitting. The fun of these scenes, which have the same sort of dynamics as the Hal-Falstaff exchanges, is to see just how Braunkopf will keep his flag flying in the face of being caught out in the most flagrant prevarication, the most abject waffling, or the most crushing humiliation.

The Da Vinci Gallery is first introduced in *A Private View* (U.S. title: *One-Man Show*). It is an establishment with all the trappings of art, yet operated like a used-car lot. The face it ordinarily strives to present to the world is one suggestive of Bond Street: a few "dim and darkened pictures, bearing labels which for the most part took the form of honest doubts and frank disclaimers," even so far improving upon "the accepted convention in these matters as to indicate the degree of his establishment's dubiety over its treasures by a system of multiple quotation-marks: *Studio of Rubens? Possibly by a pupil of Dirck Hals?? El Greco????*" In *A Private View* this effect of vintage art and ponderous academicism is conveniently renounced in favor of a trendy modernism when Braunkopf corners the market on a recently deceased abstract painter and mounts a posthumous one-man show.

This is not the only time the Da Vinci and its proprietor undergo an opportune metamorphosis. In *Money from Holme* Braunkopf has the luck to corner the market on another contemporary artist suddenly deceased, this time an artist of powerful tropical scenes reminiscent of *le douanier* Rousseau who has been assassinated in an African revolution. So of course, the "voonderble vorlt of art" being what it is, Holmes is now quite definitely hot; as one well-heeled customer explains, "the stock selling like hot-cakes, eh? . . . This fellow Holme, it seems, was knocked out while still among the young entry. By niggers, too, somebody said. Poor show, eh? But as soon as Debby told me the story I got on the blower. When a *great* painter dies at that age — well, you damned well can't go wrong. Eh?" (p. 9).

But after the sensational success of the Holme exhibit, Braunkopf and the Da Vinci can revert to their true pretentious and slightly suspect form: a subdued dignity, a few quattrocento pictures sparely on the walls. Until, later in the same chronicle, the Da Vinci puts on yet another turn: "The *trecento* and *quattrocento* had vanished. The walls had been hung with a faintly damasked paper of pale lavender. The collection on view appeared to be made up entirely of contemporary English watercolours" (p. 146).

The most striking of these quick changes of merchandise and decor

is reported in *A Family Affair* (alternate title: *Picture of Guilt*). Here
again the Da Vinci, with an assemblage of works allegedly by Tor-
rigiano, at first presents its austere, pseudoscholarly pose (labels that
read: "Possibly an *atelier* piece"), with its proprietor adopting as an
appropriate persona a "muted and hieratic stance which his intimates
understood to be modelled upon the late Mr. Berenson" (p. 45). But
the next time the gallery is visited, all is drastically transformed; the
visitor is greeted with what appears to be an enormous blowup from
a comic strip: the face of a lady done in stipple dots the size of sixpence,
posed pensively on a manicured hand, "and lest one should miss the
implication of this brooding guise, there was a wavy line ascending
from the crown of her head to a bubble in which was inscribed the
single word THINKS." As Appleby readily recognizes, the Da Vinci
has gone pop — and along with it, Braunkopf, who, instead of Saville
Row, seems to have betaken himself to Carnaby Street and is now except for his years and his figure "indistinguishable from one of those
almost young gentlemen who alternate minstrelsy for the million with
the final summits and acclivities of mystical experience."

The passage does give Innes's only reference, oblique though it
is, to the Beatles, but it must be said that all this attention to the Da
Vinci Gallery is really just an occasion for fun. Innes loves art, in a con-
servative sort of way, and knows it very well, and likes to tease those
who deal in art as a commodity, and especially with some of the more
trendy aspects of the contemporary scene. None of this is precisely ger-
mane to the mystery plots of the novels in question, but they do lend
a playful authenticity to the settings. The same is true for the cameo
appearances of Braunkopf himself as a Falstaffian butt of ridicule.
Braunkopf's leitmotif is a particular brand of fractured English; as Appleby notes, "Mr Braunkopf must have enjoyed his nativity in the
recesses of the continent and come thence to England by way of New
York" (*A Private View*, p. 9). As one either enjoys dialect humor or
doesn't, it is likely that the reader either will find Braunkopf very tedious indeed, or he will enjoy the constant stream of language gags
and one-liners in his scenes. Two-liners, to be more precise, for first
comes the malapropism, often wholly mystifying, and then the amusing clarification. On one occasion Braunkopf says to the Duke of Horton, with reference to bringing his current exhibition directly to the
nobleman's country seat for inspection:

"The Da Vinci is always doing pig affairs that sort. I got three five
pig pantechnicons perpechal carrying selek private views gentle-
mens' and nobles' bottoms."

"Bottoms?" The Duke was rather dazed.

"The Limbert private view arrive Scamnum, your stately bottom, middle nex week. No deposit."   (Ibid. p. 69)

Later, in conversation with Appleby, Braunkopf is recounting how the
late painter, Limbert, had come unexpectedly upon the shady art
dealer Steptoe in the latter's shop, "busy with his privates." That is,
as Appleby translates, "What we call his private affairs" (p. 74). Elsewhere, speaking of the affairs of a couple, Braunkopf says, "she and
her husband were deranged." When asked if they were really *both*
deranged, he answers, "But natchally. . . . He was deranged from her,
so she was deranged from him. But there was no divorcings" (*Money
From Holme*, p. 22).[2]

Even when attention is not focused on the egregious Braunkopf
there is still plenty of scope for effective social satire and satire ger-
mane to the mysteries in somewhat the same way that the portraits
of pretentiousness of one sort or another were always clues to the
villainy in the Peter Falk *Columbo* series of television. Perhaps Innes's
finest success along these lines occurs in the opening scene of *A Private
View*, recognized by reviewers and critics immediately as a tour de
force.[3] Lady Appleby has invited her husband to attend a private view
(an invitational preview) of the posthumous one-man show of the
abstract painter, Gavin Limbert. Braunkopf has seized the opportunity
presented by Limbert's violent death to make this *the* event of the London gallery scene, replete with a scholarly lecture to lend weight to
the occasion. The lecturer, Mervyn Twist, "was a youngish man, with
an indeterminate face suggestive of an underexposed photographic
plate, and a high, screaming voice. If one listened for long enough,
Appleby supposed, some semblance of intelligible utterance, some
rough approximation to the divine gift of discursive speech, might piece
itself together amid these horrible noises" (pp. 7–8). But all that does
emerge is a "mush of arbitrarily associated words":

heroic era of the first *papiers collés*; his second and third ego wres-
tling with the demon; correspondence to a sublime internal necessity. . . .

Appleby, in self-defense and out of policemanly habit, occupies himself with observing the audience of this extraordinary performance:

> While all had the appearance of following Mervyn Twist, a large majority was in fact exclusively concerned with disposing and maintaining the facial muscles in lines suggestive of superior critical discrimination. Some put their faith in raised eyebrows, thereby indicating that while they approved of the speaker's line as a whole, they were nevertheless obliged, in consequence of their own fuller knowledge, to deprecate aspects of it. Others had perfected a hovering smile, indicative of discreet participation in some hidden significance of the words. Yet others contented themselves with looking extremely wooden, as if conscious that the preserving of a poker face was the only safe and civil way of receiving observations which their uninhibited judgment would be obliged to greet with ridicule. Appleby found the spectacle depressing.   (p. 7)

Amidst all this nonsense, the reader sees Appleby's wholly natural and spontaneous enjoyment of what Limbert's real gift has apparently been, for lurking in Limbert's abstracts are after all reminiscences of things known outside both studio and classroom:

> The pure ellipses could be felt as yearning after the condition of Rugby footballs; and slanting across several of the canvases was a diminishing series of white rectangles from which Appleby was disposed to infer that at one time a principal ambition of young Limbert's had been winning the under-fifteen hurdles.   (p. 6)

They are paintings, in short, that "hinted at a more catholic enjoyment of created things than they were prepared openly to admit."

There is detection in this group of novels, to be sure, but there is much more not only of satire but of action and the thriller. Innes has virtually invented or at least perfected a subgenre: the *comic art thriller*. Reviewers on the whole welcomed these volumes as a relief from the baroque intricacies of Innes's fantasias of the forties, the Cloudcuckooland mode as several reviewers had called it. By contrast to such fantasias as *Stop Press, Appleby on Ararat, Appleby's End*, and *The Daffodil Affair*, these novels are relatively straightforward and are in a sense less demanding of the reader. On the other hand, each of these stories does constitute an intricately worked-out puzzle with, in each case, some ingenious double twist thrown in.

The mystification in *A Private View* begins when, after the appalling Mervyn Twist lecture, the prize painting of the opening, an enormous abstract by Gavin Limbert called "The Fifth and Sixth Days of Creation" is stolen at the crowded reception right from under Appleby's nose. Before long, the situation proves to be much more complex than a matter of a spectacular heist. For "The Fifth and Sixth Days of Creation" has, unwittingly, been overpainted on a stolen Vermeer; the thieves of the Vermeer have laid a neutral ground over that masterpiece and by a stroke of ill luck Limbert has unknowingly walked off with that reconditioned canvas from the art-supply store the thieves used as a front. But a further weird revelation is that Limbert has never actually painted on that canvas; rather, an old art-school chum, now turned espionage agent, one night holed up in Limbert's studio and, after killing Limbert, painted the secret plans of a new military complex on the canvas, disguised as the abstract Braunkopf later dubs "The Fifth and Sixth Days of Creation."

Thus, in the chase sequence that develops, there is the ultimate Keystone Kops situation of two rival espionage gangs pursuing the canvas as a disguised secret document, a gang of art thieves pursuing it as their overpainted Vermeer, and Braunkopf pursuing it as his stolen Limbert abstract! The climax of this chase is a violent but highly theatrical bit of melodrama enacted in the amphitheater of a quarry, in which the canvas — and Appleby — are rescued by none other than the Duke of Horton, owner of the stolen Vermeer and Innes's archetypal country squire.

Money from Holme, the second Braunkopf story, is a straight art thriller, without any real detective element involved. The plot concerns a fantastic but diabolical scheme perpetrated by an uninspired abstract pointillist painter and hack art critic named Mervyn Cheel. The story is interesting as a narrative told from the point of view of a scurrilous, low-life character; in it Innes achieves the Browningesque trick of conveying his satirical vision obliquely through the point of view of its object. It is a masterful portrayal of how a thoroughly vulgar, low-minded, and mean-spirited person, snubbed and avoided by nearly everyone, nevertheless can continue to present himself as an elevated but wounded character.

Cheel's unexpected opportunity to get back at life arises when at a private view at the Da Vinci Gallery of a one-man show of Sebastian Holme, a painter supposed to have perished, along with many of

his greatest works, in a hotel fire in Africa, Cheel makes the astound-
ing discovery that the deceased painter is actually in attendance in
disguise. It turns out that Holme, as desperate people sometimes do,
has found it convenient to be dead, while continuing to live quietly
as his brother (the one who really died in the fire), at least to the extent of signing his brother's checkbook from time to time.

Almost at once Cheel smells the possibility of blackmail and hits
upon what can only be called a diabolically clever variation of the impersonation theme. He half-coaxes, half-bullies Holme into *impersonating himself*, but only on canvas. That is, Cheel will provide the
studio, the materials, and some loose change, and the opportunity of
recommencing the one activity that matters to Holme — and Holme
will oblige him by reproducing or rather replicating the famous lost
paintings of the African hotel fire.

It is an ingenious sort of forgery and indeed it works well for a
time, as Cheel slips one after another of the "salvaged" paintings on
the market. Cheel's nastiest moment comes when Braunkopf, who has
been purveying these works for Cheel, turns up one day with one of
the original paintings that actually did survive the fire. Thus Cheel
is confronted with two "Clouded Leopards Playing" paintings, and furthermore, an expertise that has determined that Cheel's version is a
recent painting and therefore self-evidently a forgery!

Thus the scheme rapidly unravels. The briefly resurrected Holme,
now out from under Cheel's thumb, decamps, and Cheel is left at the
mercy of the equally unscrupulous artist who exposed him, an artist,
moreover, whom Cheel the critic has mercilessly pilloried in print. A
social/industrial realist, the artist sets Cheel to work as *his* captive
assistant, filling in the details of two immense canvases commissioned
for the Wamba Palace of Industry: "Her Majesty the Queen reading
the Speech from the Throne on the occasion of the State Opening of
Parliament"; and "The Opening of the new Road Bridge over the Firth
of Forth viewed from the East through the Cantilevers of the old
Railroad Bridge." The faces of the Commons in the one, and the rivets
in the other, are the task Cheel is set to. As his captor explains: "I flat-
ter myself that the design is intricate and pleasing. But, of course, the
number of rivets requiring representation is almost burdensomely large.
No doubt you will pass alternately between the rivets and the faces
of the M.P.s. They are about equally expressive, after all" (p. 170).
And so the abstract pointillist is set to work and, as in Dante, punish-

ment is really nothing other than getting a pretty stiff dose of what you asked for in the first place.

As an anxiety tale based on the theme of impersonation and exposure and the inexorable unraveling of a scheme, *Money from Holme* is most closely related to the thrillers *A Change of Heir* and *The New Sonia Wayward*.

Silence Observed concerns an altogether higher class of art skulduggery, partly in the exalted setting of the National Gallery itself. The book begins with one of those seemingly irrelevant Innes conversations, witty and entertaining but seeming to lead nowhere. In the sedate setting of a London club, a fellow member is telling Appleby about a wonderful find he has just made in an antiquarian bookshop. He begins reading some verses that Appleby, who confesses to having "a very fair memory for verse," recognizes as from Meredith's "Phoebus with Admetus"—except that some of the lines seem unfamiliar, and inferior. What Gribble seems to have in hand is a holograph manuscript of the poem that includes lines subsequently rejected by the poet. Appleby is impressed at this but then is taken aback as Gribble announces, "Forgery, my dear boy. . . . Every sheet of it!" (p. 9). But Gribble is not complaining, he is *gloating*—over having acquired one of the works of the master forger, Geoffrey Manallace. Then comes the real twist: as they are examining the sheets, Gribble suddenly gives a howl of rage, for he has noticed on one sheet a watermark that first appeared in 1924. For this is not merely a rare slipup by the forger—because Manallace himself died in 1924. What Gribble has in hand is therefore *a faked forgery!*

As the narrator points out, policemen are pleased when "one damned thing leads to another"—it's how cases are solved. And so it is that in rapid succession a series of obscurely related events takes place that ultimately produces a coherent picture, centered on a shop (the antiquarian bookseller, of course) that is the headquarters of an extensive art and literary forgery operation. A number of subplots, and for good measure a romance, are woven together in this story, and once again it ends in a melodramatic chase—this time with Judith Appleby, rather than Inspector Appleby, theoretically in a position of risk.

Most reviewers took the story as a plain good read, even something of a relief from some of Innes's "more elaborate mazes" (*New Statesman*, 27 Oct. 1961, p. 620). Some, however, like the *TLS* reviewer, felt that the story was not only contrived and overloaded with coincidence, but even frivolous as well: "Mr. Innes has long ceased to take himself or his readers seriously. He seems to act the tongue-in-cheek part of Henry James at Scotland Yard [the name of one of the policemen in the story] with half his mind elsewhere; but his entertainments are still very pleasant and civilized" (Oct. 6, 1961, p. 669). In a way the comment begs the question: he takes himself and his readers seriously in what way? If the aim was to produce a humoresque comic thriller, a fantasia compounded of comedy of manners, intellectual satire, and crime/suspense elements, then Innes has kept his bargain with the reader.

With *A Family Affair* (alternate title: *Picture of Guilt*) Innes is wholeheartedly back in the world of agreeably entertaining comedy of manners. The story, which will concern a series of bizarre art thefts, is set in a wonderful assortment of English country houses, with a donnish prologue and a dramatic epilogue set in Oxford, where the Applebys' son Bobby is currently ensconced as an undergraduate.

As *Silence Observed* began with an extended conversation on forgery, striking the leitmotif of that book, so the bellwether discussion here is on the subject of practical jokes. Appleby is the elderly guest of honor as Bobby and his friends celebrate an evening of wine and good talk. As is their wont on such occasions, their conversation is pursued with rather a heavy formality; their topic for the evening is practical jokes. After the conversation meanders through labyrinths of mock scholarship and learned and labored allusions, talk eventually does get round to the subject of college rags and finally to an account of what proves to be the first of the series of mysteries with which the novel is concerned. Young Lord Oswyn tells a family anecdote of a rag perpetrated donkey's years ago on his father, Lord Cockayne of Keynes: it was an elaborately mounted impersonation of a visit from a "royal personage" who, as social custom dictated on such occasions, simply walked off after tea with her choice memento from Keynes, in this case a Duccio Madonna. Needless to say, in the following days there appeared no notice in the Court Circular of any such visit by anyone connected with the royal household. And the ultimate effectiveness of the scheme was that the whole thing was just too embarrassing for Lord Cockayne to make a fuss about, especially, as he sees it, just over a bit of old canvas.

The narrative unfolds, unveiling a long, intermittent history of similar ingeniously simple thefts, perpetrated only about once in every five years — a patient, quinquennial art racket! — and in each case, perpetrated in such circumstances that, for one reason or another, the person defrauded or imposed upon would feel ridiculous or humiliated in raising a complaint and is a person of sufficient means to afford a loss and even accept it as a cruel prank. In one case a country squire was robbed of a Roman era statue that had been converted by one of his forebears into an embarrassingly indelicate garden *pisseuse*, and in another, a dealer, thinking he was buying on the q.t. a piece of high-class erotica, has ended up with a copy. In such instances it is just not something one would care to raise a hue and cry over.

Most of the rest of this wonderfully talky novel consists of a series of visits to the various gulls, each presenting a special problem of approach, in terms of how to get them to discuss these old and long-suppressed embarrassments. Inspector Appleby, Bobby, and Judith (hence, "a family affair") each take on a different conversational challenge. Bobby is able to gain admission to the residence, and the confidences, of a particularly crusty old recluse on the strength of a suddenly discovered mutual interest in Rugby, while Judith, thoroughly well versed in the byzantine subtleties of rural social graces, is more than equal to the task of bringing casual polite conversation round to the topic of the pilfered *pisseuse*. These sequences represent some of Innes's most remarkable conversational *passages*.

With these interviews accomplished, the evidence is all in, the inventiveness of the tale played out. Someone must be guilty, and by the rules of detective fiction, it must be someone encountered by the reader, but of course there's no way in the world for the reader rationally to solve this puzzle. This sort of Innes book is not really detection at all, but a comic thriller that just moves along from one intriguing conversational exchange to another. So here all that remains is straightforward revelation of who the villains are, delivered at an appropriately dramatic moment.

Ultimately the thieves are lured into making one more attempt; they are, after all, a species of practical joker and will rise to the challenge. The trap is set at Oxford under the guise of a college rag. A mock funeral is staged for a student who is supposedly being sent down; he is carried to the river in a rare Romano-Christian sarcophagus (in ancient times it had been converted from Bacchic to Christian use, a process the present occasion will reverse!). It is a valuable object whose ownership happens to be hotly disputed by two Oxford colleges. That unseemly dispute, plus the embarrassing use being made of it in this undergraduate prank, make it an effective lure for the rather fantastically minded art thieves, leading to the novel's tragicomic conclusion. When the funeral procession enters its water phase — the launching of a Beowulfian funeral ship on the Isis — the conspirators suddenly pull out in a motor boat, followed hard by a police launch in hot pursuit. The ensuing chase on the Isis ends in a fatal crash for the thieves, because they are unfamiliar with the twists and turns of Oxford's sacred river. A fitting end, it may be said, for a crew of villains who are led by a Cambridge man!

From *"London" Far*, 1946
(alternate title: *The Unsuspected Chasm*)

Among all Innes's art-related novels, the foremost among them may be the unjustly overlooked early masterpiece *From "London" Far* (1946), written and set in the year Europe emerged from the unspeakable murderousness of World War II. It is perhaps Innes's most direct response as a storyteller to the devastating threat to civilization represented by the war. Characteristically, Innes makes only very indirect, although unmistakable, allusions to the historical situation; in fact, it is that very reticence that enables the story to take on the deep allegorical coloration that it does.

The novel begins with a mellow, meditative overture in which a number of literary threads, seemingly of no great consequence but of great ultimate moment, are delicately interwoven. After some opening reflections on the question of sheer chance versus inevitable but unperceived causality in life, the narrator introduces Richard Meredith, a blameless classical scholar of orderly life at work in the British Museum Library, engaged in "the austere pleasure which workers in such places know" — he is collating a manuscript of Juvenal lent him by the Duke of Nesfield. As he finishes his labors, he stretches in the warm October sunlight and murmurs "happily with Chaucer, 'O Juvenal lord, true is thy sentence'" (p. 10). As usual, it is helpful to consult the full reference: "O Juvenal, lord! trewe is thy sentence, / That litel wyten folk what is to yerne / That they ne fynde in hire desir offence; / For cloude of errour lat hem nat discerne / What best is"

(*Troilus and Cressida* IV, 197–201), lines taken out of Juvenal's Tenth
Satire and aptly paraphrased again a few centuries later by Dr. Johnson as "The Vanity of Earthly Wishes." This Juvenalian theme will
be important later on, but for now it is enough that the train of association puts Johnson in Meredith's head, in particular another of his
Juvenalian paraphrases, "London. A Poem."

As Meredith walks through the streets of Bloomsbury, reflecting
that he would soon be traveling north, he quotes to himself scraps of
Johnson's denunciation of the treacheries and ills of urban life (for here,
Johnson, lover of London that he was, was following his Juvenal):

> Resolved at length, from vice and *London* far,
> To breathe in distant fields a purer air. . . .
> Here malice, rapine, accident conspire,
> And now a rabble rages, now a fire. . . .

Meredith enters a tobacconist's shop and the tobacco jars and adver-
tisements of smokers in their frozen gestures lead him, comically, from
Johnson to Keats's "Ode on a Grecian Urn," with its images of "pipes"
and "parching tongue" as well as its frozen figures of flight and pursuit. Later the imagery of Keats's ode will recur, but meanwhile, at
this point Meredith mutters aloud what was first in his head; "London. A Poem" — and the tobacconist immediately replies, "Rotterdam's
gone," springs open a trapdoor before Meredith, and bids him hurry
down. Incredible as this is, Meredith tumbles almost instantly to the
fact that this seemingly benign merchant has believed himself to hear
the password "London's Going," and so immediately has given the
counter reply. The nature of the password and the reply indicate that
what is afoot is a nefarious international conspiracy.

And just here is where *character* comes into play, for *From "London" Far* is decidedly not a novel of sheer coincidence. First of all, it
is far from random accident that Meredith has uttered the words he
had; "the words were of a piece with the man; one of the major interests of his life echoed in them, however idly" (p. 9). Secondly, having
uttered this Open Sesame and tumbled to the truth, however obscurely, Meredith is confronted, literally as well as figuratively, with a passage to the underworld, and with a sure mythic sense he apprehends
that there is something here that he must *do*.

The paths of night and day sweep close together — but at their nearest a step remains to be taken. There is always a moment of decision, and it is through some assertion of the will that we either stay cautiously put or move from the old world to a new. So with Richard Meredith, a scholar in his fiftieth year. Suddenly a strange path opened — opened at the distance of one vigorous stride. Literally it was like that; and literally — as if for further drama — it came in the shape of an unsuspected chasm at his feet. Meredith stepped forward and down.   (p. 9)

It is Meredith's decisive step through the wardrobe or the looking glass or, more aptly, down the rabbit hole; in epic terms, it is his descent into the underworld. And as it happens, this unassuming, fiftyish scholar is precisely the person whose character will effectively set itself against the dark forces at work in that underworld.

What Meredith encounters, fantastically, beneath the tobacconist's shop are the operations of a multinational conspiracy to plunder the art treasures of Western Europe during the chaos brought about by the war. His first glimpse, though, is merely a mild embarrassment: in the dim light he sees a lady reclining on a divan wearing a tiara, three strings of pearls, and not a stitch of clothes — and worse yet, to this man of orderly life and conventional views, she seems *familiar*, which is disconcerting to Meredith until he realizes she is the Venus painted by Titian that he had often seen in the Duke of Horton's collection. Meredith is lost in rapt contemplation of the splendors of this work — until he realizes that the painting ought to be at Horton House, not in this den of thieves! Soon he is made aware of the scale of the thing: from the still-smoking ruins of Europe, this organization is gleaning the El Grecos of Toledo, the Tiepelos of Budapest, the Rembrandts of Amsterdam. . . .

What follows for the next 150 pages is a magnificent Buchan-style thriller that brings Meredith and the alert and courageous girl he has rescued at last to an interview in a remote Scottish fastness with one Don Perez Sierra y Campo, the apparent mastermind of the Society for the Diffusion of Cultural Objects. Meanwhile, Meredith's habit of mind has been seen to lie in an unassuming sense of simply doing the right thing; he shows constant preoccupation with ethical questions: having gotten the drop on a thug or plug-ugly threatening his life, can he still rightfully dispatch the man?

Meredith's overwhelming concern for the safety of the Duke of Nesfield's Juvenal manuscript leads him to another ethical question: Godwin's parable about the burning house from which you must choose to rescue the philosopher Fenélon or his housemaid. Godwin maintained that it was one's duty to rescue Fenélon before attempting to rescue the maid, or even one's mother, "because the philosopher had more potential ability to benefit mankind than the prettiest girl or most estimable old woman" (p. 151). Meredith recalls how Bishop Butler long ago evolved an argument to dispose of such quandaries: "Men are quite without the sort of prescience which can determine what amount of human happiness a specific action may ultimately achieve, and before the burning house conscience will be a surer guide than any attempt at utilitarian calculation" (p. 152).[4]

All this prepares us for Meredith's encounter with Don Perez over brandy and cigars, during which Don Perez sets forth a leisurely philosophy of cultural despair, a glimpse into the chaos, the acknowledgment of the decline of the west, as Europe has embarked on final self-immolation:

> "On the one hand, we see the smouldering ashes of a million destroying fires. We see shattered cathedrals; whole cities surviving from the Middle Ages only to be flattened from the air; canvasses, which enshrine not individual genius alone, but centuries and centuries of the very mind of Europe, huddled in salt mines or trucked about as some war lord's booty. It is a veritable *Götterdammerung* — "
> "Quite so," said Meredith. "And an *Untergang des Abendlandes*. And *Blick ins Chaos* we have already had." (p. 168)[5]

Undaunted by or unaware of Meredith's irony, Don Perez continues with the idea that "Everywhere public order perishes, and civil polity has become but a historical phenomenon." But the conclusion Don Perez draws from this sense that "things fall apart / the center cannot hold" is only the decadent one that what remains is wine and flowers — and the conveniently self-enriching mission of shipping as much of the artistic stuff off to America as possible to reduce the balance of debt and let things start up anew. "For the populations of Europe will be no more than a peasantry and a wandering banditti. And thus when these works of art are brought forth from their half-century of seclusion men will no more think to inquire of their former owners' rights than they do of tom-toms and totem-poles in some museum of Polynesian anthropology" (p. 170). For what is provenance, he adds, but the history of acquisition and theft?

Don Perez's Mephistophelian purpose is to recruit Meredith to his organization by holding out the delights that untold wealth can bring. But he must, "Meredith reflected, have a thoroughly stupid side to him or he would scarcely imagine that a middle-aged man with whom orderly living had become second nature was to be won over by a little blarney and a little wine" (pp. 182–83). He talks on into the night. "He talked women. He kept on talking women with all the freedom and erudition of an Aretino" and Meredith must worry about his ability to resist such subliminal persuasion. But his scholarly habit of mind saves the day:

> For the simple truth was that not even the Aretino of the *Sonnets* — and certainly not Don Perez Sierra y Campo himself — could hold a candle in all this to Meredith's virtuous old Romans once they were in their slippered and smoking-room vein. Meredith therefore . . . found himself listening to Don Perez with substantial if academic, interest. It was like watching a slightly inferior examination candidate cover familiar ground — not an absorbing activity, but one offering reasonable scope for the exercise of the judgment.   (pp. 185–86)

At bottom, Don Perez's argument is a perversion of Pater's aestheticism, the idea that "your business in life was to burn with a hard, gem-like flame" (p. 178), and here is where Keats's "Ode on a Grecian Urn" comes in again. For that poem also preaches a kind of aestheticism — "'Beauty is truth, truth beauty' — that is all / Ye know on earth, and all ye need to know" — and in particular holds out the idea of the superiority of its frozen art images over the feverishness and mutability of mere sublunary love. Taken with ponderous classroom literalness, this could come across as the same sort of sophistry as Don Perez's exposition of Pater — while a hearty intrusion of life can laugh such sophistries out of court. And precisely this happens now. In a fantastic reversal of the terms of the ode, the urn figures suddenly appear in the flesh as a Celtic lad chases a maenadlike housemaid through the study. This real-life comedy breaks the spell of Don Perez's conjured fantasies and provides the immediate distraction that enables Meredith to make his escape.

While Meredith is engaged in this episode, his partner in adventure, Jean, finds herself captive in a U-boat commandeered by Captain von Schwiebus, a muscular counterpart of Don Perez, and a group of "broken soldiers, surplus war material — what you will," who are the transportion arm of the Society for the Diffusion of Cultural Objects. Von Schiebus is prone to putting on a turn as the world-weary antihero, but "Jean found the noble melancholy of this German ex-sailor not particularly appealing" (p. 217). Nevertheless, she finds that barbed references to the inevitable literary associations — Captain Nemo, the Byronic outlaw — are the readiest way to goad this self-consciously satanic figure:

> "What is wrong with many Germans," she said, "is nothing particularly Germanic. It is simply reading too much Byron. Why is so mediocre a poet celebrated all over central Europe? And you, my dear Captain, devoured him. The fluency of your English attests it. And I was told how you delighted in the outcast hero role." (pp. 218–19)

Once again, these literary allusions serve to highlight the moral allegory unfolding; nor does the melodramatic nature of these allusions undercut this function, indeed, it underscores the märchen-like quality of Innes's tale.

The end of part 2 finds Meredith and Jean reunited aboard this Flying-Dutchmanlike U-boat. With the easy dispatch by which Hamlet, offstage, extricates himself from the death trap aboard ship with Rosenkrantz and Guildenstern, and simply reappears as the liberated Hamlet of Act V, so through providential mischance to von Schwiebus's ship, Innes blithely frees Meredith and Jean from their captors, and as part 3 opens they have made their way, with a thin disguise readily dispensed with, to the destination of the precious cargo of the Society for the Diffusion of Cultural Objects: the fabulous Michigan estate of the barbaric American art collector Otis K. Neff.

Neff is the perfect dragon of Germanic mythology: not actively nefarious himself (he disapproves of hanging paintings with violent scenes "if you are a man of peace same as I am" [p. 257]), he is unimaginably wealthy and a quintessential Hoarder. His mansion is a magnificent emblem of the futile and ultimately ludicrous effort to "collect" culture. Rather like Freud's image of Rome, whose historical strata he saw as analogous to the layers of the human psyche, Neff's mansion is conceived as the ontogeny that recapitulates the phylogeny of art history. Assyrian in its foundations, it rises through a Norman crypt to a ground floor modeled on Hampton Court, a second story modeled on the extravagant Wollaton Hall, and culminates in four Queen Anne mansions atop each of the four towers, with a central tower after Le Corbusier. Among its amenities are a front door bell that activates a golden cuckoo and "the muted strains of massed choirs singing the 'Jerusalem' of William Blake" and an express elevator "appropriately embellished with a massively-sculptured Ascension after Bernini" (pp. 232–33). Neff calls it Dove Cottage.

Neff is at once more imposing and formidable, and yet less intimidating than Meredith's earlier adversaries. In fact, he is not really an adversary at all; like Tolkien's Gollum, he is a mere hoarder and it is an essential feature of Innes's myth-making that this Lucifer-figure at the center of the pit is, finally, a comic figure. For one thing, Neff is almost as huge in his innocence as in his wealth. He is a ruthless enough captain of enterprise, of that one can be sure; the prize feature of his prodigy house is a tank of sea creatures left to their own Darwinian survival of the fittest ("In Mr Neff's view, fish-life was peculiarly well calculated to illustrate progress—particularly on that side of struggle, supercession, and rugged individualism which is one of the most salutary revelations of the evolutionary hypothesis" [pp. 235–36]; the smooth irony of the narrator here is a wonderful reminder of the vision of the Attendant Spirit who guides the reader through the narrative). But Neff's naïveté is even more apparent. From top to bottom, Dove Cottage blazons forth that, as Meredith notes, "it is demonstrable that he doesn't have a scrap" of artistic appreciation. Yet Meredith is somewhat hasty here, for Neff does "get" art, as he puts it, and the discovery is as hugely wondrous to him as Tamburlaine's discovery of the power of beauty in Zenocrate: "Haven't I found I understand art same as a kitten understands milk?" (p. 279). So "Mr Neff, then, was a Dragon after all—a Dragon with pronounced if untutored aesthetic sensibilities and no morals whatever. He knew that art was beautiful. And he helped himself" (p. 259).

Neff's outer halls are hung with hundreds of Rembrandt etchings, but nothing, he says, really big: "Quiet and in good taste. Nothing to catch the eye, but the quality right. Same as if you had a custom-made suit with a neat pin stripe—nothing loud or dressy" (p. 256). But his primitive aesthetic sense is clear when he explains why he prefers Rembrandt to Goya:

"It just seems that this Rembrandt got more art all the time. It's
the way the lines go across the paper." Mr Neff offered this accurate
if unsurprising information much as if it were his own unassuming contribution to aesthetic theory. "That and how the light comes
here" — he made a curiously subtle gesture — "and here. . . . And
why is this Rembrandt still most the same van Rinjn even if you
hang him topside down? Just because he got more art all the time.
Step back folks, or we'll be late for the soup." (p. 257)

But Mr. Neff does have a dark secret. In his dragon lair this enigmatical
Bluebeard has a forbidden locked room that houses his unimaginably
rich collection of some of the world's greatest paintings. But no one
is ever allowed in to see these "coloured ones," as Neff calls them. It
is not just that they are ill-gotten goods; there is something really
mysterious about the way Neff's assistants feverishly try to keep him
from showing the collection to anyone. Are the pictures fakes? or is
it a matter of the Emperor's New Clothes, as Jean wildly guesses — no
pictures at all, just some hypnotic delusion? What is it that would kill
the goose that lays the golden egg, as Neff's suppliers fear, if anyone
should enter that room with Neff?
    Nevertheless Meredith and Jean do manage to accompany Neff
on a tour of his Carpaccios, Palma Vecchios, Titians, and Velazquezes
and all his other "coloured ones." Again, Neff's untutored but uncan-
ny feeling for art is apparent; before a Masaccio Madonna he tries to
explain his feelings:

> It's as if you were exploring it with all your muscles ever so slight-
> ly moving, so that there's a sort of dance going on way inside
> yourself that's like all the movements in the picture. Isn't that so?

But then he adds a bizarre footnote:

> And then — quite suddenly — it's not like that any more. The
> dance kind of loses itself, and you feel like coming down stairs in
> the dark and taking a step that isn't there. That right? (pp. 278–79)

Something for Neff is radically and unaccountably wrong with all these
paintings. For the simple truth, which his suppliers feared his ever
discovering, but which is now apparent, is that the Dragon is *color-
blind* and thus radically unable to appreciate his hoard!
    When that realization dawns on Neff, the *götterdammerung* com-

mences. The dragon in a demented rage pulls Dove Cottage down around him, hurling to destruction the "junk" that has so cruelly betrayed and mocked him: a "monstrous funeral procession of pigment and bronze and marble, this glyptic and plastic twilight of the gods" (p. 288). Meredith's last glimpse of him is of "Mr Neff himself insanely dancing beneath the portico, his gold and ruby dove hovering above him while the solemn strains of William Blake's 'Jerusalem' floated down through the air" (p. 289).

Fortunately, Meredith and Jean are able to make an airborne escape, salvaging many of the precious art objects. The three airmen who pilot the plane — hale, muscular young Americans — quite surprisingly break into verse as the plane climbs away from the scene of destruction:

> Before the starry threshold of Jove's court
> My mansion is, where those immortal shapes
> Of bright aerial spirits live insphered
> In regions mild of calm and serene air,
> Above the smoke and stir of this dim spot
> Which men call earth.   (p. 295)

(The pilot has an interesting patriotic explanation for this ready poetic facility: "Airmen, you see, must have a great deal of poetry by heart if they're not going to go to sleep. That's why between us we beat the *Lüftwaffe*. They didn't have nearly enough poetry to keep awake on. Not even when they stretched a strict Aryan point or two and included Heine." [pp. 295–96].)

At any rate, what the three airmen, "as beautiful as singing angels by Botticelli," are chanting are the opening lines of Milton's *Comus*, and if the reader continues a few lines, he will find that the Attendant Spirit goes on to speak of the tormented earth as unmindful of "the crown that Virtue gives," save that

> Yet some there be that by due steps aspire
> To lay their just hands on that golden key
> That opes the palace of Eternity:
> To such my errand is.   (ll. 12–15)

In *Comus* the person so protected is the Lady, and her golden key is Chastity, that much misunderstood Spenserian and Miltonic virtue.

Meredith has it too; it is simply purity of heart. The golden key, on the märchen level of the story, is that bit of paraphrase of Juvenal by Johnson that admitted Meredith to the Underworld just as the golden bough did Virgil, or the moly Odysseus. It admits him, one might say, down the rabbit hole, where subsequently, to continue the analogy, he brings down the whole false house of cards. He accomplishes the *geste* by virtue of who and what he is — it is "a fact of character," for "Meredith himself was a cultural object" (p. 208). In fact, Innes had already in the British Museum Reading Room given Meredith the nimbus of sainthood: "when at lunch-time the farthest-creeping shaft of golden light touched his high forhead crowned with its untidy hair" (p. 10).

In case the allegorical intent of Innes's novel is not sufficiently clear at this point, one need only attend to the comic epilogue, in which the reader learns what happened, back in Scotland, to the mastermind of the Society for the Diffusion of Cultural Objects. A local character, Captain Maxwell, reads it as a news item in the *Oban Argus* ("a journal o' opinion . . . a wee bit more circumscribed than the *Scotsman* or *The Times*"): the man known as Don Perez has been crushed to death by a falling statue being transported to one of his ships; a witness noticed

> that at the moment of his death the deceased had apparently been reading *Der Untergang des Abendlandes* of the German ideologue, Oswald Spengler. Mr Fairweather then identified the statue. It proves to be by a well-known contemporary Yugoslavian sculptor, and is an allegorical group known as the *Europa Rediviva*, or Europe Restored.   (p. 300)

Captain Maxwell, taking off his spectacles and folding the paper, aptly has the last word in the novel: "'What they ca' *The Decline of the West*,' he said. 'And then *Europa Rediviva*. Now, would ye no' be thinking there was some inwardness in that?'"

It is surprising that such a wonderfully written book should as yet have failed to gain the literary reputation it deserves. Except for Will Cuppy, who was a persistent admirer of Innes in the pages of the *New York Herald Tribune* in the thirties and forties (see *NYHT Book Review*, March 3, 1946, p. 26), the reviewers seem not to have been enthusiastic about *From "London" Far*. The *New Republic* reviewer called it a "particularly extravagant extravaganza" and judged that "Mr. Innes has never been more recondite or long-winded, and the few moments of fun or excitement he provides . . . are hard bought" (March 11, 1946, p. 358). Moreover, the work has been unaccountably ignored in the modern select surveys of detective fiction, even those, such as Symons or Routley or Barzun and Taylor, that accord Innes an important place. The one exception is Professor Volker Neuhaus's very perceptive recent scholarly article (in German) on From "London" Far as game and as glass-bead game.[6] It is to be hoped that with the book back in print in paperback, it will attract the new readership it deserves.

Honeybath

Before leaving the subject of Innes's art-related novels, a note should be added about the recent group whose protagonist is the elderly establishment painter, Charles Honeybath, R. A., yet another variant of that favored Innes type, the mild-mannered, eminently affable but surprisingly resourceful culture-hero. The Honeybath novels are quite like the latter-day Appleby tales and are distinguishable only in being, if anything, even more gently mannered and in offering more continuous occasion for pleasant talk about art. Indeed, one of these chronicles, Lord Mullion's Secret (1981), does not even nod in the direction of detection, nor even of any real mystification, being essentially an Edwardian-style family intrigue. The only real mystery in the story is why Honeybath, invited to Mullion Castle to do a portrait of Lady Mullion, appears to be deftly discouraged by the local vicar from inspecting too closely one of the chief art treasures of the castle, a tiny ancestral portrait executed by the great Jacobean miniaturist Nicholas Hilliard, and why, as Honeybath is able to detect in any case, what resides within the tiny frame is an excellent reproduction rather than an original. And that gives rise more to suspicions about some discreet sale of heirlooms necessitated by penurious circumstances than to any notion of theft.

To the contrary, very early in Lord Mullion's Secret it becomes clear that the basic situation of concern is the fact that Mullion's daughter has fallen helplessly in love with the family gardener, a fragrantly sweaty, golden-skinned nature god straight out of D. H.

Lawrence. The all too evident complication, beyond the obvious social one, is that the garden lad, Swithin Gore, projects a distinct image of being a little more of kin than of kith to his employer's family. The vicar, as it turns out, is the custodian of the secret of Swithin's ancestry, and therein lies the answer to the small mystery of the Hilliard portrait: by a freak of heredity, that Jacobean ancestor was an embarrassing spit and image of Swithin Gore. To keep the painful implication from the family, the vicar has substituted another miniature for the genuine Hilliard, but upon Honeybath's arrival, the vicar realizes that the Royal Academician will immediately spot the deception and thus unwittingly stir up the whole uncomfortable situation.

The other three Honeybath novels are closer to detective interests, and in fact ring amusing changes upon some well-worn themes. *Honeybath's Haven* (1977), for example, plays a bizarre variation on that favorite Innes motif, art forgery, somewhat along the lines of *Money from Holme*. Again, hitherto unknown masterpieces or presumed lost works from a great contemporary artist's most productive period mysteriously begin turning up. Here it's not an artist, presumed dead, being constrained to recreate great lost masterpieces (the situation in *Money from Holme*), but rather a sadly deteriorated painter, Edwin Lightfoot, now living in a sanitarium, who is periodically taken back under hypnosis to his years of greatest creativity in order to produce, unbeknownst to himself, more valuable "early Lightfoots." Honeybath's clue to the situation is a satirical sketch by Lightfoot that seems to reflect some dim apprehension of his plight: it is a caricature of his therapist, titled "Signor Cipolli," an allusion to a stage hypnotist in a story by Thomas Mann. Actually, this matter of the satirical drawing connects directly with what does turn out, after all, to be the murder mystery. After Lightfoot is found drowned, in a shallow pool of seaweed, it turns out that his habit of making satirical sketches has proven fatal — one person in the sanitarium has had special reason for not wanting a sketch made and promulgated.

The first of the Honeybath stories, *The Mysterious Commission* (1974), is a takeoff on Conan Doyle's "The Red-Headed League." Honeybath is called upon to execute a portrait of a mysterious "Mr. X" under conditions of absolute secrecy and anonymity. Honeybath is driven blindfolded and drugged to a great country house where he spends two weeks as a virtual prisoner doing a portrait of an evident lunatic in the custody of very suspicious caretakers. When the job is done, he is dumped unceremoniously on a motorway in the middle of the night. Back in London, he discovers that in his absence a gang has used his studio as a base from which to tunnel into a neighboring bank.

Honeybath helps the police run the bank-robbers to earth, but he is not convinced that this is the whole truth to the strange episode — moreover, he wants to recover his portrait of Mr. X because, incredible as it seems, he realizes that his portrait of the unknown lunatic is the masterpiece of his career. Honeybath does some ingenious detective work of his own to track down the location of the mysterious country house, aided by a British Rail timetable and the remembered offnote of a steeple chime. A line from Eliot's *The Waste Land*, about how S. Mary Woolnoth keeps the hours "with a dead sound on the final stroke of nine," causes him to recall a similar effect in the vicinity of his captivity. When he does, Honeybath finds himself caught in the middle of a war between rival gangs — the trump card of one gang had been to prove, by way of Honeybath's portrait, that a certain crucial character was in their hands, but without revealing that he had become a lunatic. At the end there is a kind of siege and a great conflagration at the mansion, and Honeybath risks his life by charging into the burning building to retrieve his "Portrait of an Unknown Gentleman" — and a Monet that he had earlier observed in the house. This wasn't heroism, or foolishness; Honeybath was only acting according to his nature: "Perhaps it was equally rational simply to stand by the way you were made. The way God had secretly made you — deep inside Honeybath, successful R.A." (p. 186).

Finally, *Appleby and Honeybath* (1983), perhaps Innes's finest work of the last decade, brings Innes's two protagonists together in a playful revival of some favorite devices and a gentle sendup of the whole genre. The opening pages establish a country-house situation in which a body is found in the library in a takeoff of the classic sealed-room mystery.

Honeybath, once again on commission to do a portrait of a landed gentleman, has decided to take a look at the long-disused library as a possible, though unlikely, setting for the work (his host, Grinton, a hunt-loving squire, having nothing but contempt and distaste for his James Gibbs-designed ancestral library), only to find a body propped in a chair and fixed with an expression of malicious glee. Honeybath leaves, locks the door, and fetches Appleby, an old friend and also a weekend guest. They return to find no sign of a body, but on investigation do discover a hidden door in the farther wall that leads to a sort of shabby utility shed in which they find a kind of tramps' hangout: a bed, a table, and a stove with a bit of rarebit still warm. They relock the doors and return a third time, with the local police inspector, and this time find that not only has the body disappeared, but the tramps' setup as well.

Throughout the rest of the narrative, Appleby and Honeybath, together and separately, set about elucidating the mystery, which, as in *The Ampersand Papers*, revolves around a double treasure hunt, one literary and one artistic. For as various old family papers reveal (compare *Christmas at Candleshoe* and *Old Hall, New Hall*), the house might well contain a hidden cache of drawings by the great painter Claude, and a possible holograph manuscript by Alexander Pope of a hitherto unknown satire directed against this very household, somewhat in the manner of the Timon's Villa section of the "Epistle to Burlington." Indeed, the body Honeybath saw eventually is found and identified as that of an American scholar who, with the butler's connivance, had been camping out in the digs behind the library, searching out the Pope manuscript. But as Appleby and Honeybath come to realize, several different sets of house guests, independently, have been on the trail either of the Claudes or the Pope, and a farcelike madhouse of secret comings and goings is eventually unraveled by the investigators, including a veritable corpse's ballet with the body of the scholar — all rather reminiscent of the lunacy chronicled in Innes's first work, *Death at the President's Lodging*.

The gist of all this is that both sets of treasure have apparently been found, and on the same stroke of inspiration, Blake's "fearful symmetry" or — more pertinently — Pope's "Grove nods at grove, each Alley has a brother": that is, several treasure hunters have independently hit upon what must have been James Gibbs's principle of neoclassical symmetry in the design of the library, that is, a balancing *second* hidden door. (All this, including the Pope quote, had been used before in *Appleby's Other Story*.) The American scholar was the first to find the second door and the Pope manuscript, but the excitement was too much for him and he died on the spot, clutching the manuscript. At any rate the Claudes prove to be probably an irretrievable loss — whoever found them has promptly mailed them out of the country — but the Pope poem is yielded up and handed to Grinton, its rightful owner. But no sooner does the squire read, for the first time, Pope's devastating mockery of his ancestral home and forebears, than Grinton turns purple with rage — and hurls the manuscript into the fire. And so, Pope scholarship need not be revised after all!

In any case, the real interest in these genial stories is the cultured conversation and civilized viewpoint of Honeybath himself, who, self-effacing as he is, would, as we have seen, unhesitatingly risk his life to save a Monet. The inner character of this elderly Innes alter ego is, finally, that he is a passionate lover: each artistic project he approaches with a lover's reverent sense of mystery, "since that is what painting the portrait of another human being involves. Or painting a kitchen chair or an old pair of boots for that matter. You have to love the things, and achieve an obscure act of possession, and the result is that you have brought a minute speck of light into the vast darkness in which we move and have our being" (p. 58).

6

Comedy of Manors: The Country-House Stories

Stop Press
Country-House Weekends
Fearful Symmetry

> Of all the great things that the English have invented and made
> part of the credit of the national character, the most perfect, the
> most characteristic, the only one they have mastered completely
> in all its details, so that it becomes a compendious illustration of
> their social genius and their manners, is the well-appointed, well-
> administered, well-filled country house.
>
> — Henry James, *English Hours*[1]

In a recent brilliant study of the English country house and the literary
imagination, Richard Gill has shown how persistent and how important the country house is as a locus and a symbol in English literature,
particularly in the novel. Based on the medieval manorial system, and
thereby different in character and role from Continental equivalents
such as the French château or the Italian villa, the English country
house is, according to Gill, "even more than an ancestral home and
family seat: it is—or at least has been—a social, economic, and cultural
institution, inextricably linked with the surrounding landscape and
profoundly affecting not only those living under its roof but those
within its purview as well,"[2] and as such has been an important motif
in English literature from the seventeenth century to the present.
Beginning with Jonson, Carew, and Marvell, a distinct subgenre of

151

English lyric poetry has grown up around the theme of the well-ordered country house as the Great, Good Place—and the denunciation of the corruption of that ideal as in Pope's description of Timon's Villa in *Epistle IV. To Burlington.*

Gill argues that the prominent place of the country house in English literature, especially in modern fiction, has to do with the polarity of isolation and community. As isolation is conveyed through the literary use of such emblems as islands and locked rooms, so the theme of community or communion has been most frequently conveyed through images of social gatherings—

> Which brings us to the significance of the country house in modern fiction. Of all the available symbols of community, the outstanding one for the English novelist is obviously the country house. As an institution representing the structure and traditions of English society, it is a microcosm which has the advantage of being public and familiar, yet malleable enough to serve the protean interests of individual novelists . . . [who] have all found in the country house a means of embodying the qualities and values of community, whether in a state of decay, transformation, or renewal.[3]

As to *why* the country house should be favored as an image for the theme of community, one must turn not only to its role as a socio-economic institution and social microcosm already alluded to, but to its physical nature as well. On this score the great house and its attendant parks and gardens is a convincing stage that offers sufficient scope for the full range of ordinary social intercourse. The gardens and parks provide a variety of terrain and allow for reclusive perambulations or intriguing trysts in a natural setting; the labyrinth of rooms, corridors, staircases, and terraces allow for all manner of comings and goings, meetings and separations; and the great public gathering places, the great hall and the long gallery and the library serve as centralizing spaces that draw all the parties together.

Perhaps even more important is the role of the country house as a place where fundamental life rhythms and rituals transpire: the great passages of individual and generational life (births, marriages, deaths), the ephemeral passages of arrivals and departures, and above all the conventional diurnal social round of breakfasts, teas, dinners, of dressing and retiring, of meeting for parlor games, billiards, or cigars and brandy. Thus, as an overwhelmingly social environment, the country-house setting has lent itself particularly to the tradition of the novel of manners.

There have been many critics who have regarded the country-house tradition in literature as essentially snobbish,[4] but one thing that has tended to blunt a sharply negative view is the dismantling in real life of much of the actual power and status of the traditional country house. It has become virtually a *pastoral* symbol, in contrast to images of the harsh realities and brutalized relationships of the contemporary urban world. Until it is violated by the intrusion of bloody murder: and there the detective novel comes in. For it was in just that historical milieu — the breakup of the old order between the wars — that the formal detective novel of manners flowered into its Golden Age. It has frequently been remarked that this species of popular fiction nostalgically preserved that vanishing order and, exactly as a kind of modern fairy tale, showed in one country-house story after another how this comic yet idyllic world is preserved by the intervention of the Prospero-like Great Detective.[5] The appeal of the formal detective novel resides in the reader's desire for reassurance and order — after first enjoying the thrill of disorder and confusion for the first 200 pages or so! — and for the reaffirmation that all — but one — are truly innocent.

The reasons suggested above for the prominence of the country house in English fiction generally apply with particular appositeness to detective fiction, and indeed houses are as prominent in the titles of detective novels as they are in the titles of mainstream novels of manners.[6] Innes himself in a recent essay has succinctly put the reasons for the prominence of the country house setting in his own tales. One reason is technical, as he calls it, having to do with the great house as a *physical environment*:

> The mansion, the country seat, the ducal palace, is really an extension of the sealed room, defining the spatial, the territorial boundaries of a problem. One can, of course, extract a similar effect out of a compact apartment or a semidetached villa. But these are rather cramping places to prowl in. And in detective stories detectives and their quarry alike must prowl. At the same time, they mustn't get lost. And this fairly spacious unity, the Unity of Place in Aristotle's grand recipe for fiction, conduces to an observance of those other unities of time and action that hold a fast-moving story together.[7]

In this respect the country house is the prototype of those other variants of the closed setting that delimit the scene of action and the cast of characters — the ship, the railroad train, the snowbound ski lodge, the college quadrangle, the cathedral close — but it has the advantage over those others of incorporating a greater range of social types combined with a greater cohesion.

This leads to the second and perhaps most significant reason Innes offers for favoring the country-house setting, that having to do with it as a *social environment* ("Roofs seem to give rise to situations," as Ivy Compton-Burnett has a character say[8]). Innes, not surprisingly, invokes the microcosm idea:

> In serious English fiction, as distinct from a fiction of entertainment, the great house has long been a symbol — or rather a microcosm — of ordered society; of a complex, but on the whole harmonious, community. . . .
>
> Something of this has rubbed off on the novel's poor relation, the detective story — the more readily, perhaps, because in England itself that sort of story was in its heyday rather an upper-class addiction.[9]

For Innes this is indeed a literature of nostalgia, his characters operating "within a society remembered rather than observed — and remembered in terms of literary conventions which are themselves distancing themselves" as their creator works. What Innes is defining here is what Hanna Charney later would denominate as "the detective novel of manners." In such a work detection does go on and is the means of bringing about the ritual expulsion of the villain and the restoration of communal order, but as Innes says about his manners hero, "Appleby is as much concerned to provide miscellaneous and unassuming 'civilized' entertainment as he is to hunt down baddies wherever they may lurk." Hence, too, Appleby "becomes rather fond of talking, or at least of frequenting the society of persons who prefer amusing conversation to going through the motions of being highly suspicious characters, much involved with low life and criminal practice."[10]

Since the ruling ethos of the novel of manners lies in an assumed equivalence between the social and the moral codes, it is precisely the detective's comfortableness in this high-toned milieu and his ability to discriminate between the authentic and the bogus that is his surest intellectual and moral weapon. The detective's oft-mentioned simple pleasures—his delight in his pipe or a glass of port or a favorite painting—are not a mere colorful divertissement but rather serve as signifiers or emblems of the good, well-ordered life on whose behalf his operations are conducted.[11]

Innes's comedy of manners approach to the detective novel is apparent in his first book, *Death at the President's Lodging*, an academic puzzle story in which the College of St. Anthony's takes on some of the functions of the country house. But his second novel, *Hamlet, Revenge!*, is a full-fledged country-house mystery centered on the device of a play-within-a-play in the form of a private theatrical. Innes was to use the great house, in one form or another, as the setting or at least as *a* setting in most of his succeeding narratives.

Stop Press, 1939
(alternate title: *The Spider Strikes*)

After the impressive start represented by the first three Appleby novels, Innes turned decisively to a comedy of manners approach and produced what has remained his most ambitious novel and arguably the best country-house mystery ever written: *Stop Press* (1939).

From the point of view of literary texture, of the capacity of the text to sustain repeated rereading with enhancement rather than diminishment of aesthetic pleasure, *Stop Press* is virtually without parallel in detective fiction. It is a novel proportionally far less dependent than most mysteries on sheer plot—on ingenious crime and ingenious solution—than on the richness and subtlety of the prose and the wit of the dialogue for its effects. It is closer to the great tradition of Austen, Trollope, and Henry James than to the tale of ratiocination inaugurated by Poe and Conan Doyle. In fact, unlike the backward plotting characteristic of most mystery novels, *Stop Press* is forwardly plotted in the manner of traditional straight fiction and concerns itself with an unfolding of events rather than with the reconstruction of a crime.

Especially notable is the way *Stop Press* becomes a masterly study in the handling of point of view. The third-person narration is not omniscient but rather follows intermittently the viewpoints of a limited number among an exceedingly large cast of characters. When Innes is following one of these "open" characters the reader sees what he sees and hears what he hears, whereas the other characters are presented only behavioristically. The voice of the narrator tends to adopt, chameleonlike, the style and vocabulary of the current open character, but without any direct or implicit identification of narrator and character.

For instance, in a railway conversation between Timmy Eliot, an Oxford student, and his tutor, Gerald Winter, it is clearly from Winter's point of view that the reader gets the scene:

> Timothy Eliot, curled comfortably in a corner of the compartment with his exeat in his pocket, seemed aware of the symbolism of the accelerating train. . . . Winter, whose breakfast had been more hurried than he would have wished, peered over *The Times*. . . . Timothy stuffed the pipe — with one of those nameless but expensive mixtures, Winter noticed, which Oxford tobacconists delight to compound for the young on the bespoke principle.   (p. 30)

The distinctions are slight but decisive: Timothy "seemed" but Winter "noticed," and the narrator silently adopts Winter's mode of expression, in which tobacconists "compound" mixtures on the "bespoke" principle. And it is always clear that the narrator is simply *adopting* this or that manner, as when he slips into a clearly independent point of view — and says, for instance, that "Winter looked gloomy."

This complex interplay of point of view serves to establish a careful balance of empathy and distance that adds up to a perspective similar to the novel of manners. Indeed, *Stop Press* is a perfect example of the "detective novel of manners" as Charney and George Grella have aptly defined the form.[12] At its center is a country-house gathering with a surplus of characters of Jamesian sensitivity and a plot that follows the archetypal comic pattern of an idyllic order threatened and restored.

Moreover, because in this novel the central protagonist is himself a writer of detective fiction, and because the mystery involves an enigma having to do with his writings and the occasion of the house party is a literary anniversary, *Stop Press* is a very self-consciously *literary* novel, full of bookish talk, quotations, allusions to poetry, and self-referential comments about detective fiction. Indeed, *writing* proves to be almost obsessively the subject.

The central situation focuses on Richard Eliot, a would-be Pope scholar who has made a success as a mystery writer and been thereby gradually seduced from his initial vocation and been in a sense taken over by his creation, the Spider. A prologue to the novel — written from the point of view of the objective narrator — first introduces the Spider, chronicling his evolution from a gentleman master criminal ("Sitting in a library of old books the Spider controlled from afar a nefarious organization of surprising complexity") to a sort of Robin Hood outlaw and finally to a formidable private detective marked by severely ortho- dox moral views and marked literary predilections. In his progress from Scarlet Pimpernell and Arsen Lupin to Sherlock Holmes, the Spider has acquired striking resemblances to his creator; "He was fond," for instance, "of quoting from the poet Pope — of whose tangled bibli- ography he had a connoisseur's knowledge" (p. 7). In the end, this dominant creation got quite a hold on his creator's psyche, and the Spider began in his narratives to embark on projects and deliver him- self of disquisitions that seemed rather to belong more to Mr. Eliot's sphere of interest. Indeed, "It is certain that in the Spider's final phase the Spider and Mr Eliot became a little mixed up. . . . This was the situation when the thing happened" (p. 12).[13]

"The thing" turns out to be that uncomfortable Pygmalionesque situation of a creation that comes to life. First, someone in the char- acter of the Spider plays a series of pranks in the neighborhood; in the most striking incident, a very Victorian lady traveler and author named Mrs. Birdwire is burglarized and some uncouth graffiti left on her garden wall showing Mrs. B. in pith helmet finding her husband in a secretary's arms and saying, "Mr. Birdwire, I presume?" Rather more alarming, certain episodes are acted out and even found on typed sheets inserted into Eliot's typewriter — episodes from stories Eliot has never published nor even written down, but which he *has* thought of and recognizes as incidents he someday intended to make use of! So dis- concerting are these manifestations and so alarming the possible in- terpretations of them that Eliot, brought to the verge of nervous break- down, is on the point of renouncing any further work on the Spider stories. This prospect naturally alarms his publisher and the various relatives and associates who have come to depend on the income from the Spider.

All this comes to a head at the weekend house party at Eliot's estate, Rust Hall, held to celebrate the Spider's twentieth birthday. The household consists of Eliot, his daughter Belinda, son Timmy, and an aged aunt who never leaves her room. The guests include Eliot's two cousins, Rupert, who presents himself as a rough and tumble man of the world, and Archie, a failed engineer; Gerald Winter, Timmy's Oxford tutor; Mrs. Moule, a psychic; Miss Cavey, a writer of popular romances; and a variety of professional people associated in one way or another with the Spider enterprise. There is the publisher Wedge, the actor Peter Holme who plays the Spider in films and feels typecast and trapped in the role, the ghost writer Kermode who adapts the Spider stories and is contracted to continue the series whenever Eliot gives it over. Another guest happens to be a friend of Belinda's named Patricia Appleby, the sister, of course, of John Appleby.

Events unfold during this quintessentially British long weekend amid a ceaseless flow of witty conversation; Julian Symons, in judging the book as "perhaps the best" of all Innes's works, noted how its plot is "balanced on little jets of unfailingly amusing talk."[14] After a wonderful opening scene in Oxford, a train journey brings Timmy Eliot and his tutor through Innes's favorite landscape of imagination, a "heart-of-England" countryside marked by such towns as Warter, King's Cleve, Low Swaff'ham, Pigg, Little Limber, Snug, and Cold Findon, to arrive finally at the Eliot estate, Rust Hall. Like most of Innes's country houses, Rust Hall is an imposing, isolated antiquity, demonstrating a confusing succession of architectural styles ranging from the Tudor through the neoclassical, with winding corridors and staircases offering ample scope for the physical demands of mystification.

Despite the awkward circumstances created by the seemingly independent existence of the Spider, and by Eliot's apparent imminent decision to give up his detective writing career, the literary party goes forward. Naturally much of the table talk is about literature and ranges from Winter's facetiously donnish monologue on the esenoplastic power of the imagination ("the esemplastic power, as the shaky scholarship of Coleridge called it") to Wedge's idea that the important thing is to keep the presses rolling. There is also an Auden-like discourse on the rules of detective fiction by Mrs. Moule, the psychic and actress:

Mr Eliot's later books are successful because everything is subject to rules which the reader knows. There is generally a puzzle which the reader can solve by means of the rules — and that implies that in the little universe of the book the reader is master. The books — though the reader is hardly aware of it — cater for the need of securi-

ty. Real life is horribly insecure because God is capable of keeping
a vital rule or two up his sleeve and giving us unpleasant surprises
as a result. Mr Eliot isn't allowed to do that. In a puzzle-book the
surprises are always pleasing because it is implied that our intelligence is really superior to them.   (p. 64)

Kermode's account of detective fiction is simpler: it's just juvenile imagination not let go of: "If you grow up, you find that the simplest solution's the booze. But if you stick at the age of ginger-pop — well, there's
nothing much for it but to scribble away" (p. 221).

The real business of the weekend turns out to be ongoing manifestations by the mysteriously vivified Spider, announced by notes from
a mysterious clarinet playing the Spider's theme. The first time it
heralds a peculiarly pointless-seeming prank: across the architrave of
one front of the house, the guests find, in red paint, the words "This
is Folly Hall" writ large. This leaves Eliot, who has been planning to
use the name Folly Hall in an as yet unpublished story, thoroughly
demoralized and bewildered. Subsequently the house is repeatedly
plunged into utter darkness, a childish trick that nevertheless has an
effect of producing incrementally heightening tension. The second such
manifestation occurs during a game of hide and seek (parlor games being an expected part of the proceedings of such a weekend), and here
the house plays its part:

> Though not rambling, it was confused; though long since fallen into
> some sort of harmony to the eye, it was yet incoherent and baffling
> to the exploring foot: an aggregate of improbable angles and broken
> lines, like a crystal which has been damaged in the slow process
> of accretion. . . . Rooms unexpectedly intercommunicated, pas-
> sages branched and united again, loft ladders and a brace of spiral
> staircases offered unlooked-for opportunities for reversal and sur-
> prise.   (pp. 125–26)

But the circumstances of the attendant blackout leave Eliot reso-
lute rather than confused. He now knows for certain that a whole set
of his ideas for a mystery story, *ideas he has never set on paper*, are
in the process of acting themselves out. In fact, he is able to predict
that the next step will be the theft of a valuable painting and, sure
enough, when the guests rush to the gallery they find that a Renoir

nude that Eliot gave Belinda as a present is indeed missing — and thus does the unwritten plot seem to be coming to life.

However, when the missing painting turns up the next morning in the bed of the footman Joseph, found by the chagrinned servant himself upon awakening next to the ample nude — in a bizarre recreation of a scene from *Joseph Andrews* — Eliot suddenly rallies. Something in the disposition of the event has reassured him, and from then on he is as a man suddenly transformed, no longer frightened nor bewildered.

Meanwhile, a private theatrical has been planned for the weekend — the play-within-a-play theme yet again — in which everyone gets wholesomely involved. The performance itself proves to be a monumental fiasco. First, the locals pronounce the "neo-academic" entertainments to be "very clever, indeed" — which is their most damning expression of disapproval. Next, Miss Cavey's absurd one-woman melodrama, "A Haworth Saturday Night," is interrupted by a crude practical joke when three stuffed dogs hung from nooses and a fourth transfixed by a butcher's hook are lowered onto the stage. At midnight a shot and an agonized scream brings everyone racing back to the theater. This time the curtain is raised to reveal a steady dripping of blood coming from a figure dressed in evening trousers twisting slowly in the darkness of the rafters. The mood of terror and anxiety turns to disgust when the body on the butcher's hook is lowered to the floor and proves to be that of a middle-black pig.

Amid the general revulsion, Appleby (who by now is on the scene) sees the exact character of the demonstration: it is at once a macabre practical joke and a murderous gesture — that is, it is the clear expression of thoroughly murderous intent momentarily forced to redirect itself away from its wished-for target. It is a manifestation of the perverse operation of the pleasure principle, the reality principle having been for some reason effectively baffled. Appleby is able to surmise accurately at this point that some plan A having failed, a plan B involving a murder is now being mounted — *and he thinks he knows broadly why, but not by whom or of whom*, except that Eliot himself is no longer to be threatened (p. 302). Appleby is not being coy; he is only exercising that natural sensitivity to nuances of word and situation, while awaiting enlightenment, that Winter jestingly calls Appleby's "wise policemanly passiveness" (p. 197).

The last third of the novel shifts from Rust Hall to the neighboring Shoon Abbey, to which Eliot's house party is invited to inspect the rare-book collection. Shoon Abbey is essentially a reconstruction scarcely a decade old. Jasper Shoon, its proprietor, is a financial tyro, a former gunrunner in the Near East and currently an international arms supplier in a big way — but the personality he sails under in the neighborhood is that of a collector and amateur scholar. He is president of a bogus learned society called The Friends of the Venerable Bede, a group of individuals with similar backgrounds and interests. Shoon Abbey thus has the very smell of inauthenticity about it — at least to the sensibility oppositely attuned to the genuine. The place is in fact nothing other than a gigantic replica, a replica not of medieval gothic, but rather of eighteenth-century picturesque "gothick," complete with artificial ruins, chinoiserie, labyrinthine natural garden, all composing "a sort of dream-Gothic, the Gardens of Idea — gloomy groves, murmering streams, sequestered grots, root-houses, urns, dells, denes, dingles — all these revealed themselves from this height in one extensive, costly, and subtle statement: a yearning after a past age which had yearned after a past age" (p. 265).

The heart of this falsely medievalizing place is Shoon's rare-book collection, for this too, valuable though the collection really is, exudes the very spirit of falseness. There is, for instance, the Coleridge Collection, purchased on the strength of Shoon's "successful flotation of the Medicinal Opium Company (China) Limited"; the Wordsworth Collection, fruit of a trust whose finances grew out of a series of bankruptcies, alimonies, and other domestic calamities; and the Milton, Cowper, Byron, and Shelley libraries, forming the nucleus of Shoon's section on English Literature and the Voice of Liberty, purchased on the strength of an operation supplying African labor to employers in central Arabia. Shoon's literary manuscripts include a collection of *parerga* — posthumous fragments, false starts, unpublishable snippets, and clippings — which Wedge labels "English Literature and the Wastepaper Basket." Each acquisition is expensively bound and stamped with a hyena rampant, Shoon's coat of arms. In general, the chief impression emanating from the collection is the smell of a well-conducted mortuary.

The big surprise of the Shoon collection, and the treat that Jasper Shoon has reserved for his neighbor's literary anniversary, is that he has in a special section all thirty-seven volumes of the Spider mysteries, uniformly bound in vellum and stamped with a gilt spider. And not only does he collect them, Jasper Shoon assures his guest, he avidly reads them, and he announces how eagerly he awaits the next volumes in the series, *Murder at Midnight* and *A Death in the Desert*, on which Eliot is currently at work. Meanwhile, more mysterious manifestations of the Spider redivivus occur at Shoon Abbey, but this time in the form of death threats against Eliot's cousin Rupert.

Toward the end of his visit to Shoon Abbey, Appleby is quite confident that a murder has been arranged, and why, and he is even sure who the two principals are, but does not yet know which will be the intended victim and which the would-be murderer. The day's visit ends with a confusing mélange of violent actions under cover of darkness, culminating in a violent explosion and Appleby's announcement that Shoon has been killed.

At this time Appleby presents his solution of the case, including an explanation of the apparent preternatural clairvoyance of the Spider prankster. Eliot, like his cousin Rupert, was once in the Near East and, Appleby hypothesizes, came to know of some damning act of villainy on the part of Jasper Shoon. But Eliot fell into a terrible illness that created an amnesia blocking all memory of Shoon. Shoon's great fear is that Eliot will unconsciously dredge up recollection of those forgotten events and work them into one of his mysteries. The forthcoming *A Death in the Desert* has seemed particularly threatening. Hence Shoon's campaign to drive Eliot into giving up his Spider publications. Secondly, how was Shoon able to recreate incidents based on unpublished plot ideas? They must simply be plot ideas that Eliot in his delirium gave utterance to and that were overheard by Shoon. Appleby concludes that instead of succeeding in his murderous attack Shoon has been hoist by his own petard in some infernal explosion.

Hearing this incredible explication, and able to confirm certain objective features of it, Eliot is shaken and appalled, and cries out, "Never again will I put pen to paper as a writer! This is the end." At this, Rupert abruptly turns on his cousin: "You fool . . . you soft fool. . . . Will you give over thousands of pounds a year just because — "(p. 350).

With that, Appleby slaps his hand on the table and announces that the case is solved. The entire preceding analysis has been nothing but a trap to trick Rupert into giving himself away. Now that Shoon is pronounced dead (Appleby's fabrication), Rupert, who all along has been urging Eliot to give up the Spider, suddenly wants Eliot to carry on after all.

The truth is that Rupert is the villain. How did Rupert know about unwritten plot ideas in Eliot's head? The key was spoken by Kermode when he contemptuously dismissed detective writing as juvenile fantasies not let go of. Eliot was not so much inventing as *remembering* juvenile fantasies long forgotten but stored deep in the mind; furthermore, these were fantasies *shared* by Eliot with his childhood companion Rupert, and of which Rupert retained better conscious recollection.

Eliot was the first to suspect Rupert as the source of the Spider pranks when Rupert reenacted a set of their old joint fantasies that seemed to be the inexplicable coming to life of Eliot's plot for *The Birthday Party*, a mystery involving blackouts and the theft of a picture. When the trick was given the additional uncouth twist of pitching the Renoir nude into the footman's bed, Eliot recognized in this the personality of Rupert. The subsequent threats against Rupert at Shoon Abbey were Eliot's attempts at retaliation.

Appleby's explanation that Shoon feared disclosure of something in one of Eliot's novels was bogus. It was Rupert who feared the disclosure of something, and specifically *to* Shoon. When Rupert failed to deter Eliot from further publication and his cousin mysteriously rallied, Rupert's recourse was to attempt to murder Shoon. Murdering Eliot would have been futile since *A Death in the Desert* was already in the publisher's hands. What Rupert feared was that the forthcoming *A Death in the Desert* would reveal a bizarre murder method that the two cousins had dreamed up as children — *and which Rupert had later actually used in an attempt to murder Shoon in the Near East*. Shoon might recognize the device, associate it with Rupert, and exact terrible revenge.

The ingenious murder method? To poison a camel's hump so that when the creature started feeding off its fat on a long desert journey, the animal — and its rider — would perish!

Such, more or less, is the mystery plot of *Stop Press* — except that there is the Oxford subplot involving the possession of a valuable codex. In fact, the first Spider prank, the burglarizing of the explorer, Mrs. Birdwire, was actually the work of the don, Gerald Winter, as his part in that academic melodrama — and it was that jest that put into Rupert's head the idea of bringing the Spider to life in order to terrorize Eliot. As a murderless detective novel of manners *Stop Press* can perhaps best be compared to Sayers's *Gaudy Night*, and like that novel, its real pleasures lie in the literary texture of the narrative, especially the endlessly inventive conversation on literature and art.

Nor can one ignore the striking literary role of the narrator in this novel. For just as Eliot and the Spider have gotten themselves mixed up, so too have the narrator and his protagonist, Mr. Eliot, the detective writer and would-be Pope scholar. Not only is the narrator a teller of a mystery, but he offers it amid a veritable thicket of eighteenth-century quotations and poetic allusions and incorporates into the text in his own donnish voice mini-lectures on such topics as landscape gardening (p. 268) and offers extraordinarily elaborate and learned descriptions, such as that of Shoon's highly ornamental carved bookcases (p. 294), a passage which is an excellent academic exercise in the minor classical literary form known as *ecphrasis*.

Moreover, this narrating persona also manages to present the whole narrative of *Stop Press* within a framing structure that is a remarkable pastiche of Pope's *Rape of the Lock*. There are numerous allusions throughout the text to Pope (at one point the literary gathering puts Appleby in mind of *The Dunciad*) and to *The Rape of the Lock* in particular. Eliot's daughter is named Belinda and during the nocturnal hide and seek game Appleby humorously warns her not to stain her new brocade; on another occasion he trades quotations from the poem with Peter Holme. But all this allusiveness merely serves to point up the narrator's larger imitative purpose, that is, to tell the story of *Stop Press* in a manner imitating Pope's comic imitation of classical epic, giving us something like a mock mock epic. *The Rape of the Lock* is a "comic-heroical" poem in five parts, with each part introduced by an epic description of the sun, successively recording its progress from dawn to sunset over the Thames valley. Just so does the *Stop Press* narrator, in introducing the four parts of his story, offer four wonderfully purple passages marking the course of the sun over his scene.

The first such passage is a richly melancholy description of a November evening in Oxford, marked by a mood of gentle decay. Part 2 of the novel begins with an epic-scale description of the dawn rising progressively over the face of England, from Canterbury to Westminster and Oxford, and finally touching the remote western coun-

tryside of our tale, awakening the towns of Pigg, Wing, Snug, and
Rust:

> Dawn came to Wing; to Low Swaff'ham morning; there was com-
> mon day at Pigg. In Wing the medieval glass glowed rich and dark;
> the mist stirred and drifted by the sallows of Low Swaff'ham; and
> the temperance institute at Pigg cast its diurnal challenge at the
> credence of the sun. . . .
> England heeled over and the sun threaded the steel-spun ruins
> of Shoon Abbey itself. . . .
> It was Saturday morning.   (pp. 158–59)

Similarly, part 3 begins with an abbreviated description of just such
another dawning day, and calls attention to the inimitable particulari-
ty of "just this November day":

> England, unwearied and infinitely various mistress, had turned
> again from darkness to the sun. Never had she yawned and stretched
> herself in just these diaphanous robes before Time. . . . Time had
> never witnessed just this configuration of light and shadow, just
> these driftings of mist and vapour over the land; had never garnered
> in its winter harvests just this November day.   (p. 255)

And finally, part 4 begins with a rolling apostrophe to the descent of
evening over that same deep-rural English landscape:

> Evening, like a gallant enfolding his lady in some finespun shawl
> of Kashmir or Ispahan, dropped its shadows over England. . . .
> The shutters were up in Snug and Warter; in Low Swaff'ham it
> was time to open the Five Mows of Barley; around the church at
> Wing the Martyrs slipped from their torments with a yawn and a
> stretch, the Fathers laid down their pens and idled, heaven and hell
> blended and faded, Judgment was suspended until dawn. . . . One
> further heave eastwards and rural England would be in bed, draw-
> ing about itself an eiderdown of stars.   (p. 313)

Pope, too, provides the aptest word for the plot of *Stop Press*, a
line often quoted in the story: "a mighty maze, but not without a plan"!
Or, as the narrator explains early on, this will be an affair of comedy,

"And the comedy was to be of the classical sort which is based on character" (p. 20).

Two other Innes novels that turn on the theme of stories unaccountably come to life are *Appleby's End* (1945) and *Appleby's Answer* (1973). These two are not, strictly, country-house stories, but are both set in that deep rural "womb of England," as Innes calls it, which is the usual surrounding environment of the classic country-house story.

Appleby's End has a certain importance for the fictional biography of John Appleby; in it, he will not die — as the title might suggest — but he *will* meet and marry Judith Raven, and at twenty-nine this "prematurely senescent" detective will already begin thinking about retiring to the life of a country gentleman. It is in this novel, written at the end of Innes's ten-year expatriation in Australia, that the Innes canon becomes firmly anchored in his favorite imaginative landscape — the quintessentially English deep rural countryside surrounding Long Dream Manor, home of the eccentric Raven family, Appleby's future in-laws, which will become Appleby's home after his marriage and eventual retirement. This deep rural environment, the "womb of England," is Innes's equivalent of Yoknapatawpha County, recurring again and again in many subsequent narratives. The precise topography and geographic location of this imaginative terrain, which one comes to know as Appleby country, is never made quite clear: in this novel it seems to be in East Anglia, although in later novels it seems rather to be in Wiltshire or Berkshire, somewhere in the environs of where Innes himself eventually settled (in what he describes as his personal dream country), amid the gently rolling downs southwest of Oxford. At any rate, one knows he is in Appleby country whenever one hears of pigs called Gloucester Old Spots and sturdy rural gentry called "stones-in-the-rain," and whenever the place names sound like they have come out of Edward Lear: Abbot's Yatter, Drool, Linger, Boxer's Bottom, Sneak, Snarl.

The story begins with one of those classic Innes railway journeys, the first two chapters comprising perhaps his most successful evocation of the peculiarly atmospheric quality of a rail journey through the remote English countryside.[15] It is a late Sunday afternoon midwinter journey through flat, dreary plowland, in which "here and there cattle stood steamy and dejected, burdened like their fellows in Thomas Hardy's poems with some intuitive low-down on essential despair" (p. 7).

Appleby finds himself ensconced with an extremely bizarre and rather sinister, mad-hatter collection of individuals who turn out to be members of one odd local family, the Ravens. ("A gifted family running to eccentricity," pronounces the local inspector later on, "Just the place to look for trouble, if you ask me.") When Appleby is unable to make connections for his original destination, he is forced to accept the Ravens' hospitality. Early in the inauspicious-seeming trip to the Ravens' Long Dream Manor, the carriage that has fetched them from the station founders in a flooding stream, and suddenly John Appleby and Judith Raven find themselves alone in the coach, stranded in midstream, with everyone else on either bank. No sooner do the two succeed in clambering atop the carriage than it breaks free of whatever has obstructed it and begins to drift downstream. Eventually the stream joins the river and Appleby and Judith find themselves part of an eerie winter nocturne, floating silently down the River Dream, bathed in moonlight and with the snow gently drifting down — as if, as Appleby drily remarks, they were in some fantastic vision of Shelley.

It is the beginning of a romance that will proceed apace through an innocent night in a shared haystack (though this quickly becomes a local romantic legend of Wagnerian proportions) and the succeeding couple of days at Long Dream during which Appleby solves a series of weird cases that have begun to swirl around the Raven family. The plots of melodramatic regional tales written long ago by the father of the current Raven clan — Ranulph Raven — seem to be disturbingly coming to life.

Appleby is not for a moment mystified by any of this (nor should he be, as the detective who had unraveled the mystery of the Spider in *Stop Press*), for he immediately tumbles to what must have been the secret behind Ranulph's "prophetic" powers: Ranulph's mode of research has apparently been to extract people's most cherished wishful fantasies and use them as the basis of his plots. In later years, enough of these deep-seated fantasies and obsessions were acted out by these simple rural folk to create Ranulph's reputation for prophecy. And, as Appleby soon sees, the reoccurence of this phenomenon so many years later is to be explained by nothing more mysterious or sinister than the state of the economy of the Raven household, which has rapidly been sliding from genteel poverty to actual penury. The recent rash of Ranulph-stories-come-to-life, Appleby sees, have all been staged by the family as a publicity stunt, in the modest hope that such a sensation will create a demand for a new edition of the out-of-print stories, thus keeping the wolf from the door just a little bit longer.

Around this huge maguffin swirl other mysteries, equally fantastic, including a neighboring farm where animals and even a half-wit stable boy seemed to have been turned to marble, and a true Victorian family intrigue involving matters of secret marriages and questions of legitimacy that might mean the ossified or disappeared half-wit stable boy was the legitimate heir of Long Dream Manor. (When the laconic farmer Hoobin is questioned by Appleby about the half-wit's parentage, the following interesting exchange takes place: "'Be I the one that got t'half-wit?' he said. 'That's what I'm asking.' Mr Hoobin considered. 'Mister,' he said heavily, 'did 'ee ever see a saw?' 'Dear me, yes.' 'And would 'ee ask which tooth cut board?'")

What is of lasting significance about this whole fiasco is that in it the reader is introduced to the Raven family and to Long Dream, not to speak of the future Mrs. Appleby, all of which are to remain hallmarks of "Appleby country" in many succeeding narratives. Judith, of course, becomes a prominent companion in many later narratives, especially those which are art-related and in the country-house stories, for she is an afficionado of house touring and conducts her explorations on the notable principle, "Go on till you're stopped," a useful device for getting a number of stories going. Judith's conventional country-dame façade effectively conceals the intellectual, artistic, and passionate temperament that are apparent in this, her first appearance.

Beyond these family matters, *Appleby's End* offers us a number of Innes's most characteristic recurrent motifs: bookish, literary sensations; stories that come weirdly to life; and above all, the idea of statues and people changing places, a fantastication of the whole art vs. life preoccupation of so many of Innes's — and Stewart's — fictions. Indeed, a good deal of this will be seen again, about thirty years later, in *Appleby's Answer*, similarly set in Appleby country and prominently involving the plot idea of fiction unaccountably coming to life.

Appleby's Answer (1973) — the bland and conventional title belies the book's real interest — is a minor Innes classic. Well-written and particularly satisfying for its cleverly amusing characterizations and sustained atmosphere, the general qualities of the book are well summed up in Newgate Callendar's review: "The book is very, very British and very, very traditional. And, as in all this author's mysteries, urbane, civilized and scrupulously fair to the reader" (*NYTBR*, 27 May 1973, p. 18).

The book touches in a comic way upon a number of themes demonstrably important to Innes, themes that constantly recur in his stories. Perhaps the most evident of these is the self-referential device of having one of the fictional characters be himself or herself a writer of mysteries. Miss Priscilla Pringle is the dizzy and rather vacuous authoress of an absurd series of detective novels all distinguished by their ecclesiastical settings and alliterative titles (*Vengeance at the Vicarage; Poison at the Parsonage*). This circumstance occasions some amusing talk in the novel about detective fiction and about writing in general. As in *Stop Press* and *Appleby's End* this narrative plays on a related theme — the idea of fictional plots unaccountably coming to life and realizing themselves in actuality. This is more than an interesting plot idea, for it seems to touch on a genuine moral concern about crime fiction: that ingenious ideas in a crime story might actually be expropriated for real-life criminal purposes.

As in the case of *Appleby's End*, this "very, very British" detective story opens on a quintessentially traditional note, with a section entitled "British Rail," and yet another Innes variation of the classic encounter of strangers on a train. In this opening scene Miss Pringle meets in her compartment a tweedy and distinguished-looking elderly gentleman whose bearing indicates somebody "flawlessly bred." As she mentally phrases it: "That air of aloofness and perfect diffidence which marks an English gentleman" (p. 12).

Before the journey is over, however, this perfect gentleman, Captain A. G. de P. Bulkington, headmaster of "Kandahar," has revealed himself to be either simply slightly mad or slightly mad and quite malevolent as well. Under the guise of a queer proposal that they collaborate on a mystery, Captain Bulkington has quite transparently endeavored to pump her for ideas about how to perpetrate an ingenious murder. The matter is left hanging as Miss Pringle parts awkwardly at Paddington Station from her late admired gentleman. In a succeeding scene at the mystery writers' luncheon (the Crooks Colloquium) — at which John Appleby happens to be a guest speaker — the reader learns that other writers have been similarly approached in a suspicious manner. The difference is that Miss Pringle will "take the bait."

Part 2 of the novel takes place, with wonderful oxymoron, in "Darkest Wilts," that innocent rural heart of England that Innes is so fond of converting into sudden unexpected sinisterness. It is the sort of country where Judith and John Appleby — and Michael Innes — make their home, and where many Innes novels are set. Here, to the

village of Long Canings, has come Miss Pringle to, as they say, "gather
material." Two things draw her to Long Canings: a vague intent to
follow up the enigmatic Captain Bulkington's proposal of collaboration, and to learn more about the mysterious death of Bulkington's
predecessor, the previous headmaster and rector who, it has been
rumored, was drowned in a well at the Old Rectory. She is sure he
was murdered: "It is quite notable how seldom this happens to clergymen in real life, so an authentic instance is naturally of interest" to this
author of sensational ecclesiastical murder mysteries.

"Kandahar," Bulkington's name for the Old Rectory, turns out
to be a sprawling Victorian pile in the Gothic taste, originally built
as a rectory but now set up as a "crammer" school, a place where failed
public-school boys are given another whack at qualifying for the university or Sandhurst. In fact what Miss Pringle finds at Kandahar is
perhaps the most bogus school in English fiction; the whole operation
consists of one staff member, Captain Bulkington himself, and his two
pupils, a pair of brutish youngsters whom he passes off as scions of important families but whom the local gentry at Long Canings think of
as a couple of Borstal boys over whom Bulkington has some sinister
hold. Later it develops that Bulkington keeps them under his thumb
by blackmailing them over a sexual misadventure he himself set them
up for.

When Bulkington welcomes Miss Pringle, he picks up right where
he left off, inviting her more specifically to come up with an ingenious
"plot idea" for murdering the local squire at Long Canings, a man
Bulkington despises. Miss Pringle has decided to play along and lead
Bulkington on, letting him think he is leading *her* on. On the feigned
understanding that they are collaborating on a mystery plot, Bulkington offers her five hundred pounds for the "technical know-how for
a single simple murder," the planned death by fire of Squire Ambrose
Pinkerton.

Miss Pringle also has a private conversation with Bulkington's two
charges, and from them she gets not only a sense of their contempt for
him and their conviction that he's a sham, but also their belief that
he's a homicidal maniac who did in his predecessor, Dr. Pusey, and
is planning to murder the squire. Thus armed with this alarming con-
firmation, Miss Pringle's idea is to construct her plot, lead Bulkington
on, and at the last moment intervene and bring in the police, while
gaining spectacular publicity for herself and her latest book.

When Squire Pinkerton actually does start receiving ghoulish
death threats pointing to an impending death by fire, Appleby arrives
on the scene to investigate. By this time, however, Miss Pringle has
been brought to the realization that in her idea of leading Bulkington
on and turning the situation to her advantage, the shoe all along has
been precisely on the other foot. It is Captain Bulkington who is now
prepared, on the eve of the expected conflagration at Manor House,
to blackmail Miss Pringle. He has understood completely her idea of
somehow manipulating him. "You thought of me," he tells her, "as an
unbalanced sort of chap, who had developed a senseless hatred of that
idiot Pinkerton, and who might be coaxed into the commission of
nothing less than *un crime gratuit*. . . . Your idea was that, if you
played your cards cleverly, there would be either the most splendid
publicity in the affair or a good round sum in your pocket to induce
you to keep me out of the picture. . . . What you failed to consider
. . . was that the endeavor to coax me into crime might well be criminal in itself" (pp. 183–84).

When Appleby finally intervenes and provides his "answer" to the
mysterious affairs at Long Canings and to the old mystery of the death of
Captain Bulkington's predecessor, the situation has more or less resolved itself; this is one of those stories in which Appleby plays an essentially passive role. The last section is titled aptly, "The Dénouement
Will Not Take Place." A fantasticated melodramatic ending ties up all
the loose ends in the final page or two. The real interest in the novel
is in its character as a variation on the stories-come-to-life theme, and
as a sort of parable on the subject of the relation between detective
fiction and real crime and the propriety of turning the serious and sordid business of crime to the purposes of light entertainment.

Country-House Weekends

The classic country-house situation in British detective fiction is the
famous "long weekend," in which a group of family and guests gather
for a few days in the relatively isolated setting of a great country house,
sometimes further isolated by a snowstorm or some similar device. The
carefully designed mixture of social and personality types and their virtual isolation make the country-house weekend gathering an effective
microcosm of society at large. The group, of course, is usually large

and diverse enough to allow for maximum character interest and intrigue, but small enough to constitute a coherent dramatis personae
for the mystery.

In *The Bloody Wood* (1966) the country-house setting and the attendant social rituals of the milieu are particularly prominent and play
a significant part in the design of the mystery. The plot in *The Bloody
Wood* involves a particularly nasty bit of domestic violence, aptly introduced with an epigraph from T. S. Eliot's "Sweeney Among the
Nightingales":

> . . . And sang within the bloody wood
> When Agamemnon cried aloud,
> And let their liquid siftings fall
> To stain the stiff dishonoured shroud.

An elderly couple, Charles and Grace Martineau, are quietly living out their mellow and devoted last years at Charne, their country
estate — or rather, their last days, as Grace is acknowledged to be in
precipitously declining health. Their habit is to walk in their garden
each afternoon and sit for a while in the picturesque belvedere, a spot
associated with their fondest romantic memories. This situation of gentle, private pathos is complicated, however, by a disturbing divergence
of views about the future. Charles would like to see their nephew Bobby marry his cousin Martine and both eventually inherit Charne.
Grace, however, disapproves of the brash Bobby and would rather see
Charles himself marry his niece Martine, after her own death, and
have the offspring and heirs she has not been able to bear him.

At a small weekend gathering of family and a few friends Sir John
Appleby, a neighbor and guest, senses: "Charne was, of course, a place
where a raised voice, an impatient tone, an ill-chosen phrase tended
to reverberate — this simply because the house itself gave the impression of having been murmuring for generations that the paramount
duty of its inhabitants was to consult the social ease of their fellows"
(p. 59). The ripples of conflict, however slight, cause Appleby to remark to Judith, "What if we're slipping sedately into one of those well-
bred English detective novels of the classical sort? *Death at Charne
House*" (p. 62).

Improbable as such intimations of violence are made to seem, part

1 of this narrative does end with the shocking announcement that Grace Martineau has been found drowned in the garden pond, and Charles shot to death in the house. Did Grace drown accidentally and Charles subsequently commit suicide out of grief? Did Grace herself commit suicide, and then Charles? Did Charles perform some act of euthanasia and then take his own life? Was there some awful fatal quarrel between these two gentle souls over their different plans for the future of Charne? Was another party involved in one or both of the deaths?

As the investigation in part 2 begins, the narrator, reflecting Appleby's viewpoint, comments that "A notable English novelist — one bearing, indeed, the highest of contemporary names — has exhibited Muddle as the archenemy of human happiness." In the hypothetical mystery novel *Death at Charne House*, he reflects, it would all be handled neatly: the dramatis personae would advance one by one and under the penetrating gaze of the Great Detective the guilty party would stand revealed. "Sir John Appleby knew that at Charne matters weren't going to be conducted after this fashion. He was to be confronted by Muddle" (p. 85). The investigative muddle is heightened by the design of the house itself and the indeterminate movements of everyone within it, as the local constable notes: "The design of the house — or at least of the ground floor — is a kind of dream setting for this sort of thing. Several routes from any one point to any other. . . . So many wheels within wheels in this place, if you ask me, that one can pretty well hear the damned things whirring all the time" (pp. 112–113).

The telling piece of evidence proves to be a lie — a rather pointless lie, it appears — that the butler seems to tell about hearing Charles and Grace converse in the belvedere just at a time when Grace was known to be elsewhere. Moreover, he testifies, oddly, that this conversation was "exactly as on the previous night." The explanation is not far to seek. A tape recorder is found in the belvedere, with a blown fuse. When it is repaired, the device proves to contain the conversation that the butler heard. Soon Appleby is able to propose a solution: Charles's plan was to carry out a mercy killing of his wife, but to protect himself by playing the taped conversation as the butler passed and then joining him so as to maintain an alibi until the body is discovered. This was the plan; what the butler reported hearing was a rehearsal of it.

But on the critical day, in a stroke of infernally bad luck, the fuse blew, destroying the carefully prepared alibi. Hence, Charles subsequently committed suicide.

But, as so often in Innes, this is only the penultimate explanation. It is what the killer *meant* the police to conclude. The killer did indeed take the idea from Charles's own use of the tape recorder, but all that Charles had been taping and playing were songs of the evermore scarce nightingales at Charne, a loving deception designed to offer this innocent pleasure and satisfaction to his dying wife. Indeed, in the first pages of the novel, as the group gathers on the patio, one of the guests had called attention to the song of the nightingale, which "has sung tonight exactly as last night."

The particularly mellow atmosphere of *The Bloody Wood* derives from the emphasis in the narrative on the regularity of Charne — the regularity of its Palladian design and its formal gardens, and even more the regularity of the rituals that govern the life of the house, without which, as one guest says, all would be a hopeless muddle ("One must, after all, continue to observe the forms. Fail in that, and chaos is come again" [p. 95]). It is that very regularity that gives rise to the ingenious murder scheme.

There Came Both Mist and Snow (1940; alternate title: *A Comedy of Terrors*) is another quintessentially British country-house weekend story. It is a straight comedy of manners novel whose interest overridingly lies in the literate and amusing talk of a cleverly conceived collection of character types gathered for a weekend party at a grand country mansion. As reviewers noted, interest in the witty conversation here far outweighs any serious interest in the rather whimsical mystery element. *The New Yorker* mischievously summarized: "A member of the gathering gets shot, thus saving himself from being bored to death. Lots of words in this one for highly educated readers who find them soothing, but featherbrains may fall asleep" (22 June 1940, p. 16).

Innes's familiar Jamesian manner has in this novel the added verisimilitude of being produced by an identified first-person narrator and principal in the action, a novelist of manners named Arthur Ferryman, who is one of the group of relatives and friends of the owner of Belrive Priory gathered for a Christmas house party. When Ferryman is twitted by his younger relatives for being a disciple of Henry James

and is parodied for his "who-goes-with-whom" social narratives, he
rather stiffly reaffirms that he will indeed continue to endeavor to write
stories about people who "are exceptionally aware both of each other
and of the world around them" (p. 164). Appleby himself is credited
by Ferryman with a quality rather like that of Henry James's hero,
Strether (in *The Ambassadors*), of being one upon whom nothing is
lost: "I looked at him with new respect," Ferryman says at one point;
"It was plain that of every word that eddied around him he missed
just nothing at all" (p. 149). In turn, Appleby recruits Ferryman as
a useful Watson for that same quality of careful observation and attentive listening.

As for the plot of *There Came Both Mist and Snow*, it is one of
Innes's more whimsically ingenious mystifications. A group of relatives
have been brought together by Sir Basil Roper ostensibly for a simple
Christmas family gathering at Belrive Priory, a gathering at which the
liveliest activities on deck appear to be games of quotation-capping
(bells in Shakespeare), billiards, and revolver shooting. The group includes a good range of comic types: the narrator himself; Lucy, a
cousin, who is also a writer but of the romantic, melodramatic school
and without any pretention to Jamesian subtlety; Basil's cousins, Wilfred, a banker and Cecil, his brother, a hapless schoolmaster; Hubert,
another cousin, and Geoffrey, his son, both painters, who are engaged
on an absurd portrait of Cecil (it is to be a picture of Cecil in bed with
a mule — with a lady's slipper, that is — and utilizing multiple mirror
effects); Dr. Wale, Cecil's personal physician, who seems never to let
Cecil out of his sight and also seems to hate him; a couple of industrialist neighbors, Cudbird, the charming owner of a brewery, and
Cambrell, the not so charming owner of a nearby "dark, Satanic mill."

The situation that sets the drama going is Basil's proposal to sell
Belrive to finance some sort of scientific expedition. The two local in-
dustrialists are both prospective buyers. Naturally the plan appalls the
other relatives, all of whom in one way or another would stand to lose
their continued connection with — or in some cases prospective inheritance of — the family estate. This tension is exacerbated by various old
and new family quarrels that are the mainstay of such family reunions.

The incident that constitutes the mystery is that Wilfred Foxcroft,
the banker, while sitting at cousin Basil's desk in the library, is shot
at close range from the terrace and almost killed, the bullet passing

through the right side of his chest. Those circumstances, plus various built-in family complications, raise an essentially comic host of possibilities with regard to a solution, or interpretation, of the event.

To begin with, it is not at all clear *who* the intended victim was really meant to be; it could have been Wilfred, the man actually shot, or it could have been his look-alike brother Cecil, the schoolmaster; or — if the villain did not get a good look through the curtains of the French window — it could have been Basil, whose study after all it is. Each of these possibilities needs, then, to be explored: was someone trying to kill Basil to prevent the sale of Belrive, or to insure that the property would pass to someone who would dispose — or not dispose — of the property as that someone desired? or was Basil trying to kill Wilfred — or Cecil — to eliminate one source of opposition to the plan?

A pertinent question about the shooting is why the victim was shot so ineffectively: why, that is, at such close range he should have been shot on the *right* side of the chest? Was it because the intent was to wound and frighten, but not kill, the intended victim — perhaps so that he would live to change a will? Was it because the assailant used a gunman's trick of shooting behind his back with the aid of a mirror, thereby confusing left and right? Was the assailant one of the painters, so confused by his complicated use of mirrors in the portrait of Cecil that he had gotten facial symmetries, identities, and left and right all mixed up? Or was it because the assailant had reason to believe that his intended victim was dextrocardiac?

Appleby proposes a convoluted but intriguing solution involving Dr. Wale's Faustian obsession with obtaining the abnormal heart of his patient Cecil. After Appleby has provoked an admission of this horrid motive and seemingly sealed a case against Wale of having shot Wilfred, mistaking him for Cecil, the situation is thrown into further confusion by new admissions of concealed evidence and two fresh accusations — by Hubert and narrator Ferryman — against one another. This in turn leads to the final deduction by Appleby, who has confidently orchestrated this whole series of false dénouements. With the possible exception of *A Night of Errors*, this is the most complicated and double-crossing "final explanation" scene in any Innes mystery. In it, he has pushed detective story convention about as far as it could possibly go.

Another country-house story that uses the device of a distinctly identified narrator who is a principal in the case is *What Happened at Hazlewood* (1946). To be more accurate, the novel has two such narrators, a woman named Nicolette who is the wife of Sir George Simney, the baronet, and who narrates parts 1 and 3; and Harold, a young policeman who assists Inspector Cadover and serves as his admiring Watson, and who narrates the middle section. *What Happened at Hazlewood* is an Edwardian-style family melodrama, written in rather a different narrative voice than is usual in Innes. Harold is straightforward and naive in his section, and thoroughly artless and open-mouthed about the high-toned but crass social environment in which the case has landed him. Nicolette, for her part, though far from artless (she is, after all, an ex-actress), speaks in a narrative voice that is a combination of frankness and coyness, sophisticated awareness, and huge self-ignorance.

The plot itself is a combination of a very complicated sealed-room sort of mystery, with an equally complicated Victorian family melodrama, complete with elaborately detailed subplots. The murder occurs in the context of a very uncomfortable family gathering at the home of Sir George and Lady Simney, a gathering that includes a pair of cousins and their sons, and a group of kinsfolk from Australia — Sir Hippias and his son and daughter-in-law — whose arrival puts the Simneys' surley and evil-looking butler in a panic. This butler, Owden, happens to have a son who is an embarrassing spit and image of one of the Simney cousins. As Sir George has taken to favoring this lad to wait on the family at table, the awkwardness is constantly intensified; had Owdon once had a liaison with a Simney female? had Sir George himself fathered the boy?

The marriage between the profligate Sir George and the coolly indifferent Nicolette is a thinly disguised battleground, a scandal to the neighborhood, and the despair of the local vicar, Reverend Deamer. The surly butler seems to have some evil hold over his employer — or why else would he be kept on? The interactions among the cousins and their sons, and Sir George and Lady Simney, seem to consist entirely of jealousies, resentments, disapprovals, and backbiting. Finally, when the Australians arrive, the ghastliness is multiplied: the reader learns that Sir George and a younger brother of his named Denzell have once been involved with Hippias in thoroughly criminal activities in Australia involving slaving and murder, and that in a final catastrophic melée, Hippias escaped, leaving George and Denzell to die, but that George in fact escaped as well, leaving Denzell to die. Subsequently, it seems, George turned up and "diddled" Hippias and his son in some kind of land deal over a place called Dismal Swamp. As if these old quarrels are not enough, Sir George has an immediate go at an affair with Hippias's daughter-in-law, while a former lover of Lady Simney's seems to have turned up in the vicinity.

Such is the situation when "the thing" happens:

> In fact this bad baronet has died true to the traditions of his kind — mysteriously in his library, at midnight, while a great deal of snow was falling in the park outside. . . .
> George's end was ugly. Even if the back of his skull was not as I now saw it to be, there would have been something peculiarly horrible about that sprawl across the table. . . .   (pp. 8, 93)

The circumstances of what proves to be a classic sealed-room mystery occupy the patient Inspector Cadover at great length, until he hits upon the truth of what proves to be an extraordinarily confused situation centering on Lady Simney's bold scheme to confront her husband with the convincing bluff of a plan to murder him unless he gives her her freedom — a plan that involves her disguising herself as a Caravaggio Venus! A fantastic plan which fatally misfires.

Here is, once again, a country-house novel of manners without a real murder — although in this one there is villainy enough and more than just villainy of the domestic sort. Sir George Simney's death has something of the character of nemesis; Cadover manages to elicit long-hidden truths about a mystery in Australia that explain the peculiar hold Owdon seems to have over Sir George Simney as well as the remarkable Simney physiognomy of Owdon's son Timmy. The younger brother Denzell, left to die in Australia by George, did not, in fact, die but eventually made a very awkward reappearance. Both brothers — along with cousin Hippias — committed capital offenses of one sort or another, but Denzell's cards, so to speak, were the stronger. Denzell has actually adopted the identity of George — so that "Sir George" has really been Denzell all along! — while George was forced all these years to play the role of Owdon the butler (the hold has thus been over "Owdon," not the other way around). The one "bright note," if there can be said to be such a thing in such a sordid family saga, is that the charming Timmy, "Owdon's" son, now proves to be the legitimate heir of the estate.

What Happened at Hazlewood thus plays upon several favorite Innes themes: the Victorian theme of a servant who proves to be a true heir; the idea of a servant seeming to exercise mastery over his employer; and the plot device of one brother assuming another's identity, the latter used again with extraordinary complexity in *A Night of Errors*.

Over the years, reviewers have often enough commented that the complications of Michael Innes's plots are apt to make one's head spin, but in *A Night of Errors* (1947) Innes produced a country-house murder mystery so complicated and so fantasticated that it may lay fair claim to being the most *migrainous* detective novel ever written. The *Saturday Review* summarized it as a "Completely fantastic mystery involving three identical brothers, shocking death-roll, veritable corpses' ballet, and solution that sets head spinning" (1 Oct. 1947, p. 26), while Ralph Partridge grumbled at the idea that "If identical twins make a good joke as well as a good plot, then identical triplets should be half as funny again. So runs the arithmetical reasoning in *A Night of Errors*." The book is "a huge joke," he concludes, " — at the reader's expense" (*New Statesman*, 12 June 1948, p. 482).

This work was indeed conceived in the spirit of a joke. Innes began work on it the night after he was inducted into the Detection Club of London. One of the rules of initiation was the taking of an oath not to transgress certain "rules of fair play," one of which was not to write a detective story turning on the plot device of identical twins. "Being donnish and intellectually arrogant, I thought poorly of this; indeed, the next day I started *Night of Errors*, a mystery novel turning on triplets,"[16] and taking off on *A Comedy of Errors*.

The background of this country-house story of a murdered baronet is provided in a satirical prologue that offers a summary of the history of the Dromios, a Mediterranean family that naturalized itself in England in the sixteenth century and subsequently married into such distinguished families as the Moneytraps, the Overreaches, and the Whorehounds. The key thing about the family is an unfortunate tendency to produce triplets, a propensity particularly awkward with regard to inheritance laws.

The previous baronet, Sir Romeo Dromio, forty years earlier found himself faced with both a ruinous financial position and a brand new set of triplets. One night a terrible fire at Sherris Hall decimated the nursery wing, from which Sir Romeo was able to rescue but one infant. Shortly thereafter Sir Romeo died mad.

Now, forty years later, his widow, a vague and confused sort of woman, lives at Sherris with Oliver, the remaining son, and also with Lucy, an adopted daughter, a rather mysteriously discontented and sharp-tongued young woman. Also on the scene is a rude and scoundrelly Uncle Sebastian and Mrs. Gollifer, Mrs. Dromio's best friend, a widow who lives with her son Geoffrey. Completing the household are Swindle, the laconic aged family retainer, and Grubb, a stupid and belligerent gardener.

It takes about a hundred pages or so to complete the sense of the complications that exist among these people. The matter is built up effectively, and incrementally, through a series of small but revealing domestic scenes. First, Mrs. Dromio has always suspected that her other two sons are really alive, that Romeo Dromio would never really have contrived to murder his own children. Her great fear is that the two bodies found in the fire may represent her husband's cold-blooded murder of two other substitute infants. While it turns out to be true that the bodies were not those of the Dromio infants, her worst suspicion proves to be unfounded. A game-keeper and his wife had had stillborn twins at the same time; they were persuaded by Dromio to give him the bodies and to bring up the two Dromio boys anonymously somewhere in America. Only now, forty years later, has Mrs. Dromio taken the opportunity of a trip of Oliver's to America to write him about the existence of his long-lost brothers. Oliver is expected back at Sherris Hall, and already there are rumors of "two Olivers" having been seen in the neighborhood.

On the home front, Oliver, a notorious womanizer, has been playing a thoroughly dastardly role. He has been abusing the affections of his adoptive sister Lucy, who has tragically fallen in love with him. Worse yet, Oliver has discovered that Lucy is actually the daughter of Mrs. Gollifer, his mother's friend, by a previous liaison; he has been blackmailing Mrs. Gollifer to keep silent about the fact.

As the narrative begins, Geoffrey Gollifer, who is earnestly in love with Lucy himself, makes the crushing discovery on his own not only that Lucy is his half sister, but that Oliver has been toying with Lucy's feelings and has been blackmailing Geoffrey's mother over the secret of her birth.

This is the heavily complicated emotional situation at Sherris that prevails on the eve of Oliver's return as all these personages are assembled. That event, not surprisingly, proves to take the form of a grisly act of violence. Late at night a loud crash calls attention to the vacant library, and a terrible smell emanating from it. What is discovered is the body of Oliver Dromio, killed by a vicious blow to the head, lying sprawled on the hearth, his arms actually burning in the fireplace. It is distinctly one of the more unpleasant murder scenes in Innes, and the effect is heightened by the callow manner of the young doctor who examines the body along with Appleby and Hyland, the local inspector. The doctor comments about the dead man, "And I doubt if he had the stuff of martyrs in him. Take a pinch at the buttocks here and you'll see he was a flabby sort of cove" (p. 66).

Yet, for all that, it is, as Appleby says, "a beautiful murder," that is, a case worthy of and demanding the most intense ratiocinative powers. It looks at first like a case of retributive justice delayed for forty years, the circumstances inevitably suggesting Romeo Dromio's fire and the presumed infanticide of Oliver's two look-alike brothers. Almost immediately, however, the initial situation is further complicated: the gardener Grubb is found on the grounds with the murder weapon (a great decanter), and after an absurd chase through a formal garden labyrinth, just as he is apprehended and about to pronounce some decisive word about the case, he is shot dead by a purportedly confused Uncle Sebastian. And no sooner has that transpired than Geoffrey comes forward to confess killing Oliver — but it seems a patently false confession, as he claims to have killed Oliver on the terrace (Geoffrey is ignorant of the circumstances of the actual discovery of the body). To add to this confusion, Lucy testifies that the body is *not* Oliver's after all! At that announcement, Geoffrey makes a spectacular, panic-stricken exit into the night, a fittingly melodramatic conclusion to what might be called Act III of the drama.

At this point, Appleby takes stock of the evening's events (remember, all this has transpired and will transpire in one evening!), and reviews the bewildering possibilities: is the body Oliver's after all? Or is it one of the other two brothers? Was Sebastian trying to protect himself — or someone else — by killing Grubb? Is Geoffrey's confession to be taken seriously, or is *it* an attempt to protect someone? Did the murderer aim at killing Oliver, or one of the other brothers? Who *was*

killed and was it the right party? Did one or another of the two unknown brothers kill the other, or Oliver? Did Oliver kill one of them,
and then stage the death as his own?

Inspector Hyland flings his arms despairingly in air: "Madness!
. . . The whole thing is a nightmare. Three identical brothers creeping round the place with each other's dead bodies! It's like a drunken
hallucination" (p. 127).

Appleby rather agrees, noting that the real trouble is that he can't
even tell what the murderer *intends* him to think. But the affair takes
yet another dramatic turn when Sherris Hall is set on fire and becomes
a mighty conflagration. By the time the blaze is brought under control, the greater part of the house, including the body, has been destroyed. At this, Appleby takes fresh stock of the situation: it seems that
what he has is the case of a body partly burnt, so that a particular identification would be made, and now destroyed completely, presumably
because the murderer knew that that identification would ultimately
not hold up. But in fact the original identification of the body (as
Oliver) did *not* hold up — so was the destruction of the body by fire
in vain after all? This last point, at least, is definitely established: dental
evidence confirms that the body recovered from the fire is not Oliver's.

One further point Appleby's investigation does establish: the gaso-
line used to start the fire was not taken from what was in fact the most
convenient storage space — a place known only to the members of the
household. Thus it seems certain that the arson, and presumably the
murder, was perpetrated by an outsider. What this adds up to is the
rather confusing conclusion that the body is not Oliver's, but also that
Oliver did not commit the crime.

Meanwhile, Appleby's imagination is haunted, seemingly irrel-
evantly, by the image of Lucy as she jumped free of the burning
building, falling through the air with her skirt up around her head.
It is no sort of erotic fascination, but unaccountably it seems to present itself to Appleby as some sort of clue. . . .

In a final melodramatic development, Oliver actually makes an
appearance behind the burning house in the distance, laughing maniacally. He then leads police on a wild, pyromaniac chase, setting fires
here and there across the countryside in a seemingly random pattern.
It seems a final madness. At this point, however, Appleby announces
he has solved the case, and predicts that the fugitive's ultimate object
is, in the words of the old sea chantey, "fire down below." And sure

enough, in the final encounter, Oliver is seen poised above a fire he
has set in a quarry, again laughing maniacally, and a moment later
his body is seen hurtling through the smoke into the quarry. Soon
thereafter Oliver's — and it really *is* Oliver's — burned and battered
body is recovered from the quarry.

Hyland is pleased to regard the maddening case as now closed.
Oliver, he concludes, killed one of his brothers, but tried to make it
look as if he himself was killed. Thus Oliver arranged it so the hands
would be burned, eliminating any immediate evidence that the body
was not his own, and then destroyed the house and evidence entirely
to prevent any revision of that identification. But, Hyland concludes,
when Oliver learned that the revised identification was already made
(to be verified by dental evidence), he went mad and destroyed himself
in the quarry.

Appleby congratulates Hyland on his reasoning and announces
that the only flaw in it is that it happens to be untrue, although it is
precisely what the murderer *intended* the police to believe! The truth
is *one step more complicated* than the case Hyland has made out.[17]

Geoffrey Gollifer *did* quarrel with Oliver on the terrace, and there
struck him on the head and left. At that point Oliver's twin brother
Jacques, who had come back from America with Oliver, found the
body and contrived an ingenious plan: to let the body be identified *at
first* as Oliver's (which it was), but with the idea that on closer examination it would be thought *not* to be Oliver's after all. The police
were meant to think — as Hyland did, in fact — that Oliver killed his
brother, hoping to suggest that it was he himself who had been killed.

The reason Jacques could count on the body ultimately *seeming
not* to be Oliver's was that in America Oliver had been hospitalized
and bedridden, thus undergoing a subtle change of physique. His consequent flabby buttocks were counted on as a misleading telltale sign
here, for Oliver had always been very fit and vain about his appearance
(this was the clue that kept tugging at Appleby's mind in the image
of Lucy's inelegant plunge). The burning of the hands prevented any
easy identification through fingerprints.

But Jacques realized that professional examination even after the
fire would eventually show that the body really was Oliver's after all,
so the next step was to plant a substitute body in the house, so that the
remains, after the fire, would indeed be verified as *not* being Oliver's.
The body he provided was none other than that of Geoffrey Gollifer,

whom he killed in the garden after Geoffrey had bolted; nice poetic justice, in that Geoffrey was, after all, the original murderer. Then Jacques, posing as Oliver, staged his mad pyromaniac act, while actually driving about the countryside with Oliver's bashed and partially burned body, until finally he found a place where he could contrive the necessary situation — "fire down below" — a fire at the bottom of the quarry. There he played mad Oliver one last time and then, under cover of the smoke, pretended to leap into the flames, while actually hurling Oliver's body into the quarry. Thus, in short, *his idea was to stage the murder of himself and follow it with the apparent suicide of Oliver*, after which he could make his appearance *as the third brother* and claim the Dromio estate for himself!

This almost impossibly convoluted plot demonstrates Innes's technical ingenuity, here exercised as a sort of defiant trick played on the Detection Club, and illustrates his own prowess in the sheer technical invention that is the hallmark of the puzzle story. The novel also serves as a reminder, with its hall of mirrors proliferation of possible solutions, that one's primary interest in a detective story cannot realistically lie in the reader's attempt to outwit the author by anticipating his solution. For the author's solution is, after all, arbitrary, in that he could simply have chosen to give one more twist or one less to the intentions of the protagonist, requiring a comparable hermeneutic hitch or adjustment. A *Night of Errors* is not, therefore, a "joke at the reader's expense," as Partridge fumed; rather it is a work whose ingenuity frees the reader from the absurd notion that interest in detective fiction has to do with competitive puzzle-solving, and allows the reader to recognize that our interest is, finally, literary and lies in the pleasures of reading the text.

Fearful Symmetry

In addition to those country-house stories built on the classic situation of the weekend gathering of family and friends, there are a number of other Innes stories in which it can be said that the country house functions as a sort of protagonist in the action. One social institution associated with the country house that serves as a useful plot device is the country fête in which the owner of a manor house opens his grounds as a charitable occasion for the benefit of the parish and brings together the population of the village within the confines of the manor park, creating yet another version of the effective social microcosm. The character of such occasions is nicely captured in a passage in *Appleby at Allington*:

> The men came to shoot clay pigeons under the superintendence of Owain Allington's keeper, and also in the hope that one or another of their children would win not a lollipop or a comic but a bottle of whiskey or gin from the threepenny lottery. The children came to ride the ponies of their more fortunately circumstanced contemporaries, to scream, to run, to collide with each other and with the adults, and occasionally to fall into the lake. The women came to gossip — and in the perennial hope that the gentry, whether in miserable ignorance or to curry favour, would be selling their fruit-cakes and chutney and jam well below market prices. These may be declared the main motivating forces at play within this wholesome English festival. (pp. 38–9)

Two Innes mysteries are built around this distinctly British institution, the novel quoted above and the recent *Sheiks and Adders*.

Sheiks and Adders (1982 — the name is intended as a pun on the children's board game, Snakes and Ladders) is one of Innes's shortest detective novels, and one of the simplest in conception. Appleby, strolling in the woods, suddenly encounters a dolorous maiden copiously weeping beside a pond in a glade — as in some scene out of Spenser or Ariosto.

> It wasn't precisely that there was anything theatrical about it; yet it did hauntingly suggest some familiar deliverance of art. Whether in poetry or in painting — or even, conceivably, in music — he couldn't tell. . . . There ought to be a rock — Appleby suddenly told himself — of bizarre configuration unknown to geology, and this young person in mediaeval dress ought to be chained to it. A dragon — preferably rather a comical dragon — ought to be breathing fire in the background. (p. 17)

In fact, however, the girl's adolescent pique proves to be over nothing more momentous than her father's refusal to countenance her boyfriend's dressing as a sheik for their upcoming garden fête. "Why can't I have my own way?" she pouts. But when Appleby himself attends that fête, there turns out to be more than Victorian prudery in her father's opposition to her young man's bedouin costume. For the fête is the chosen occasion for some important negotiations with a very powerful real sheik who happens to be the target of various terrorist opponents. However, the sheik is a man of royal Arab demeanor who would never stoop to hiding or appearing in disguise. Hence, the usefulness of the fête, which proves to be swarming with sheiks: the genuine article, a sort of doppelgänger bodyguard, numerous masquerade sheiks "planted" by the host (on the Ali Baba principle of marking all doors with an X), plus a number of enemies who have infiltrated also under the guise of sheiks.

The situation is rife with bewildering possibilities. Look at any given Arab chieftain and "He might be pretending to be Lawrence of Arabia pretending to be a real sheik. And here a kind of infinite regress became theoretically possible." The sheik's situation is as delicate and demanding as that of a Shakespearean boy actor playing the part of a woman disguising herself as a boy. And yet, Appleby realizes that this elaborate exercise "had really been mounted to *obviate* the real sheik's need to disguise himself" (p. 83).

When the crisis finally comes and the garden fête is actually under violent siege, the sheik, with Appleby's help, will make his escape by "pretending to be a plebeian pretending to be a prince. It is a fitting end to the very great piece of nonsense perpetrated here this afternoon" (p. 117). The scene ends in grand Appleby-induced chaos and farce: the terrorists are diverted by a contingent of boy scouts on maneuvres and a bagful of snakes let loose by an Oxford herpetologist as Appleby and the sheik make their escape in a hot-air balloon. As the sheik said, a "very great piece of nonsense," but amusing nevertheless.

The other garden fête story, *Appleby at Allington* (1968 — alternate title: *Death by Water*), begins *after* the fête in question, a *son et lumière* performance at Allington Park. The proprietor, Owain Allington, is entertaining his neighbor, Sir John Appleby, late the following evening, with sociable drinks and conversation by the fireside. The evening ends with Allington showing Appleby the *son et lumière* mechanism, inviting his guest to play about with the electrical switches in the gazebo erected for the purpose. This neighborly occasion ends when Appleby discovers a dead tramp in a dark corner of the gazebo — electrocuted.

The dead tramp proves to be only the beginning of the mystery.

That same night Allington has been expecting the arrival of a ne'er-do-well nephew who is his only heir. The young man never shows up, but the next day, the nephew's car — and his body — are fished out of the large lake that dominates Allington Park. Why did the young man drive straight off the road and into the lake? Here the formal Georgian design of the house and especially of the elaborately symmetrical grounds laid out by Repton seem to come into play. One of Repton's devices for symmetry was to place two identical gates at the entrance of the park, some distance apart. One gate leads to the main drive, the other to a winding cart track. If someone mistakenly takes the second — if it has been left open and the other shut — and drives straight on assuming it is the main drive, he will in fact go straight into the lake.

Appleby's investigations follow this intriguing line for much of the narration and indeed it seems to be a case of murder by Palladian symmetry. However, that hypothesis eventually crumbles, and the truth proves to be an even more fantastic consequence of the layout of the estate. Allington admits he knew all along how his nephew died: Appleby himself had inadvertently killed the man! It was all a matter of "twelve o'clock and two o'clock" — that is, in the military map sense of the phrase. When Appleby was playing with the *son et lumière* device the lights momentarily sprang up across the lake while the house itself was plunged into darkness — and at exactly that moment, by a horrible mischance, the nephew entered the drive and, misled by the lights, took a wrong turn in the darkness straight into the lake.

It is one of Innes's most delightfully ingenious infernal machines — although as is so often the case, it is not quite the final truth. It is indeed the mechanism by which the nephew was killed, but not in fact *how* it was carried out. Appleby was led to toy with the switches only as a blind. Actually, Allington himself had deliberately employed the same device some fifteen minutes earlier by remote control right from his own living room.

In one other tale, *Appleby's Other Story* (1974), the symmetry of a Palladian mansion proves to be the key to the solution of an ingenious murder. In this mystery, a swindling baronet who has been stealing his own paintings and collecting on the insurance is murdered by his accomplice, his efficient secretary, who seems to have an air-tight alibi. In the course of showing a guest around the house, the murderer ushers the guest into the baronet's study, a sparsely furnished room. Finding the room empty, they leave, continue their tour, and return fifteen minutes later to discover the baronet's body. A tiny shred of a high-quality art production is for Appleby the key to the mystery: the murderer prepared a whole duplicate study on the floor immediately above and led his unwitting guest first into the dummy room and then a few minutes later back into the real study with the baronet's body. The deception works because of the confusing layout of halls, corridors, and stairs and, above all, because of the elaborate symmetry of the overall design.

This all sounds far-fetched in a typical Ellery Queen sort of way, but actually Innes had prepared for it ingeniously, and on sound if playful artistic principles. Elvedon Court is a Palladian mansion, house and grounds built upon principles of elaborate symmetry. The "clue" is provided in the opening paragraph as Appleby, viewing the house from the overlooking Palladian bridge, is moved to quote a bit of Pope: "Grove nods at grove, each alley has a brother, / And half the platform just reflects the other." The lines are from *Moral Essays. Epistle IV. To Burlington*, 11. 117–18 and are part of the description of "Timon's Villa," Pope's fictional example of a pretentious house built without good Sense and on pseudo-Palladian principles. It is an apt introduction to the superficial order but underlying moral disorder of Elvedon Court; the whole of Pope's *Epistle* is relevant. Appleby's country colleague, Colonel Pride, whom one expects to have nothing but Kipling in his head, surprisingly comes back with a clever rejoinder out of Blake:

> "Ah, a bit of poetry." Pride nodded. He was seemingly gratified
> at having got, as he would have expressed it, right on the ball. "And
> I see what the chap means. All a bit formal, I agree. What another
> of those long-haired chaps calls fearful symmetry."   (p. 5)

Thus the ingenious murder is ultimately solved when Appleby follows up these original nudges to his aesthetic sensibilities. The title *Appleby's Other Story* proves, then, to be an outrageous pun — it refers not only to the element of subplot in the tale, but to the deceptive "other story" of the Palladian house itself.

Finally there is *The Open House* (1972), a work more whimsical thriller than detective story — and a Palladian thriller, at that. The initial situation is rather fantastic and has an eerie märchen-like quality about it.[18] In the opening pages Appleby finds himself stranded at midnight on a remote country road, his car stalled, and his flashlight dead. As he makes his way gropingly along the road he is confronted with a suddenly spectacularly illuminated mansion, every window uncurtained and all simultaneously illuminated. The effect is profoundly reminiscent of some spectacle out of childhood drama — The Palace of the Fairy Prince." Even more disconcerting, the house is blatantly *open* — and empty, although drinks and food have been set out and in a bedroom pajamas and soap and towel are laid out and welcome fires are blazing. Now the effect is rather like that in Cocteau's *Beauty and the Beast*.

Eventually someone does turn up, the extremely eccentric and doddering proprietor who stages these dramatic effects every year on the birthday of his nephew, the true owner of the house. The nephew, a black sheep who has been living in South America, has promised to return some year, on his birthday, and so his uncle maintains these grand welcoming demonstrations. Not surprisingly, the long-absent squire does make his appearance, but it is only to be found brutally slain at the moment of his homecoming.

The crime resolves itself into another of those family inheritance disputes on which Innes plays so many variations, but here complicated by a second factor — a gang of South American terrorists who have their own quarrel with the young man and are intent on retrieving some crucial papers from a safe in the house. The latter plot element leads to a fantastic chase through the house, a chase in which Appleby's knowledge of conventional Palladian layout proves to be most helpful:

> The house perched, as such places do, upon a basement storey out of which alone a good many reasonably commodious dwellings might have been carved. There was a dominating central block with a Corinthian portico, and on each side of this quadrant corridors connected with substantial and symmetrical wings. It seemed probable that the same effect was repeated at the back — in which case what one would view from the air would be something like a giant crab or sprawled four-footed beast.   (p. 13)

When the chase develops, Appleby is at a distinct advantage:

> Knowing, for example, that he was now on the first floor of the main building, and that the outer wall was on his right, he knew that eventually there must be a left turn which would prove to be

a cul-de-sac. Stateliness has to be paid for by inconvenience; the hall and saloon between them, thrusting up the full height of the building from façade to façade, must cut the entire formidable structure into two symmetrical and self-contained halves, between which the only communication would be at basement level or through the hall or saloon themselves. It might be possible to corner a fellow who didn't realize that.   (p. 105)

Unfortunately, Appleby loses this advantage when he corners his adversary in a hall of mirrors, and with dust in one eye he has lost his depth perception vision and so cannot distinguish the flesh-and-blood fugitive from his numerous reflections! And yet "this situation was insusceptible of indefinite continuance — if only because of the frangible quality of what encapsulated the contents." That is, the glass starts to shatter around them as they thrash about. And with that last bit of whimsical verbiage, the reader should be pretty well aware of where he is with Innes — and where he has been in most of these Palladian house tales. It has all been a gigantic lark in which the house itself has become a kind of comic protagonist. As Ivy Compton-Burnett had said, "Roofs give rise to situations."

Epilogue: Educating Our Emotions

Any concluding description of the mystery novels of Michael Innes must once again have recourse to the by now familiar adjectives: donnish, erudite, bookish, witty, mannered, farcical, bizarre, fantasticated — and to Innes's own description of them as "a diversion to be lightly offered and lightly received." Innes's version of the Great Detective, Inspector Appleby, who started out as a more or less conventionally ratiocinative detective, has over the years grown more and more intuitive, more and more dependent on a "mysteriously acquired familiarity with recondite artistic and literary matters," and finally has become "as much concerned to provide miscellaneous and unassuming 'civilized' entertainment as . . . to hunt down baddies wherever they may lurk."[1]

As these comments by Innes imply, the real pleasure to be sought in these books is the pleasure in the storytelling itself, or, as Erik Routley put it, "the pleasure of the story rather than the pleasure of the chase," adding that in an Innes novel "narrative is vastly more important than plot and character."[2] Splendidly recreated conversation, in the best comedy of manners tradition, is a hallmark of every Innes tale, and yet even more basic to our literary pleasure is the reassuring voice of the narrator himself, the reader's constant companion through almost fifty novels that span half a century. In Routley's words, "The impression you always get is that of a first-class senior common room raconteur with a sense of humour, to whom you listen just for the pleasure of hearing it happen."[3]

Like John — and Judith — Appleby, and numerous other Innes protagonists, the narrator in these tales is demonstrably someone who is
exceptionally aware of the world and the people around him, someone
on whom nothing is lost, who has cultivated a wise passiveness and
reserve, and developed a tentative and contemplative habit of mind,
combined with a schooled but still free intelligence, and a humane and
compassionate sensibility. Once again, one is put in mind of Madame
de Sévigné's remark about Montaigne (quoted by J. I. M. Stewart in
his introduction to an edition of Florio's Montaigne): "Ah, Charming
man! What good company he is!"

Far from anything like the gritty mean streets, the tough guys and
the "curvicaudate" blondes of the hard-boiled detective story, let alone
the sordid realism of "docu-drama" crime fiction, the Innes mystery
clearly is the stuff of comedy, as the headnote to *Death at the President's Lodging* said so many years ago: these dons, with their "endearing and always innocent foibles" are "persons such as comedy would
choose; it is much easier to give them a shove into the humorous than
a twist into the melodramatic." And as far as any notion of "realism"
goes, he concludes, these "Fellows are fantasy all — without substance
and without (forbearing Literary reader!) any mantle of imaginative
truth to cover their nakedness. Here are ghosts; here is a purely speculative scene of things." Innes commented about these words many
years later: "Notice how I'd already got the habit of parentheses. Notice
that the last clause smuggles in a quotation from Charles Lamb. And
notice that this mannered and wholly artificial approach to guilt and
misery made my modest fortune, such as it was to be."[4]

Innes has consistently maintained that comic approach
throughout his career, and he has nicely articulated the theory behind
it in an essay that in effect serves as his rejoinder to Raymond Chandler, "Death as a Game" (1965), in which he maintains that his "mannered and wholly artificial approach" is mandated simply because the
world of actual violent crime is merely squalid and disgusting. As a
Sergeant Cuff (!) explains to Freddie, the mystery writer who is the
subject of J. I. M. Stewart's short story, "The Man Who Wrote Detective Stories," and who has trafficked in murder in high-toned society
against a background of English country-house life, "You'd say it was
unbelievable, if you didn't know the background. Sexual promiscuity,
drink — and of course a very low mentality all round. That's the main

positive correlation with homicide, you know, sir: very low mental development" (p. 80).

This point was brought home to Innes by two incidents in his own life which, he says, had for him the power of moral parables; he recounts them in the "Death as a Game" essay, and presents fictional renditions of them in the Stewart story mentioned above and in the mystery *Appleby's Answer*.

The first incident was a conversation with a judge and a geologist during a railway journey in Australia, shortly after the first Innes novel had been published but before the identity of its author was generally known. The judge enjoyed mystery stories, he said, and liked them to be realistic in matters of criminal proceedings. Innes argued against this heresy, as he conceived it, and so the geologist was appealed to — but the latter said he didn't read detective stories.

> The judge railed him on this. They are first-rate entertainment, so why didn't he? The geologist was also an explorer; he had performed notable feats of endurance and heroism in the Antarctic; he was a most impressive person all round. And now he flushed and hesitated like the inarticulate English gentleman he was — and finally he muttered that after all, you know, when you come to think of it, murder is a pretty rotten sort of thing.

The second incident occurred many years later, on the occasion of Innes's induction into the Detection Club of London, at that time presided over by Dorothy Sayers. Innes reports that he was not bothered by the jesting macabre trappings on the dinner table, a skull and a coil of hangman's rope, but that the speaker of the evening, a distinguished barrister, cast a different light altogether on the proceedings:

> He told us how, as a young man, he had once defended a woman charged with murder. His plea failed, and she was sentenced to death. It was a small assize court in a provincial town, with inadequate accommodation, and there was some hitch about getting the condemned woman off to prison. Her howling was audible in court throughout the rest of the day.

The incident seemed to Innes to be "a parable about holding cheap what is most dear; about scrawling one's superficial fictions over the surface of such deeps." Such howling as that of the condemned woman, for Innes, is fatal to the purposes of detective fiction. Real crime, and real guilt, and real misery, like that, are properly the fit subject, he says, for such as Aeschylus, or Shakespeare, or Dostoevski — not for the writer of detective entertainments.[5]

Hence, for Innes, the propriety of the non-serious, comic approach to detective fiction. And for technical reasons as well Innes believes that detective story methods are incompatible with those of straight fiction: the requisite manipulations of character and situation in the former are inconsistent with the *caring* about a character and the disinterested exploration of character and situation that are the marks of the serious novel, whether tragic or comic or any other mode.

But this mannered and comic approach does not imply that the Innes mysteries are inconsequential as literature, nor even that they do not instruct or edify. It was one of the frustrations of the Man Who Wrote Detective Stories, Freddie Seston, an Innes alter ego, that he wished he could edify as well as entertain, and that perhaps because his stories displayed talents beyond what the genre required, he had squandered his gifts. To the contrary, the Innes mysteries not only offer the innocent pleasure of any good detective-story read, they also, precisely because of the literary qualities of the narrative, "educate our emotions."

In an address entitled "Educating the Emotions," delivered by J. I. M. Stewart in 1944 in Adelaide for the New Education Fellowship,[6] he analyzes the modern dissociation of emotion and intellect and the almost exclusive attention paid to educating and developing the practical intellect at the expense of the emotions and the foundations of values. In this, Stewart argues, we are truly carrying out Francis Bacon's program of attempting *to effect all things possible* — the Prometheus Project — and without at all developing a commensurate sense of *why* and *for what*. The universe we have come to regard as something we learn to exploit and to shove about to the best of our technical abilities — in which respect, scientist and businessman alike have this in common: they are "remorselessly on the make." Values in this system are relegated to the "merely subjective," and art and aesthetics to the status of trifling luxuries. Not surprisingly Stewart notes that the one figure of modern literature to achieve mythic status is Sherlock Holmes, a virtual ratiocinating machine for whom emotion was just so much "grit in a sensitive instrument."[7]

But our emotions, Stewart argues, which are the tribunal of our values, are indeed educable, precisely in terms of the Arnoldian idea of liberal education — of attempting to see things as in themselves they really are. In heightening our capacity to be not merely observant (the work of the practical intellect) but aware or *mindful* of the things about us, according to their own uniqueness and integrity, we derive a very special kind of pleasure — the pleasure that comes from discerning, and conforming ourselves to, reality, or "holy fact," as Charles Williams called it. And then, Stewart adds, this "contemplating the universe with appropriate emotion" may pass even into what can only be called communion. At this point, true, disinterested love becomes possible: "Truly, we do not love because our beloved makes us 'feel good' but because our beloved is loveable, and because God of His bounty has revealed this to us" (p. 7).

What enables us to educate our emotions in this direction is precisely, according to Stewart, what Matthew Arnold called the cultivation of the best that has been known and thought in the world — a recourse, that is, to the great traditions of art and literature, and to "the beautiful and permanent forms of Nature, when these are carried alive to the heart in passion" (p. 18).

In their modest fashion, Innes's own narratives provide just that sort of pleasure to the receptive reader. Not only do they add to the world's stock of entertaining mystery stories, but through the flow of the narrative we are continually being made aware of ourselves and of the people and things about us; as readers we are in conversation with someone who is gracious enough to expect us to bring the best of ourselves to that encounter. And, specifically, all that comfortable-seeming and allusive talk in these stories about literature and art, far from being a matter of frivolous erudition or snobbery, is a continual playful reminder of what, after all, is our shared sense of the best that has been known and thought in the world, of what, finally, we set store by. Innes does for his readers what the best sort of don should do: makes us feel, rightly, that these things, and the pleasures they bring, are rightfully ours.

To return to our starting point in this study, Innes's mysteries are not, then, merely the "texts of desire" that detective stories generally are, that hold our attention only in the unsatisfied longing or suspense, and leave us feeling sated and without interest, and perhaps rather let down at the end. Instead, like all real literature, Innes's novels are "texts of pleasure," whose pleasure resides in the reading — and the rereading — itself.

Notes

Preface

1. Dawson Gaillard, *Dorothy L. Sayers* (N.Y.: Frederick Ungar, 1981), p. ix.
2. Dennis Porter, *The Pursuit of Crime/Art and Ideology in Detective Fiction* (New Haven: Yale University Press, 1981), pp. 257–58.
3. Quoted in Porter, p. 246.
4. Michael Innes, "Death as a Game," *Esquire*, 63 (January 1965), p. 55.
5. Erik Routley, *The Puritan Pleasures of the Detective Story* (London: Gollancz, 1972), p. 161.

Chapter 1

1. Michele Slung, entry on "Michael Innes" in *Twentieth-Century Crime and Mystery Writers*, ed. John M. Reilly (N.Y.: St. Martin's Press, 1980), p. 847; H. R. F. Keating, ed. *Whodunit? A Guide to Crime, Suspense and Spy Fiction* (N.Y.: Van Nostrand Reinhold, 1982), p. 187; Julian Symons, *Mortal Consequences* (N.Y.: Harper & Row, 1972), p. 126; Routley, p. 160.
2. Autobiographical note quoted in entry on "J. I. M. Stewart" in *Twentieth Century Authors*, ed. Stanley J. Kunitz & Howard Haycraft (N.Y.: H. W. Wilson, 1942), p. 1349.
3. Michael Innes, "John Appleby," in *The Great Detectives*, ed. Otto Penzler (N. Y.: Penguin, 1979), p. 13.
4. Innes, "Death as a Game," p. 56.
5. J. I. M. Stewart, *The Man Who Wrote Detective Stories and Other Stories* (London: Gollancz, 1959), p. 80.

6. Innes, "Death as a Game," p. 56.
7. Robert Graves and Alan Hodge, *The Long Week End/A Social History of Great Britain 1918–1939* (N.Y.: Macmillan, 1941), p. 290.
8. Routley, pp. 161, 158; cf. LeRoy Panek, "The Novels of Michael Innes," *Armchair Detective*, 16 (Spring 1983), pp. 122–126.
9. Innes, "Death as a Game," p. 55; also see Panek, "The Novels of Michael Innes," p. 116.
10. The most important published sources of information on Stewart/Innes, aside from the standard contemporary author reference works, are an essay by Stewart: "An Edinburgh Boyhood," *Holiday*, 38 (August 1965), pp. 60–70 & 101; and the two Innes essays cited above: "John Appleby" and "Death as a Game." In addition, I have drawn upon an interview granted by Professor Stewart at his home in Wantage in June 1982.
11. Innes, "John Appleby," p. 13.
12. Ibid.
13. Autobiographical note in Kunitz & Haycraft, p. 1348.
14. Stewart, "An Edinburgh Boyhood," p. 60. The information, quotations and page references in the succeeding half dozen paragraphs all derive from this essay, unless otherwise noted.
15. It is interesting to note that Innes attributes the same childhood expectations about making the rail crossing over the Firth of Forth Bridge to his heroine Sheila Grant in *The Secret Vanguard* (1941), p. 37.
16. Autobiographical note in Kunitz and Haycraft, p. 1348.
17. Stewart, Introduction, *Montaigne's Essays*, trans. Florio (N. Y.: Random House, [1931]), p. vi.
18. Autobiographical note in Kunitz and Haycraft, p. 1348.
19. Innes, "Death as a Game," p. 55.
20. Innes, "John Appleby," p. 13.
21. Autobiographical note in Kunitz and Haycraft, pp. 1348–49.
22. Innes, "Death as a Game," p. 55.
23. Innes, "John Appleby," p. 13. See Panek, "Novels of Michael Innes," pp. 126, 130.
24. Innes, "Strange Intelligence" (first broadcast 30 June 1947), in *Imaginary Conversations*, ed. Rayner Heppenstall (London: Seeker & Warburg, 1948), pp. 137–151.
25. Innes, "The Hawk and the Handsaw" (first broadcast 21 Nov. 1948), in *Three Tales of Hamlet*, by Rayner Heppenstall and Michael Innes (London: Gollancz, 1950), pp. 11–73. A critical discussion of the work occurs in Horst Priessnitz, "Shakespeare-Bearbeitungen als Shakespeare-kritik: Funkspiele um Hamlet von Rayner Heppenstall, 'Michael Innes', Herbert Read und G.W. Stonier," in *Anglo-Amerikanische Shakespeare-Bearbeitungen das 20 Jahrhunderts*, ed. Horst Priessnitz, *Ars Interpretandi*, 9 (1980), 207–211.

The first production of "The Hawk and the Handsaw," starred Cyril Cusack, and Innes reports that Cusack, a Catholic, was inspired to special eloquence by the play's satire on Freudianism! But after the production, Ernest Jones wrote to Innes and they developed a friendly correspondence. Later Stewart reviewed Jones's monumental biography of Freud, and after Jones's death, Stewart was invited to give a memorial lecture to the London psychoanalytical society. His talk, Stewart says, was gently satiric and seemed to be received well — but was not published, and afterward, when he asked for a copy back, was told it had been lost.

26. Innes, "The Mysterious Affair at Elsinore" (first broadcast 26 June 1949), in *Three Tales of Hamlet*, pp. 77–89.
27. See Gaillard, p. 6.
28. Innes, "Death as a Game," p. 56.
29. Innes, "John Appleby," p. 13; authors' interview with J. I. M. Stewart, June 1982.
30. Innes, "Death as a Game," p. 55.
31. See *TLS* (25 October 1974), p. 1206, and *New Yorker*, 51 (28 April 1975), p. 138 — on *The Gaudy*; and *TLS* (6 June 1975), p. 617 — on *Young Patullo*; and, similarly, *New Statesman*, 98 (10 August 1979), p. 208, and *Observer* (19 August 1979), p. 36 — on *Our England is a Garden and Other Stories* (1979).
32. Howard Haycraft, *Murder for Pleasure/The Life and Times of the Detective Story* [1941], enlarged edition (N. Y.: Biblo & Tannen, 1968), p. 187.

Chapter 2

1. Innes, "John Appleby," p. 11.
2. James Sandoe, *N.Y. Herald Tribune BR* (24 Feb. 1957), p. 9 — on *Appleby Plays Chicken*; and Julian Symons, *Mortal Consequences*, p. 126.
3. For a comprehensive analysis of this dichotomy, see George Grella, "The Formal Detective Novel," and "The Hard-Boiled Detective Novel," both reprinted in *Detective Fiction/A Collection of Critical Essays*, ed. Robin W. Winks (Englewood Cliffs: Prentice-Hall, 1980), pp. 84–102 and 103–120, respectively; and, in a humorous vein, Marilyn Stasio and Richard Hummler, "A Slight Debate/A Hard-Boiled Fan and a Country-House Fan Discuss the Genre," in *Murder Ink/The Mystery Reader's Companion*, "perpetrated" by Dilys Winn (N. Y.: Workman, 1977), pp. 451–53.
4. Michael Holquist, "Whodunit and Other Questions: Metaphysical Detec-

tive Stories in Post-War Fiction," *New Literary History*, III (1971), pp. 146-7.

5. Grella, "The Formal Detective Novel," in Winks, pp. 85-6; also see LeRoy Panek, *Watteau's Shepherds: The Detective Novel in Britain 1914-1940* (Bowling Green: Popular Press, 1979), pp. 21-5.

6. Grella, "The Formal Detective Novel," in Winks, p. 86.

7. See Panek, *Watteau's Shepherds*, pp. 25-26; Dorothy L. Sayers, "The Omnibus of Crime" (1929), in Winks, *Detective Fiction*, p. 82.

8. Ralph Harper, *The World of the Thriller* (Cleveland: Case Western Reserve University, 1969).

9. Innes, "Death as a Game," p. 56; compare J. I. M. Stewart, "Introduction to Wilkie Collins," *The Moonstone* (Harmondsworth: Penguin, 1981), pp. 7, 20, 22.

10. See Grella, "The Formal Detective Novel," in Winks, pp. 84-102; Panek, *Watteau's Shepherds*, chapter 1; John Cawalti, *Adventure, Mystery and Romance/Formula Stories as Art and Popular Culture* (Chicago: University of Chicago Press, 1976), chapter 4; Hanna Charney, *The Detective World of Manners/Hedonism, Morality, and the Life of Reason* (Rutherford, N. J.: Fairleigh Dickinson University Press, 1981.

11. Innes, "John Appleby," p. 13.

12. Panek, on the other hand, supposes that such allusions to detective fiction conventions, within the novel, are actually distancing devices, "constant reminders to readers that *they are reading a detective story*: this is not life, they say. It is a detective story." Panek, *Watteau's Shepherds*, p. 19.

13. Innes, "John Appleby," p. 12. In *Operation Pax* Appleby is said to have been a student at Bede's College, Oxford. Also see John Neville, "Michael Innes," *Clues* (Fall/Winter 1984), p. 120.

14. Julian Symons, *The Detective Story in Britain*, Writers and Their Work, No. 145 (Longman House, Essex: The British Council/Longmans, Green, 1969), p. 29.

15. For a useful parallel account of Innes's (i.e., Stewart's) own serious academic reflections on *Hamlet* and on the "historical school" of Shakespeare criticism, see J. I. M. Stewart, *Character and Motive in Shakespeare/Some recent Appraisals Examined* [1949] (Brooklyn: Haskell House, 1977), esp. chapters 1, 4 and 5.

16. Anthony Boucher, Introduction to *Hamlet, Revenge!* (N.Y.: Collier, 1962), p. 7.

17. Melvyn Barnes, *Best Detective Fiction/A Guide from Godwin to the Present* (London: Clive Bingley, 1975), p. 63.

18. Routley, pp. 158-59. See Haycraft, who, calling it "a richly tapestried work," judged *Lament for a Maker* "not only his most mature achievement, but also one of the vividly outstanding detective novels of the

generation": *Murder for Pleasure*, pp. 188–89. Also cf. "Crime Compendium," *Spectator*, 231 (1 Sept. 1973), p. 284.
19. Routley, p. 159.
20. Ibid.

Chapter 3

1. G. K. Chesterton, "A Defense of Detective Stories," reprinted in *Detective Fiction/Crime and Compromise*, ed. Dick Allen and Allen Chacko (NY: HBJ, 1974) p. 384.
2. Jacques Barzun, "Detection and the Literary Art," [1961], reprinted in Winks, *Detective Fiction*, p. 145.
3. Alain Robbe-Grillet, "A Path for the Future of the Novel," quoted in Holquist, p. 149.
4. The phrases in quotes are from Robbe-Grillet, as cited in Holquist, p. 148.
5. Harper, *The World of the Thriller, passim*.
6. Auden, "The Guilty Vicarage," in Winks, p. 23.
7. Barzun, p. 150. Barzun and Auden on the one hand, and Chandler, on the other, in "The Simple Art of Murder," are classic statements on behalf of the two "schools" of detective fiction: the formal detective novel and the hard-boiled story, respectively. See chapter 2, n. 3 above. It should be noted that, on the other hand, Jerry Palmer argues that the distinction between the detective story and the thriller has been exaggerated — see Jerry Palmer, *Thrillers/Genesis and Structure of a Popular Genre* (N.Y.: St. Martins, 1979), pp. 93–106.
8. See Robert Champigny, *What Will Have Happened/A Philosophical and Technical Essay on Mystery Stories* (Bloomington, Indiana University Press, 1977).
9. See the chapter in Palmer, *Thrillers/Genesis*, entitled "The School of Mayhem Parva: the Classic English Detective Story."
10. Greene, quoted in Harper, p. 4.
11. The same device is used in an Appleby short story, "Was He Morton?" in *Appleby Talks Again* (1956), pp. 53–57.
12. See Richard Lister in *New Statesman*, 49 (19 Feb 1955), pp. 256–57; Penelope Houston in *Spectator*, 194 (18 Mar 1955), p. 334; James Sandoe in *N.Y. Herald Tribune BR* (10 Apr 1955), p. 7.
13. Barzun & Taylor, p. 249.
14. Routley, p. 160.
15. As Elizabeth Bullock commented in the *New York Times*: "Indeed, the story is so well swathed in blandly tortuous Innes sentences, with their

deft turns of phrase, that a reader not susceptible to the elephantine, ironic, mandarin pedantry of his style, and interested only in what happens next, may find himself daunted" — though the patient and persevering reader, she added, would be amply rewarded by one of Innes's best narratives (16 May 1949, p. 18).

16. The *Manchester Guardian* concluded that "To readers of the more sophisticated type the book will appeal enormously. But others may be inclined to suspect Mr. Innes of having this time pushed his tongue into his cheek just a little too far" (1 July 1941, p. 3). Or, as John Fairfield put it in the *Spectator*: "Rose-petal jam has charms when taken rarely, but it makes a sickening staple" (13 June 1941), p. 640.

17. Panek, "Novels of Michael Innes," pp. 122–24.

18. Barzun and Taylor, p. 250.

Chapter 4

1. Auden, "The Guilty Vicarage," in Winks, p. 18.

2. Ibid.

3. Dorothy L. Sayers, "Gaudy Night," in Howard Haycraft, *The Art of the Mystery Story* (N. Y., 1946), p. 212, 213, 216.

4. Agate Nesaule Krouse and Margot Peters, "Murder in Academe," *Southwest Review* (Autumn 1977), p. 377.

5. Marjorie Nicolson, "The Professor and the Detective," in Haycraft, *The Art of the Mystery Story*, pp. 125–26.

6. Jane Merrill Filstrupp, "The Shattered Calm: Libraries in Detective Fiction," parts 2 & 3, *Wilson Library Bulletin*, 53 (Jan. 1979), p. 397, and Part 1, *Wilson Library Bulletin*, 53 (Dec. 1978), p. 320.

7. Filstrupp, Parts 2 & 3, p. 397.

8. Chandler, "The Simple Art of Murder," in Allen and Chacko, pp. 393–95.

9. Krouse and Peters, p. 378.

10. Auden, in Winks, p. 19.

11. Sayers, "Gaudy Night," in Haycraft, p. 214.

12. Auden, in Winks, pp. 18–19.

13. Margaret Yorke, "Oxford vs. Cambridge/The Dark Blues Have the Most," in Winn, *Murder Ink*, p. 266. Cf. Panek, "Novels of Michael Innes," p. 116.

14. Krouse and Peters, p. 373.

15. The book was announced as the beginning of what was apparently intended as a series of Bobby Appleby mysteries, and indeed, in Innes's next novel, *Death at the Chase* (1970), Bobby again joins in the investi-

gation, and the next after that, *An Awkward Lie* (1971), was actually subtitled in its original Gollancz edition "A Bobby Appleby Mystery." Critics were not enthusiastic about the addition of Bobby to the stories, viewing his imprint on the stories as "distinctively neutral" (*TLS*, 3 April 1969, p. 372), even "null" (*TLS*, 5 March 1970, p. 204). "No objection to the young," Barzun and Taylor write, "but why Bobby, with its nursery connotation and poor sound pattern with Appleby?" (p. 250). In any event Innes did not follow up the use of Bobby as a protagonist beyond this brief series, though he has always remained fond of introducing "undergraduate types" into his stories.

16. See below, ch. 5, pp. 134–35. On the theme of the practical joke in Innes, see Panek, "Novels of Michael Innes," p. 124.

17. See *New Yorker* (17 Nov 1951), p. 190, and *New Statesman* (3 Nov 1951), p. 42.

18. Author's interview with Michael Innes, June 1982.

19. Routley, p. 159.

20. Panek regards *The Weight of the Evidence* as one of Innes's best books, though without explaining why ("Novels of Michael Innes," p. 130), whereas Neville, similarly without elaboration, reiterates the more usual opinion that it is "one of his less successful works" ("Michael Innes," p. 120). Barzun and Taylor, incidentally, hopelessly confuse the two red-brick tales in their notice of *Old Hall, New Hall*: "Though the contents are at first enticing—a university setting, improbable but amusing professors, and some semblance of plot (for once no Appleby)—this tale of murder by dropping weights on reclining dons is a bad jumble of old and young, prosiness and wit, action and irrelevance" (p. 251).

21. On the other hand, Partridge, Innes's generally unsympathetic reviewer in *New Statesman*, failed to see any significant connections with *Othello*: "The title," he wrote, "suggests that we are to be regaled with variations on the theme of *Othello*, but don't you believe it! The advantages of picaresque writing are that no characters introduced need be related to the plot, no orderly sequence of events is required, and no Shakespeare quotations need mean a thing except that the author is an Eng. Lit. don at Oxford" (3 May 1958, p. 576). In this case, at least, Partridge's judgment seems to be a result of hasty if not of careless reading. It is worth noting here as well that Innes also wrote a short story based on the *Othello* motif, "Tragedy of a Handkerchief," in *Appleby Talking/Twenty-Three Detective Stories* (Harmondsworth: Penguin, 1973 [orig. 1954]), pp. 68–81. The story, winner of an Ellery Queen prize, is based on the device of an onstage murder growing out of a domestic quarrel among a troup of traveling players staging *Othello*. The title is aptly derived from the eighteenth-century critic Rowe's contemptuous description of Shakespeare's domestic tragedy.

22. Charney, pp. 92 ff.
23. Stewart, "An Edinburgh Boyhood," p. 64.

Chapter 5

1. Stewart, "An Edinburgh Boyhood," pp. 67–68.
2. Panek calls attention to other Innes experiments with dialect humor (Properjohn's Yankee-Yiddish-British amalgam in *From "London" Far*, and the Welsh Vice-Chancellor of Nesfield, Sir David Evans in *The Weight of the Evidence*): "Novels of Michael Innes," p. 125; cf. Routley, who comments that the latter example is "certainly the only Innes to contain a palpable lapse in dialect-transmission: his Welsh Vice-Chancellor's speech is entirely unconvincing" (p. 159). Innes's occasional stabs at Americanism in speech could be similarly faulted, and Robert Alter has noted a similar failure in J. I. M. Stewart's *The Last Tresilians*, in the character of the American professor, Delver (*Chicago Tribune Book Week*, 22 Dec. 1963, pp. 4, 7).
3. Barzun and Taylor, for example, comment: "It begins with a stunning description of a lecture by Mervyn Twist. . . . The account of the facial expressions of the listeners is a marvel, and the ensuing events live up to this flourish of virtuosity," and they conclude, interestingly, that this is "Innes's undoubted masterpiece" (p. 251).
4. Note that Godwin's dilemma is built into the climax of Stewart's *A Use of Riches* (1957).
5. This conversation should be compared with the similar attempt by the parapsychologist Wine to convince Appleby of the immanent triumph of the irrational in *The Daffodil Affair* (Part 3, chap. 7), and with Prof. Titlow's monologue on the Decline of the West in *Death at the President's Lodging* (pp. 97–9).
6. Volker Neuhaus, "Michael Innes: *From London far*/Spiel und Glasperlenspiel in Detektivroman," *Euphorion*, 71 (1977), pp. 195–206; the article contributes a valuable analysis of the literary motifs in *From "London" Far*.

Chapter 6

1. Quoted in Richard Gill, *Happy Rural Seat/The English Country House and the Literary Imagination* (New Haven: Yale University Press, 1973), p. 19.
2. Gill, p. 4.
3. Ibid., p. 14.

4. See Colin Watson, *Snobbery with Violence: Crime Stories and Their Audience* (London: Eyre and Spottiswood, 1971); cf. the comments by Routley, pp. 201–229.
5. Symons, *Mortal Consequences*, p. 12; cf. Cawalti, pp. 95–6; Grella, "The Formal Detective Novel," in Winks, p. 100.
6. See Grella, "The Formal Detective Novel," in Winks, p. 94.
7. Innes, "John Appleby," pp. 14–15.
8. Quoted in Gill, p. xiii.
9. Innes, "John Appleby," p. 14.
10. Ibid., p. 12.
11. See Charney, p. 38; Grella, p. 92.
12. See Charney, esp. p. 78; Grella, *passim*. Charney's term is "the detective novel of manners"; Grella's is "the formal detective novel."
13. This novel is particularly rich in authorial self-reflection. As John Neville notes, "One may assume that Innes himself appears twice in this novel — once as the author who had rather write on Pope and again as the Oxford don" ("Michael Innes," p. 124.).
14. Symons, *Mortal Consequences*, p. 127; cf. Will Cuppy, *N. Y. Herald Tribune Books* (12 Nov 1939), p. 36.
15. On the atmosphere of trains in British mysteries, see Hugh Douglas, "Commuting/An Unscheduled Stop at an Isolated Junction," in Winn, *Murder Ink*, pp. 482–83.
16. Innes, "Death as a Game," p. 56.
17. As Panek notes, this kind of hyper-complication, so akin to farce, does show that "Innes finds the fulfillment of the form not in the irrefutable logic of its ending but in the free-wheeling creation of alternate hypotheses to explain away unusual combinations of facts" ("Novels of Michael Innes," p. 120).
18. A similar fairy-tale atmosphere centering on a house pervades the short story, "A Matter of Goblins," in *Appleby Talks Again* (1956).

Epilogue

1. Innes, "John Appleby," p. 12.
2. Routley, p. 161.
3. Ibid., p. 158.
4. Innes, "Death as a Game," p. 56.
5. Ibid. Both incidents reappear in the Stewart short story, "The Man Who Wrote Detective Stories." Also note the parallel incident to the Detection Club incident in *Appleby's Answer*, where it is Appleby himself who speaks to a mystery writers' group called the Crooks Colloquium about

the world of real crime. Here, you might say, Innes is rather effectively having it both ways, critiquing the conventions of detective fiction — through the agency of his own fictional detective.

6. J. I. M. Stewart, *Educating the Emotions* (Adelaide: The New Education Fellowship, 1944).

7. Ibid., citing Conan Doyle, "A Scandal in Bohemia."

Bibliography

I. ALPHABETICAL CHECKLIST OF
MICHAEL INNES MYSTERIES

Format: Title. Date of first publication. Alternate titles. Note: alternate titles and reprint anthologies are also included alphabetically, but indented, for purposes of cross-referencing (alternate titles that differ only typographically or involve only the dropping or adding of subtitles such as "a novel" or "a detective noel" are not separately listed).

The Ampersand Papers. 1978.
Appleby and Honeybath. 1983.
Appleby at Allington. 1968. Also published as *Death by Water.*
The Appleby File: Detective Stories. 1975.
 Appleby Intervenes; Three Tales from Scotland Yard. 1965. An anthology that includes *There Came Both Mist and Snow, The Secret Vanguard,* and *One Man Show.*
Appleby on Ararat. 1941.
Appleby Plays Chicken. 1957. Also published as *Death on a Quiet Day.*
Appleby Talking: Twenty-Three Detective Stories. 1954. Also published as *Dead Man's Shoes.*
Appleby Talks Again: Eighteen Detective Stories. 1956.
Appleby's Answer: A Novel. 1973.
Appleby's End. 1945.
Appleby's Other Story. 1974.
An Awkward Lie: A Bobby Appleby Story. 1971.
The Bloody Wood. 1966.
 Candleshoe. See *Christmas at Candleshoe.*
Carson's Conspiracy. 1984.

The Case of Sonia Wayward. See *The New Sonia Wayward.*
The Case of the Journeying Boy. See *The Journeying Boy.*
A Change of Heir. 1966.
Christmas at Candleshoe. 1953. Also published as *Candleshoe.*
A Comedy of Terrors. See *There Came Both Mist and Snow.*
A Connoisseur's Case. 1962. Also published as *The Crabtree Affair.*
The Crabtree Affair. See *A Connoisseur's Case.*
The Daffodil Affair. 1942.
Dead Man's Shoes. See *Appleby Talking.*
Death at the Chase. 1970.
Death at the President's Lodging. 1936. Also published as *Seven Suspects.*
Death by Moonlight. See *The Man from the Sea.*
Death by Water. See *Appleby at Allington.*
Death on a Quiet Day. See *Appleby Plays Chicken.*
A Family Affair. 1969. Also published as *Picture of Guilt.*
From "London" Far. 1946. Also published as *The Unsuspected Chasm.*
The "Gay Phoenix": A Novel. 1976.
Going It Alone. 1980.
Hamlet, Revenge!: A Story in Four Parts. 1937.
Hare Sitting Up. 1959.
Honeybath's Haven. 1977.
The Journeying Boy. 1949. Also published as *The Case of the Journeying Boy.*
Lament for a Maker. 1938.
The Last of Sonia Wayward. See *The New Sonia Wayward.*
The Long Farewell: A Detective Story. 1958.
Lord Mullion's Secret. 1981.
The Man from the Sea. 1955. Also published as *Death by Moonlight.*
The Michael Innes Omnibus. 1983. An anthology that includes *Death at the President's Lodging, Hamlet, Revenge!,* and *The Daffodil Affair.*
Money from Holme. 1964.
Murder Is an Art. See *A Private View.*
The Mysterious Commission. 1974.
The New Sonia Wayward. 1960. Also published as *The Case of Sonia Wayward* and as *The Last of Sonia Wayward.*
A Night of Errors. 1947.
Old Hall, New Hall. 1956. Also published as *A Question of Queens.*
One-Man Show. See *A Private View.*
The Open House. 1972.
Operation Pax. 1951. Also published as *The Paper Thunderbolt.*
The Paper Thunderbolt. See *Operation Pax.*
Picture of Guilt. See *A Family Affair.*
A Private View. 1952. Also published as *One-Man Show* and *Murder Is an Art.*

A Question of Queens. See *Old Hall, New Hall.*
The Second Michael Innes Omnibus. 1983. An anthology that includes *The Journeying Boy, Operation Pax,* and *The Man from the Sea.*
The Secret Vanguard. 1940.
Seven Suspects. See *Death at The President's Lodging.*
Sheiks and Adders. 1982.
Silence Observed. 1961.
The Spider Strikes. See *Stop Press.*
Stop Press. 1939. Also published as *The Spider Strikes.*
There Came Both Mist and Snow. 1940. Also Published as *A Comedy of Terrors.*
The Unsuspected Chasm. See *From "London" Far.*
The Weight of the Evidence. 1943.
What Happened at Hazlewood. 1946.

II. BIBLIOGRAPHY OF MICHAEL INNES

A. Mysteries

Format: Year of first publication. Title (including original subtitle, if any; subsequent differences in title or subtitle are noted except for the simple dropping of a subtitle). British and American publication history (other English language and foreign language editions not included): publishers and dates of editions and reprints, including alternate titles. Asterisks (*) denote edition of each title cited in the text. Series character indicators (A = Inspector Appleby; J = Judith Appleby; B = Bobby Appleby; H = Charles Honeybath, R.A.; C = Inspector Cadover; P = Sgt. Pride; Br = Braunkopf; G = Giles Gott).

1936. *Death at the President's Lodging.* Gollancz, 1936, 1984; Penguin, 1958, 1976, 1984, 1985 (*Seven Suspects*) and in *The Michael Innes Omnibus,* 1983. As *Seven Suspects:* Dodd, Mead, 1937; Doubleday/Dolphin, 1962*; Berkley/Medallion, 1965. A/G

1937. *Hamlet, Revenge!: A Story in Four Parts.* Gollancz, 1937, 1952, 1984; Dodd, Mead, 1937; Crowell/Collier, 1962 (with introduction by Anthony Boucher)*; Penguin, 1961, 1964, 1976, 1977, 1979 and in *The Michael Innes Omnibus,* 1983. A/G

1938. *Lament for a Maker.* Gollancz, 1938, 1971; Dodd, Mead, 1938 (as *Lament for a Maker, a Detective Story*)*; Crowell/Collier, 1961; New English Library/Four Square Books, 1964; Penguin, 1973, 1984; Harper & Row/Perennial, 1984. A

1939. *Stop Press: A Novel.* Gollancz, 1939, 1971; Penguin, 1958, 1960*. As *The Spider Strikes, a Detective Story*: Dodd, Mead, 1939.

1940. *The Secret Vanguard.* Gollancz, 1940, 1949, 1972; Dodd, Mead, 1941 and in *Appleby Intervenes; Three Tales from Scotland Yard*, 1965; Penguin, 1958, 1959; Berkley/Medallion, 1965; Harper & Row/Perennial, 1982*. A

1940. *There Came Both Mist and Snow.* Gollancz, 1940, 1972; Penguin, 1958; Hamlyn, 1980*. As *A Comedy of Terrors*: Dodd, Mead, 1940 and in *Appleby Intervenes; Three Tales from Scotland Yard*, 1965; Berkley/Medallion, 1964. A

1941. *Appleby on Ararat.* Gollancz, 1941, 1946, 1972; Dodd, Mead, 1941; Penguin, 1961; Berkley/Medallion, 1964*; Greenwood, 1971; Harper & Row/Perennial, 1983. A

1942. *The Daffodil Affair.* Gollancz, 1942, 1948, 1972; Dodd, Mead, 1942; Berkley/Medallion, 1964; Penguin, 1964, 1968*, 1972, 1984 and in *The Michael Innes Omnibus*, 1983; Garland, 1976 (ed. with an introduction by J. Barzun and W. H. Taylor as #29 of Fifty Classics of Crime Fiction, 1900–1950); Chivers (large print edition), 1983. A

1943. *The Weight of the Evidence: A Detective Story.* Gollancz, 1944, 1973 and in *The Second Gollancz Detective Omnibus*, 1952; Dodd, Mead, 1943; Penguin, 1961, 1964, 1965; Berkley/Medallion, 1964; Hamlyn, 1980*; Harper & Row/Perennial, 1983. A

1945. *Appleby's End, a Novel.* Gollancz, 1946, 1973 and in *The Gollancz Detective Omnibus*, 1951; Dodd, Mead, 1945, 1956; Crowell/Collier, 1965; Penguin, 1969, 1972, 1980*; Greenwood, 1970; Ballantine, 1975; Harper & Row/Perennial, 1983. A/J

1946. *From "London" Far.* Gollancz, 1946, 1949, 1973; Penguin, 1962, 1968, 1976, 1977, 1978, 1981*. As *The Unsuspected Chasm*: Dodd, Mead, 1946.

1946. *What Happened at Hazlewood.* Gollancz, 1946, 1949, 1973; Dodd, Mead, 1946 (as *What Happened at Hazlewood?*); Penguin, 1968, 1970*, 1976. C

1947. *A Night of Errors.* Gollancz, 1948, 1974; Dodd, Mead, 1947; Berkley/Medallion, 1963; Penguin, 1966, 1969*, 1976. A

1949. *The Journeying Boy.* Gollancz, 1949, 1970, 1984; Penguin, 1961, 1964* and in *The Second Michael Innes Omnibus*, 1983. As *The Case of the Journeying Boy*: Dodd, Mead, 1949; Berkley/Medallion, 1963; Harper & Row/Perennial, 1983. As *The Journeying Boy . . . Simplified and abridged* by E. J. H. Morris; illus. by Roger Payne: Longman's/Bridge Series, 1963. C

1951. *Operation Pax.* Gollancz, 1951, 1953, 1974, 1984; Penguin, 1964, 1969 and in *The Second Michael Innes Omnibus*, 1983. As *The Paper Thunderbolt*: Dodd, Mead, 1951; Doubleday/Dolphin, 1961; Berkley/Medallion, 1966*. A

1952. *A Private View.* Gollancz, 1952, 1974; Penguin, 1958, 1959. As *One-Man Show*: Dodd, Mead, 1952 and in *Appleby Intervenes; Three Tales from Scotland Yard*, 1965; Doubleday, 1952 (Doubleday's Dollar Mystery Guild

Book Club); Ballantine, 1975*; Garland, 1982 (ed. with an introduction by J. Barzun and W. H. Taylor for Fifty Classics of Crime Fiction 1950–1975); Harper & Row/Perennial, 1983. As *Murder Is an Art*: Avon, 1959, 1965. A/J/C/Br

1953. *Christmas at Candleshoe*. Gollancz, 1953, 1974; Dodd, Mead, 1953; Penguin, 1961 and (as *Candleshoe*) 1978*. As *Christmas at Candleshoe . . . Simplified and Abridged* by R. John; illus. by Robert Winklewright: Longman's/Bridge Series, 1963. Film: *Candleshoe*: Walt Disney Studios, 1978 and videodisc release: RCA SelectaVision VideoDisc, 1981.

1954. *Appleby Talking: Twenty-Three Detective Stories*. Gollancz, 1954; New English Library/Four Square Books, 1965; Penguin, 1973*. As *Dead Man's Shoes*: Dodd, Mead, 1954. Also repr. with Leslie Ford, *Invitation to Murder* and George Bagby, *The Body in the Basket* for The Detective Book Club: Walter J. Black, 1954. Title story "Dead Man's Shoes" also pub. as *Dead Man's Shoes*, ed. T. Gerighty for Cambridge English Language Learning, Level 5: Cambridge University Press, 1977; also on sound recording/cassette *Liar! and Other Modern Stories*, ed. Roland Hindmarsh: Cambridge English Language Learning, 1980. A

1955. *The Man from the Sea*. Gollancz, 1955, 1970, 1984; Dodd, Mead, 1955; Penguin, 1961 and in *The Second Michael Innes Omnibus*, 1983; Harper & Row/Perennial, 1982*. As *Death by Moonlight*: Avon, 1955, 1964.

1956. *Appleby Talks Again: Eighteen Detective Stories*. Gollancz, 1956; Dodd, Mead, 1957*; New English Library/Four Square Books, 1966; Books for Libraries Press, 1969. A

1956. *Old Hall, New Hall*. Gollancz, 1956*, Penguin, 1961, 1964, 1965. As *A Question of Queens*: Dodd, Mead, 1956.

1957. *Appleby Plays Chicken*. Gollancz, 1957, 1975; Penguin, 1961. As *Death on a Quiet Day*: Dodd, Mead, 1957; Berkley/Medallion, 1963*; Harper & Row/Perennial, 1983.

1958. *The Long Farewell: A Detective Story*. Gollancz, 1958, 1975; Dodd, Mead, 1958; Berkley/Medallion, 1963; New English Library/Four Square Books, 1964; Lythway (large print edition), 1977; Harper & Row/Perennial, 1982*. A

1959. *Hare Sitting Up*. Gollancz, 1959, 1975; Dodd, Mead, 1959*; Berkley/Medallion, 1964; Penguin, 1964; Hamlyn, 1981; Harper & Row/Perennial, 1982. A/J

1960. *The New Sonia Wayward*. Gollancz, 1960, 1976; Penguin, 1964. As *The Case of Sonia Wayward*: Dodd, Mead, 1960*, 1984. As *The Last of Sonia Wayward*: Crowell/Collier, 1962.

1961. *Silence Observed*. Gollancz, 1961, 1976; Dodd, Mead, 1961; Berkley/Medallion, 1964; Penguin, 1964; Ballantine, 1975; Hamlyn, 1981*. A/J

1962. *A Connoisseur's Case*. Gollancz, 1962, 1977; Penguin, 1966, 1968, 1971, 1977*; Ulverscroft (large print edition), 1980. As *The Crabtree Affair*: 1962; Berkley/Medallion, 1963; Harper & Row/Perennial, 1984.

Bibliography

1964. *Money from Holme.* Gollancz, 1964; Dodd, Mead, 1965; Penguin, 1. 1969*, 1976; Chivers (large print edition), 1980. A/J/Br

1965. *Appleby Intervenes; Three Tales from Scotland Yard* (a reprint an thology that includes *There Came Both Mist and Snow, The Secret Vanguard,* and *One-Man Show*). Dodd, Mead, 1965*.

1966. *The Bloody Wood.* Gollancz, 1966, 1977; Dodd Mead, 1966, 1983; Berkley/Medallion, 1967*; Penguin, 1968, 1977; Harper & Row/Perennial, 1986. A/J

1966. *A Change of Heir.* Gollancz, 1966, 1977; Dodd, Mead, 1966*, 1984.

1968. *Appleby at Allington.* Gollancz, 1968, 1977; Penguin, 1970*; Chivers (large print edition), 1981. As *Death by Water*: Dodd, Mead, 1968; Harper & Row/Perennial, 1982. A/J/P

1969. *A Family Affair.* Gollancz, 1969, 1978; Penguin, 1972. As *Picture of Guilt*: Dodd, Mead, 1969; Berkley/Medallion, 1970*. A/J/B/B

1970. *Death at the Chase.* Gollancz, 1970, 1978; Dodd, Mead, 1970*; Penguin, 1971. A/J/B/P

1971. *An Awkward Lie; a Bobby Appleby Story.* Gollancz, 1971; Dodd, Mead, 1971; Penguin, 1973*, 1974, 1975, 1977, 1979, 1985. A/J/B/P

1972. *The Open House.* Gollancz, 1972; Dodd, Mead, 1972*; Penguin, 1973, 1982. A

1973. *Appleby's Answer: A Novel.* Gollancz, 1973; Dodd, Mead, 1973*; Penguin, 1978, 1985; Chivers (large print edition), 1981. A/J

1974. *Appleby's Other Story.* Gollancz, 1974; Dodd, Mead, 1974*; Ballentine, 1975; Penguin, 1978; Chivers (large print edition), 1981. A/P

1974. *The Mysterious Commission.* Gollancz, 1974; Dodd, Mead, 1975; Penguin, 1977*, 1985. H

1975. *The Appleby File: Detective Stories.* Gollancz, 1975; Dodd, Mead, 1976; Penguin, 1978*; Ulverscroft (large print edition), 1978. A

1976. *The "Gay Phoenix": A Novel.* Gollancz, 1976; Dodd, Mead, 1977 (as *The Gay Phoenix*)*; Penguin, 1981, 1982. A

1977. *Honeybath's Haven.* Gollancz, 1977; Dodd, Mead, 1978; Penguin, 1979*, 1982. H

1978. *The Ampersand Papers.* Gollancz, 1978; Dodd, Mead, 1979; Penguin, 1980*, 1981; Chivers (large print edition), 1980. A

1980. *Going It Alone.* Gollancz, 1980*; Dodd, Mead, 1980.

1981. *Lord Mullion's Secret.* Gollancz, 1981; Dodd, Mead, 1981*; Penguin, 1983. H

1982. *Sheiks and Adders.* Gollancz, 1982*; Dodd, Mead, 1982; Penguin, 1983. A/J/P

1983. *Appleby and Honeybath.* Gollancz, 1983; Dodd, Mead, 1983*; Chivers (large print edition), 1984; Penguin, 1984. A/H

1983. *The Michael Innes Omnibus* (a reprint anthology that includes *Death at the President's Lodging, Hamlet, Revenge!,* and *The Daffodil Affair*). Penguin, 1983.

Michael Innes

3. *The Second Michael Innes Omnibus* (a reprint anthology that includes *The Journeying Boy, Operation Pax,* and *The Man from the Sea.* Penguin, 1983.
1984. *Carson's Conspiracy.* Gollancz, 1984; Dodd, Mead, 1984*.

B. Other Writings

1. Radio Plays

1947. "Strange Intelligence." First broadcast (BBC "Third Programme") 30 June 1947. Published in *Imaginary Conversations*, ed. with introduction by Rayner Heppenstall. London: Secker & Warburg, 1948, pp. 137–151.
1948. "The Hawk and the Handsaw." First broadcast (BBC "Third Programme") 21 November 1948. Published in *Three Tales of Hamlet*, by Rayner Heppenstall and Michael Innes. London: Gollancz, 1950, pp. 11–73.
1949. "The Mysterious Affair at Elsinore." First broadcast (BBC "Third Programme") 26 June 1949. Published in *Three Tales of Hamlet*, pp. 77–89.
1950. *Three Tales of Hamlet*, by Rayner Heppenstall and Michael Innes. London: Gollancz, 1950. Contains "The Hawk and the Handsaw" and "The Mysterious Affair at Elsinore."

2. Essays

1964. "A Few Words Concerning This Picture." *Esquire*, 62 (Nov. 1964), pp. 132–33.
1965. "Death as a Game." *Esquire*, 63 (Jan. 1965), pp. 55–56. Reprinted in *Ellery Queen's Mystery Magazine* (Nov. 1965), pp. 48–54.
1979. "John Appleby." In *The Great Detectives*, ed. Otto Penzler. Little, Brown, 1978; Penguin, 1979 (pp. 11–15)*.
1982. "Exploits of Edgar Wallace." *Times.* 6 February 1982, p. 9.

3. Column

"Radio Notes." Column in *The New Statesman and Nation* contributed by Innes between 29 October 1949 and 18 February 1950, as follows. In vol. 38 (1949): 29 Oct (p. 484); 5 Nov (p. 512); 12 Nov (p. 548); 26 Nov (p. 612); 3 Dec (p. 644); 10 Dec (p. 688); 24 Dec (p. 756). In vol. 39 (1950): 7 Jan. (p. 10); 21 Jan (pp. 63–64); 28 Jan (p. 98); 4 Feb (p. 129); 18 Feb (p. 188).

III. BIBLIOGRAPHY OF J. I. M. STEWART

A. Fiction

1954. *Mark Lambert's Supper.* Gollancz, 1954; New English Library, 1967.
1955. *The Guardians, a Novel.* Gollancz, 1955; Norton, 1957.

1957. *A Use of Riches*. Gollancz, 1957; Norton, 1957; Penguin, 1963; University of Chicago/Phoenix, 1983.

1959. *The Man Who Wrote Detective Stories: And Other Stories*. Gollancz, 1959; Norton, 1959.

1961. *The Man Who Won the Pools*. Gollancz, 1961; Norton, 1961; Penguin, 1963.

1963. *The Last Tresilians*. Gollancz, 1963; Norton, 1963; Penguin, 1966.

1965. *An Acre of Grass*. Gollancz, 1965; Norton, 1965.

1966. *The Aylwins*. Gollancz, 1966; Norton, 1967.

1967. *Vanderlyn's Kingdom*. Gollancz, 1967; Norton, 1968.

1969. *Cucumber Sandwiches, and Other Stories*. Gollancz, 1969; Norton, 1970.

1971. *Avery's Mission*. Gollancz, 1971; Norton, 1971.

1972. *A Palace of Art: A Novel*. Gollancz, 1972; Norton, 1972.

1972. *Mungo's Dream: A Novel*. Gollancz, 1972; Norton, 1973.

1974. *The Gaudy: A Novel*. (A Staircase in Surrey, I). Gollancz, 1974; Norton, 1975; Methuen, 1976.

1975. *Young Petullo: A Novel*. (A Staircase in Surrey, II). Gollancz, 1975; Norton, 1976; Methuen, 1976.

1976. *A Memorial Service: A Novel*. (A Staircase in Surrey, III). Gollancz, 1976; Norton, 1976; Methuen, 1977.

1977. *The Madonna of the Astrolabe: A Novel*. (A Staircase in Surrey, IV). Gollancz, 1977; Norton, 1977; Methuen, 1978.

1978. *Full Term: A Novel*. (A Staircase in Surrey, V). Gollancz, 1978; Norton, 1979; Methuen, 1980.

1979. *Our England Is a Garden and Other Stories*. Gollancz, 1979.

1980. *Andrew and Tobias*. Gollancz, 1980; Norton, 1980; Methuen, 1982.

1981. *The Bridge at Arta and Other Stories*. Gollancz, 1981; Norton, 1982.

1982. *A Villa in France*. Gollancz, 1982; Norton, 1983, Chivers (large print edition), 1984.

1983. *My Aunt Christina, and Other Stories*. Gollancz, 1983; Norton, 1983.

1984. *An Open Prison*. Gollancz, 1984; Norton, 1984.

1984. *The Naylors*. Gollancz, 1984; Norton, 1985.

B. Nonfiction

1. Books

1944. *Educating the Emotions*. Adelaide: New Education Fellowship/South Australian Section, 1944.

1949. *Character and Motive in Shakespeare. Some Recent Appraisals Examined*. N.Y. and London: Longmans, Green, 1949, 1965; N.Y.: Barnes & Noble, 1966, 1969; Brooklyn: Haskell House, 1977, 1982. Chapter "Steep Tragic Contrast" reprinted in *Shakespeare: The Tragedies*, ed. Clifford Leech. Chicago: University of Chicago, 1965, pp. 102–120. Chapter "The

Birth and Death of Falstaff" reprinted in *Discussions of Shapespeare's Histories*, ed. R. J. Dorius. Boston: Heath, 1964.

1957. *James Joyce* (Writers and Their Work Series, #91). London: Longmans, Green/ for the British Council, 1957, 1960, 1971.

1963. *Thomas Love Peacock* (Writers and Their Work Series, #156). London: Longmans, Green/for the British Council, 1963.

1963. *Eight Modern Writers* (Oxford History of English Literature, vol. 12). Oxford: Clarendon Press, 1963, 1973.

1966. *Rudyard Kipling*. Gollancz, 1966, 1976; Dodd, Mead, 1966; N.Y.: Apollo, 1968.

1968. *Joseph Conrad*. London: Longmans, 1968; Dodd, Mead, 1968.

1971. *Thomas Hardy: A Critical Biography*. London: Longmans, 1971; Dodd, Mead, 1971; Allen Lane, 1974.

1971. *Shakespeare's Lofty Scene*. London: Oxford University Press/for the British Council, 1971. (Reprinted from *Proceedings of the British Academy*, LVII, 1971, pp. 181–195.)

2. Essay

1965. "An Edinburgh Boyhood." *Holiday*, 38 (Aug 1965), pp. 60–71, 101.

3. Introductions and Editions

1931. Michel de Montaigne. *Montaigne's Essays: John Florio's Translation*. Ed. J. I. M. Stewart. N.Y.: Random House/Modern Library, 1931, 1933.

1955. Ovid. *The Metamorphoses of Ovid*. Ed. J. I. M. Stewart. Penguin, 1955, 1964, 1978.

1961. Kipling, Rudyard. *Kim*, with biographical illustrations and pictures from early editions of the book, together with an Introduction by J. I. M. Stewart. Macmillan/St. Martin's Library, 1961; Dodd, Mead/Great Illustrated Classics, 1962.

1966. Collins, Wilkie. *The Moonstone*. Ed. with an Introduction by J. I. M. Stewart. Penguin, 1966, 1969, 1971, 1973, 1975, 1976, 1977, 1978, 1979, 1980, 1981.

1966. Priestly, John B. *Thomas Love Peacock*. Introduction by J. I. M. Stewart. Penguin, 1966.

1968. Thackeray, William M. *Vanity Fair*. Ed. with an Introduction by J. I. M. Stewart. Penguin/English Library, 1968.

1970. Hardy, Thomas. *Stories and Poems*. Ed. Donald J. Morrison, with an Introduction by J. I. M. Stewart. London: Everyman's (#708), 1970.

1971. Thackeray, William M. *The History of Pendennis*. Ed. Donald Hawes. Introduction by J. I. M. Stewart. Penguin/English Library, 1971.

4. Articles

1971. "Notes for a Study of *The Waves.*" In *On the Novel: A Present for Walter Allen*, ed. B. S. Benedikz. London: Dent, 1971, pp 93–112.

1971. "Shakespeare's Lofty Scene." (Annual Shakespeare Lecture of the British Academy). *Proceedings of the British Academy*, LVII (1971), pp. 181–95. Reprinted in book form by Oxford University Press for The British Council, 1971.

1972. "Kipling's Reputation." In *The Age of Kipling*, ed. J. J. Gross. N.Y.: Simon & Shuster, 1972, pp. 153–60; also published as *Rudyard Kipling/The Man, His Work and His World*. London: Weidenfeld & Nicolson, 1972.

1976. "Who Was Shakespeare?" In *Shakespeare and Some Others: Essays on Shakespeare and Some of His Contemporaries*, ed. Alan Brissenden. Adelaide: Department of English, University of Adelaide, 1976, pp. 1–10.

1976. "The Major Novels." In *The Genius of Thomas Hardy*, ed. Margaret Drabble. N.Y.: Knopf, 1976, pp. 56–66.

5. Reviews — Stewart's numerous book review articles are not included in the present bibliography.

IV. SECONDARY SOURCES

1. Bio/Bibliographical Reference Works with Innes citations

Barnes, Melvyn. *Best Detective Fiction/A Guide from Godwin to the Present*. London: Clive Bingley/Hamden: Linnet Books, 1975. See pp. 62–63.

Barzun, Jacques and Wendell Hertig Taylor, eds. *A Catalogue of Crime*. N.Y.: Harper & Row, 1971. See pp. 248–52.

Bryfonski. *Contemporary Literary Criticism*. Ed. D. Bryfonski and P. C. Mendelson. Vol. 17. Detroit: Gale, 1977. See pp. 464–66. Second Series. Ed. D. Bryfonski and L. Harris. Vol. 14. Detroit: Gale, 1980. See pp. 511–13.

Hagen, Ordean A. *Who Done It?/A Guide to Detective, Mystery and Suspense Fiction*. N.Y. & London: Bowker, 1969. See pp. 357–58.

Hubin, Allen J. *The Bibliography of Crime Fiction 1749–1975*. Del Mar, Calif.: Publishers Inc. (University Extension, University of California, San Diego), 1979. See pp. 220–221. New edition: *Crime Fiction, 1749–1980: A Comprehensive Bibliography*. N.Y.: Garland, 1983.

Johnson, Timothy W. and Julian Johnson. *Crime Fiction Criticism/An Annotated Bibliography*. N.Y. & London: Garland, 1981. See p. 282.

Keating, H. R. F., ed. *Whodunit? A Guide to Crime, Suspense and Spy Fiction*. N.Y.: Van Nostrand Reinhold, 1982. See p. 187.

Kunitz. *Twentieth Century Authors/A Biographical Dictionary of Modern Literature.* Ed. Stanley Kunitz and Howard Haycraft. N.Y.: Wilson, 1942. See pp. 1348–49. *First Supplement.* Ed. Stanley Kunitz and Vineta Colby. N.Y.: Wilson, 1955. See p. 961.

Locker, Francis Carol, ed. *Contemporary Authors.* Vols. 85–88. Detroit: Gale, 1980. See pp. 565–67.

Melvin, David Shene and Ann Shene Melvin, eds. *Crime, Detective, Espionage, Mystery, and Thriller Fiction and Film/A Comprehensive Bibliography of Critical Writing Through 1979.* London & Westport: Greenwood, 1980.

Reilly, John M., ed. *Twentieth-Century Crime and Mystery Writers.* N.Y.: St. Martin's, 1980. See pp. 844–48 (article by Michele Slung).

Steinbrenner, Christopher and Otto Penzler, eds. *Encyclopedia of Mystery and Detection.* N.Y.: McGraw-Hill. 1976. See pp. 223–24.

Vinson, James, ed. *Contemporary Novelists,* 3rd ed. N.Y.: St. Martin's Press, 1982. See pp. 610–11 (article by H. M. Klein).

2. Critical Studies That Include Discussions of Innes

Barzun, Jacques and Wendell Hertig Taylor, eds. Preface to *The Daffodil Affair* (#29 of Fifty Classics of Crime Fiction 1900–1950). N.Y.: Garland, 1976. Reprinted in Barzun and Taylor, *A Book of Prefaces to Fifty Classics of Crime Fiction 1900–1950.* N.Y.: Garland, 1976, pp. 67–70.

Barzun, Jacques and Wendell Hertig Taylor, eds. Preface to *One-Man Show* (Fifty Classics of Crime Fiction 1950–1975). N.Y.: Garland, 1982.

Boucher, Anthony, ed. Preface to *Hamlet, Revenge!* N.Y.: Crowell/Collier, 1962, pp. 5–7.

Charney, Hanna. *The Detective Novel of Manners/Hedonism, Morality and the Life of Reason.* Rutherford/Madison: Fairleigh Dickenson University Press, 1981. See pp. xv, 64–66.

Filstrupp, Jane Merrill. "The Shattered Calm: Libraries in Detective Fiction, Part I. The Librarian as Victim." *Wilson Library Bulletin,* 53 (Dec 1978), 320–27. "Part II. The Librarian as Sleuth. Part III. Scene of the Crime." *Wilson Library Bulletin,* 53 (Jan 1979), 392–96. See p. 396.

Günther, Vincent. "Spiegelungen Hamlets im Roman und im Drama/Goethe, Innes Brešan." In *Teilnahme und Spiegelung/Festschrift für Horst Rüdiger.* Ed. Bede Allemann and Erwin Koppen. Berlin & N.Y.: Walter de Gruyter, 1975, pp. 165–172. See pp. 167–68.

Krouse, Agate Nesaule and Margot Peters. "Murder in Academe." *Southwest Review,* 62 (Autumn 1977), 371–78. See pp. 372–73.

Haycraft, Howard. *Murder for Pleasure: The Life and Times of the Detective Story.* N.Y.: Appleton Century Crofts, 1941; London: Dover, 1942. Newly enlarged edition, N.Y.: Biblo & Tannen, 1968. See pp. 186–89.

Jacobs, David C. "Photo Detection: The Image as Evidence." *Clues*, 1.2 (Fall/Winter, 1980), 18–23.

Murch, A. E. *The Development of the Detective Novel.* University of Pennsylvania Press, 1958; N.Y.: Greenwood, 1968. See pp. 239–40.

Neville, John D. "Michael Innes." *Clues*, 5.2 (Fall/Winter 1984), pp. 119–30.

Neuhaus, Volker. "Michael Innes: *From London far*/Spiel und Glasperlenspiel im Detektivroman." *Euphorion/Zeitschrift für Literaturgeschichte*, 71 (1977), 195–206.

Panek, LeRoy. "The Novels of Michael Innes." *Armchair Detective*, 16.2 (Spring 1983), 116–30.

Priessnitz, Horst. "Shakespeare-Bearbeitungen als Shakespearekritik: Funkspiele um Hamlet von Rayner Heppenstall, 'Michael Innes,' Herbert Read und G. W. Stonier." In *Anglo-Amerikanische Shakespeare-Bearbeitungen des 20. Jahrhunderts.* Ed. Horst Priessnitz. Ars Interpetandi, Bd. 9. Darmstadt: Wissenschafliche Buchgesellschaft, 1980, pp. 203–18. See pp. 207–11.

Routley, Erik. *The Puritan Pleasures of the Detective Story/A Personal Monograph.* London: Gollancz, 1972. See pp. 157–62.

Symons, Julian. *The Detective Story in Britain.* (Writers and Their Work, #145). London: Longmans, Green/for the British Council and the National Book League, 1962, 1969. See pp. 28–30.

——. *Mortal Consequences/A History — From the Detective Story to the Crime Novel.* N.Y.: Harper & Row, 1972. See pp. 126–27. Also published as *Bloody Murder.* London: Faber & Faber, 1972; Penguin, 1974.

3. Other Secondary Sources

a. Anthologies of Essay

Allen, Dick and David Chacko, eds. *Detective Fiction/Crime and Compromise.* N.Y.: Harcourt, Brace, Jovanovitch, 1974.

Ball, John, ed. *The Mystery Story.* Del Mar, Calif.: Publishers Inc. (University Extension, University of California, San Diego), 1976; Penguin, 1978.

Haycraft, Howard, ed. *The Art of the Mystery Story, A Collection of Critical Essays.* N.Y.: Simon & Shuster, 1946. Cheshire, CT: Biblo & Tannen, 1975. N.Y.: Caroll & Graf, 1983.

Landrum, Larry N., Pat Browne and Ray B. Browne, eds. *Dimensions of Detective Fiction.* Bowling Green: Popular Press, 1976.

Penzler, Otto. *The Great Detectives.* Boston: Little, Brown, 1978; Penguin 1979.

Winks, Robin W., ed. *Detective Fiction/A Collection of Critical Essays.* Englewood Cliffs: Prentice-Hall, 1980.

Winn, Dilys, ed. *Murder Ink/The Mystery Reader's Companion.* N.Y.: Workman, 1977.

b. Critical Studies

Bargainnier, Earl F. *The Gentle Art of Murder/The Detective Fiction of Agatha Christie.* Bowling Green: Popular Press, 1980. See chap. 1.

Cawalti, John G. *Adventure, Mystery, and Romance/Formula Stories as Art and Popular Culture.* Chicago: University of Chicago Press, 1976. See chap. 4.

Champigny, Robert. *What Will Have Happened/A Philosophical and Technical Essay on Mystery Stories.* Bloomington: Indiana University Press, 1977.

Gaillard, Dawson. *Dorothy L. Sayers.* N.Y.: Frederick Ungar, 1981.

Graves, Robert and Alan Hodge. *The Long Week End/A Social History of Great Britain 1918-1939.* N.Y.: Macmillan, 1941. See pp. 300–303.

Grossvogel, David. *Mystery and Its Fictions: From Oedipus to Agatha Christie.* Baltimore: Johns Hopkins University Press, 1979.

Harper, Ralph. *The World of the Thriller.* Cleveland: Case Western Reserve University Press, 1969.

Holoquist, Michael. "Whodunit and Other Questions: Metaphysical Detective Stories in Post-War Fiction." *New Literary History,* 3 (1971), 135–156.

Ousby, Ian. *Bloodhounds of Heaven: The Detective in English Fiction from Godwin to Doyle.* Cambridge: Harvard University Press, 1976.

Palmer, Jerry. *Thrillers/Genesis and Structure of a Popular Genre.* N.Y.: St. Martins Press, 1979.

Panek, LeRoy. *Watteau's Shepherds/The Detective Novel in Britain 1914–1940.* Bowling Green: Popular Press, 1979.

Peterson, Audrey. *Victorian Masters of Mystery/From Wilkie Collins to Conan Doyle.* N.Y.: Frederick Ungar, 1984.

Porter, Dennis. *The Pursuit of Crime/Art and Ideology in Detective Fiction.* New Haven: Yale University Press, 1981.

Watson, Colin. *Snobbery with Violence: Crime Stories and Their Audience.* London: Eyre & Spottiswood, 1971; revised edition, Eyre Methuen, 1979. N.Y.: St. Martins Press, 1972.

Winks, Robin. *Modus Operandi/An Excursion into Detective Fiction.* Boston: David R. Godine, 1982.

Index